MILITARISM, U.S.A.

By the same author

The United States Marine Corps

MILITARISM, U.S.A.

Colonel James A. Donovan,
U.S. Marine Corps (Ret.)

WITH A FOREWORD BY

General David M. Shoup,
U.S. Marine Corps (Ret.)

CHARLES SCRIBNER'S SONS / NEW YORK

D-11.70[C]

Printed in the United States of America
SBN 684-10128-9
Library of Congress Catalog Card Number 77-106537

To my wife, Kay

Contents

Foreword

In February of 1965 when the United States first introduced its armed forces into South Vietnam and commenced the aerial bombing of North Vietnam, the American people and their representatives in Congress were only moderately concerned about the ultimate results of our confident and aggressive actions. We were generally content to have Congress regulate this minor and relatively remote military contingency. Congress in turn, without much debate over the Tonkin Gulf resolution, placed the burden of this baby Asiatic tiger on the backs of our Armed Forces assuming that, if enough money and firepower were provided, the righteous might of American arms would prevail. The military were, as this book reveals, quite ready to intervene. As Senator Fulbright mentioned at the time, we had acquired a substantial degree of arrogance and assurance in our military power—our thriving militarism deluded us into believing we had the means to solve most of the complex world problems that came within range of our guns and dollars.

From the beginning of our growing involvement in the affairs of Vietnam, I had opposed the idea that such a small country in that remote part of the world constituted either an economic interest or a strategic threat to the welfare of the United States. In the past I have frequently expressed concern about military policies or plans which would commit American troops to a land war against the oriental peoples of southeast Asia.

By now it should be clear that the theories of counterinsurgency, graduated response, and limited war are unable to support political commitments and objectives that are not in consonance with the realities of peoples' revolutions and irregular warfare in Asia. We are faced with the hard fact that we cannot impose our will on the political and social order of Asian peoples. It is a grim revelation that there are limits of U.S. power and our capabilities to police the world.

Our original naiveté concerning Vietnam was born of the knowledge and experience gained from previous American successes in seemingly similar limited wars, small-scale incursions and interventions on foreign shores. Most Americans, military and defense leaders as well as Congressmen, foresaw this initially minor deployment in Vietnam as an honorable effort to fulfill our area commitments and as one that would end quickly when the "other side" realized that the powerful armed might of the U.S. was arrayed against them. The American people and their leaders believed that the Viet Cong could be stopped, that a settlement would quickly be made which was acceptable to South Vietnam and consistent with the long-standing U.S. policy of containing Communist aggression. American forces would then quickly return to their posture of strategic deterrence as ready instruments of our national policy.

Overlooked and considerably underestimated were the facts that the National Liberation Front and the 20 million people of North Vietnam did not have the fear of the modern U.S. war machine we anticipated; that the enemy's tenacity, perseverance, and willingness to suffer for their cause was to be far beyond our expectations; that the type of warfare our forces were to be confronted with did not readily lend itself to conventional American combat doctrine; and that the capabilities and potentials of the Army of the Republic of South Vietnam were not as promising as we had hoped.

When months passed in what soon became a frustrating, costly, and tragic war to even the staunchest advocates of our intervention, the confidence and apathy originally displayed by most Americans and their Congress changed to wonderment, disbelief and spreading concern. Many well-informed and discerning people began to speak up and express their doubts about every aspect of the protracted war, and what was increasingly apparent, the ill-calculated decisions which had led the nation into the morass.

Conscientious, patriotic, and troubled citizens across the land reviewed the policies, criticized the costly strategies and expressed their growing impatience with a limited war that lacked a clear objective, lasted too long, and continued to take the limbs and lives of too many young Americans. Rather than being considered sinistrous, apprehension and dissent over the nation's predicament in Vietnam became typical of a growing number of intelligent individuals who saw the damage and discord the war has been causing to our country.

By 1969 the bewilderment, doubts, and differences over the war rose to a high pitch among citizens—including many serving in the Congress and the administration. Americans found it difficult to understand why a war costing them $30 billions each year, over 38,000 young men killed, and fought by a most modern expeditionary force of 530,000 U.S. troops, with allies numbering almost one million men could not defeat a tenth-rate army of irregulars. The Viet Cong and the North Vietnamese main force army have seldom totaled over 250,000 troops. The enemy forces have had few of the tools of modern war enjoyed in profusion by U.S. forces and their allies. They have had no close support aircraft, no helicopter mobility, very little artillery, insignificant naval forces, few vehicles, and no armored forces. Yet in spite of losing most tactical battles and suffering heavy casualties, they remain undefeated and unbowed. There is considerable evidence that the National Liberation Front is in fact better organized and enjoys greater loyalty among the peoples of Vietnam than does the Saigon government.

The growing American frustrations and dissent over Vietnam have resulted in a rising crescendo of Congressional inquiries and hearings on defense policies, budgets, weapons programs, and related military matters. Authors, scientists, educators, and students have joined the chorus. A nation-wide series of moratoriums focused upon the Vietnam debate. The entire national military establishment has been swept into the whirlpool of recrimination, argument, and examination of our defense policies. Concerned Americans are attempting to understand the purposes and causes which brought us to Vietnam and to scrutinize the nature of American militarism.

In general, the professional military people have remained silent in public, although many are also concerned about the doctrine and policies which led them into the Vietnam war and the political restrictions which have contributed to limitations in the conduct of the war. The military now see themselves being blamed for an unhappy situation not entirely of their own making. The armed forces are undergoing a crisis of self-analysis.

The author of *Militarism U.S.A.*, a professional career officer with training and experience at the highest military levels and a long-time student of defense matters, has gathered in this book historical and analytical material about the development of American militarism, the complexities of the defense establishment, and the background of the current intervention in the affairs of Vietnam. He could not have chosen a more critical and timely subject. In fact, the topic is so current that much of the author's information and comment written months ago in drafts of this book has recently become the concurrent policy or opinion of other writers and public figures addressing these same problems.

I have known Colonel Donovan for many years. We served together throughout World War II in all of the campaigns and battles of the 2nd Marine Division, and he worked with me as a staff action officer and planner at Marine Corps Headquarters. We have discussed the topics of this book in detail on frequent occasions in recent years. He is well qualified to make such a study and the facts and information in this book are based upon his wide experience and careful research. He deserves high praise for his attempt to organize and clarify the great variety of recent and controversial material on this very important subject. Understanding these complex problems is the duty of all patriotic citizens interested in the welfare of their country. In this connection, I received a note from a member of Congress this past year in regard to some recently expressed views on the extent and products of militarism in America. He stated: "The courage of one's convictions and the willingness to speak the truth as one sees it for the good of his country is what patriotism really means—far more than flags and bands and national anthems."

The author has done a service in compiling this informative book. A thorough and sincere study of the subject matter it discusses should be a valuable assistance to Americans who desire to better judge and determine the role they want their Armed Forces and the entire defense establishment to assume in the future destiny of our nation.

David M. Shoup
General U.S. Marine Corps, Retired

Preface

Early in 1968 General David M. Shoup and I discussed at some length our deep concern about the causes of the U.S. involvement in the Vietnam affair and the related trends in the military establishment and American society. We agreed that our personal knowledge and experience with the pressures, motives and purposes at work gave cause for alarm over the evidence of a flourishing new militarization of American life.

A result was an essay I helped General Shoup put together which was published a year later in April 1969, by the *Atlantic Monthly,* under the title, "The New American Militarism." This article proved to be of considerable interest to many people in the U.S. and abroad. It was widely noted, quoted, and reprinted in editorial circles; some 30,000 reprints were ordered by various interested groups; it was read into the Congressional Record and distributed widely to members of Congress. The *Atlantic Monthly* reported that the piece incited an unusual amount of reader reaction—mostly concurring and complimentary.

This book is an expansion of the *Atlantic* essay. Many readers, as well as the publisher, desired an analysis on the current and controversial topic of the culture of militarism and the nature and the purposes of the defense establishment, which of course is the area where we must look in any study of the history and extent of militarism's influence upon the current American scene.

This book is not intended as an attack on the military profession or on any military individuals or service. I consider myself a professional militarist by training and over thirty years of active military duty or directly related study, writing and publishing. With maturity and perspective I have, hopefully, become a somewhat more objective and "reformed" militarist.

Rather, this is an analysis of the socio-economic-political influence of our immense military establishment, its civilian and uniformed leaders, and the vast complex of money, people, industry and vested interests, who make up America's "defense-industry team." This powerful combine has come under increasing scrutiny in recent months as Congressmen, journalists, educators, businessmen, and students, nation-wide, have evidenced growing concern over the major issues and problems of the day which are seemingly related to national defense—the unsuccessful, prolonged, and tragically costly war in Vietnam; the gigantic and growing expense of defense programs; the popular desire to devote more federal funds and efforts to domestic problems rather than to national defense; and the apparently wasteful or at least questionable military programs. The debatable ABM and MIRV concepts, the command and leadership fiasco of the *USS Pueblo,* the embarrassing loss of a Navy spy plane a year later in Korean waters, and the alleged assassinations and massacres of South Vietnamese nationals by American military personnel all reflect upon the defense establishment, its leaders, and their plans, policies and programs.

Then there have been the student demonstrations, moratoriums, and other protest activities prompted in part by the young peoples' rebellion against the "immoral and unjust" Vietnam war. The most popular issues for dissent are the draft, military-sponsored college research, and the ROTC program. In debating these issues, the youths relate them directly to the military "establishment" and its power.

This is not just a typical postwar public reaction against all things military such as has occurred regularly in America following each of our major wars. This is a deeper-seated and more far-reaching public concern. It may well be a debate described by *Time* magazine as "one of the most significant of the generation," and ". . . most useful, particularly if it brings about more thorough, dispassionate and knowledgeable reviews of defense programs. . . ." It will be reflected in the re-evaluation of our overseas alliances, commitments and defense strategy. It is the main consideration in the current study of the priorities of our national efforts. Its outcome will affect us all.

So, because national defense is our biggest business, no study of this aspect of our society can avoid analysis of the professional military people and their leaders. They are the architects, the managers, and the consumers of our defense effort and its products.

Professor S. P. Huntington has said that "the principal focus of civil-military relations is the relation of the officer corps and the state," and that "The social and economic relations between the military and the rest of society normally reflect the political relations between the officer corps and the state." [1]

So it is not inappropriate for a military professional to attempt an analytical study of this sort. Such a work calls for an understanding of the language, the motives, and the methods of the profession. The "defense-industry team" is too complex for most students or even for many civilian journalists. At the same time the profession cannot be considered as a fraternity with secrets no military brother should discuss in public. So this is an effort to "tell it like it is." Our defense establishment belongs to the people who pay for it—not to those who run it for the nation. American citizens need to know about the elements of our society that are expending over half of the Federal dollars.

This study is, however, in no way intended to impugn the honor, devotion, or loyalty of the U.S. military and their appointed civilian leaders. The paramount sense of duty, honor, and loyalty,

[1] Samuel P. Huntington, *The Soldier and the State,* Belknap Press, Harvard Univ. Press, Cambridge, Mass., 1964, p. 3.

which is a basic characteristic of America's military professionals, is a matter I can personally attest to. I am proud to have lived and served by these standards.

At the same time we have to recognize that service and duty to country, the creeds of honor, the devotion to standards of discipline and loyalty are not unique to America's fighting forces. We have largely taken these military codes from the traditions of the armed forces of Great Britain and from the past conduct and glories of the French armies. We have been influenced by our enemies as well as our allies: the Russians, the Germans—indeed, even the brave and disciplined forces of Imperial Japan—have all had their impact upon our military standards and philosophies. The most inspiring creeds and noble codes of fighting men are universal, ancient, and unquestioned.

Despite these long-established standards, the fact remains, however, that underneath the prestige and honor of uniforms are normal men with the same virtues, ambitions, and self-interests as their civilian counterparts. A uniform is neither protection nor insurance from human frailty. By the same token, civilians in the Department of Defense, executive officials in defense industries, and even be-medaled veterans of military service are not exempt from observation, analysis, and criticism in any honest study of our vast military and defense culture. The claims of "patriotism" and "in the interest of national defense" are not adequate explanations of the forces motivating the large and diverse groups who make up the military-oriented elements of our society. They provide too simple a camouflage of a truly complex combine of interrelated groups and purposes.

The nation's defense is everybody's business, yet it has become so vast and complicated—with its own terminology, secrets, technology, and propaganda—that most people have difficulty comprehending even a few facets, to say nothing of the many sides of the subject. So this book is an effort to inform readers by explaining the whats, hows, and whys of the current militaristic trend which has become such a dominant aspect in our culture and by describing some of the forces at work in the new American militarism.

Many good people have contributed to this work. Foremost has been General Shoup, whose interest, encouragement, and help have been invaluable. We have worked together on every chapter, and his judgment, experience, and clear insights have been impressive as well as beneficial. The comments and discussions of my colleagues, Colonel William C. Ward, U.S. Marine Corps retired and Colonel Robert E. Collier, U.S. Marine Corps retired, also verified and contributed to our ideas and information.

I am also grateful to Margaret Textor, Billie Ellis, and Marian Allen for their assistance in typing and preparation of manuscripts. All of these friends, critics and associates helped in the process of authorship, but the result is my responsibility.

James A. Donovan
Colonel U.S. Marine Corps, Retired

Atlanta, Georgia
November 1969

Chapter I

THE WARRIOR AMERICANS

"You cannot organize civilization around the core of militarism and at the same time expect reason to control human destiny."

Franklin D. Roosevelt, 1938

America has become a militaristic and aggressive nation embodied in a vast, expensive, and burgeoning military-industrial-scientific-political combine which dominates the country and affects much of our daily life, our economy, our international status, and our foreign policies.

Through most of its history, America has had a tradition which rejected militarism except under the pressures of a nationally declared general war. Now, however, there is impressive evidence that the United States is moving inexorably toward a society that is increasingly influenced by the defense establishment. Moreover, this is happening not as a result of a deliberate choice by the American people, but as a result of an accumulation of military decisions, commitments, and actions that are beyond the control of present democratic processes.

The Department of Defense has indicated that even if the Vietnam war effort was eliminated, the momentum of various weapons systems already approved or in advance planning, plus existing commitments and other rising costs, would largely consume not only savings from the decline of hostilities in Vietnam, but most of the increases in the gross national product during the coming years, leaving little to provide for the huge and incessant demands of the other pressing domestic problems.

American armed might is on frontier guard duty; patrolling the air and seas, or stationed on foreign shores around the world. It has been conducting an undeclared war for five years at a cost of 40,000 American dead, over 260,000 wounded and $104 billion spent, in a small underdeveloped country 8,400 miles from U.S. shores. In addition to the 600,000 military men in Southeast Asia, there are 300,000 U.S. Ground and Air Forces stationed in Europe and South Korea. Tens of thousands of Americans serve in warships on the high seas. There are over 1,200,000 U.S. fighting men stationed overseas at 2,270 locations in 119 countries. Additional divisions, air forces, and fleets stand by in the continental United States prepared to execute numerous contingency plans for every area in the world deemed to be of interest to the defense and welfare of the United States and its allies.

Within the Federal government, a *national security state* has evolved since the National Security Act of 1947 created the three separate armed services, the Central Intelligence Agency, the National Security Agency, and the Atomic Energy Commission. These government bodies, which, together with defense industry, academic research groups, and Congressmen with vested interests, bolster each other and receive such a disproportionate amount of Federal funds that there is no effective counterbalance or means of changing their momentum and direction. There is a growing problem of uncontrolled bureaucratic power. The principal instrument of the power of this bureaucracy is fear, fear of the hazards and disruptions which is claimed will result if the defense establishment is not provided with all that it demands.

The nation's armed forces are supported by a vast and permanent arms industry and a complex of related interests which affect thousands of communities and millions of citizens. These Americans—in uniform, veterans of military service, defense-industry employees and their dependents, defense scientists, Defense Department civilians, businessmen, and politicians—all have direct and personal interests in the nature and scope of militarism and the activities of the defense establishment. How did this militaristic society evolve? How did "peace-loving" America become a colossal war machine, and what has created the world's image of the aggressive warrior American?

Our military power ostensibly has been intended only to defend the nation and to help protect its friends and its allies from attack, yet it has become the cause of much national dissension and disagreement. It is the reason for a good deal of American unpopularity abroad. Our military power has come to be viewed by many people as a self-perpetuating force of aggression and destruction motivated by many interests beyond the needs of national defense. It has led us into the most disliked and controversial war of our history and has isolated the United States from its traditional allies and the peoples of the world. "There is not a single independent state in Europe or Asia," writes Walter Lippmann, "which follows our lead. . . . No European government could survive today if it joined us on the battlefield. . . . As for the Asian peoples we are supposed to be saving, no independent Asian state—not Japan, India, Pakistan, Burma, Malaysia, Indonesia—is giving us even token support." So our generally unpopular and independent military action in Vietnam has been in effect a form of isolationism, and the critics of militarism and the fruitless military venture in Southeast Asia have been called "neo-isolationists" by the logic of recent administrations.

The Seeds of Militarism

Militarism is new to America. Prior to World War II the regular military establishment was small and enjoyed even less prestige or influence. In 1939, after the outbreak of war in Europe there were still but 174,000 men in the U.S. Army and only 126,400 in the U.S. Navy. The Marines consisted of a force totaling 19,700, and there were all of 2,800 aircraft in the Army Air Corps. There was no permanent arms industry and little more than a concept of how it would be mobilized to support emergency defense needs. There was nothing resembling the influential combination of defense and industry such as the "team" which now looms so large in our affairs. "For in my youth," Walter Lippmann once recalled, "we all assumed that the money spent on battleships would better be spent on schoolhouses, and that war was an affair that militarists talked about and not something that seriously-minded progressive democrats paid any attention to." [1]

Now in a society whose leading industry is manufacturing the tools of war, inevitably, one of the leading professions is preparation to fight—military service. The armed forces have become ardent competitors for power in American society. The services compete with each other for new weapons systems, for missions, for commands, for funds, publicity and prestige. They seek the privilege of being "first to fight" with high states of combat readiness, mobility, and completed plans for contingencies. There is a constant urge to exercise and test the military solution to America's many foreign problems. The guiding military doctrines have hinged upon instant readiness for war—and the nation has been chronically at war, or threatening war, or being threatened with war during most of the past three decades.

In the years before World War II, America had a history of wars and violence but not of militarism. During the first hundred years of the new American republic it experienced relatively little peace and tranquillity, but most of its warfare and military action was confined to wresting the continent from the native Indian tribes and in a bloody Civil War. At sea, the young nation had quickly established itself as a maritime power beginning with the naval war with France, 1798–1801, over American versus French West Indian interests. The period saw the emergence of the U.S. Navy and Marine Corps which soon distinguished themselves in actions against the Barbary pirates, 1801–1816. It also fought the War of 1812 with some success against the mighty sea power of Great Britain, but America wasn't involved in any major military or naval operations overseas between the War of 1812 and the Spanish-American War in 1898.

In 1890, however, a new voice was heard in the writings of U.S. Navy Captain Alfred T. Mahan. In his book *The Influence of Sea Power Upon History 1660–1783*, he established naval doctrine that would guide strategists for fifty years. Mahan maintained that command of the seas—through possession of a great fleet, overseas bases, colonies, and a merchant marine—guaranteed trade, wealth, and security to a people and, thus, liberty and progress. His ideas encouraged the new imperialists and military jingoists who then led America into the "splendid little" Spanish-American War and onto the path of global power and expansion. The Spanish-American War further demonstrated the need of naval bases and coaling stations for the U.S. Navy with its new responsibilities and interests throughout the Caribbean and Pacific Ocean areas which Teddy Roosevelt dubbed our "ocean of destiny." America was now ready to "show the flag," carry "the big stick," and compete on equal terms with established imperialistic powers like Great Britain, France, Germany, Austria-Hungary, and Russia.

It was during this period that the American military professionals began to evolve and codify their service doctrines based upon possible missions against foreign enemies and for expeditionary operations overseas. At the same time, the armed forces were held generally in low esteem by civilians and were isolated from their society. Consequently the Army and Navy sought reasons to justify their existence and developed professional codes and creeds to guide their exclusive and separate societies. The withdrawal of the military from the distractions and materialism of civilian society at the end of the nineteenth century, however, resulted in the high standards of dedication and professional excellence exhibited by military leaders in the successful wars of the first half of the twentieth century. The period also saw the emergence of professional military organizational concepts, professional schooling, and the military ethics which provided the soil and the seeds for the growth of militarism after World War II.[2]

Interventions and Expansion

The turn of the century found American fighting forces in action or on expeditionary service in such widely separated areas as Puerto Rico and China in continuation of intervention and "expansionist" policies stimulated by the recent war with Spain. Between 1900 and 1941, American military forces—Army, Navy, and Marines—were involved in more than twenty-two expeditions, interventions, and small or major wars. The year 1900 saw U.S. Marines occupying Puerto Rico, and U.S. Army and Marines engaged with an allied force in the relief of the Peking Legation from siege by the Boxer Rebels in North China. American troops were still occupying Cuba. Army and Marine forces were fighting guerrillas in the Philippines. Brief interventions by U.S. Navy and Marine forces took place almost continuously throughout the Caribbean area; Panama, 1903; Dominican Republic, 1904; Cuba, 1906; Honduras, 1909. Some interventions lasted many years: Haiti, 1914–1934; Dominican Republic, 1916–1924; Nicaragua, 1922–1924 and 1926–1933. In the summer of 1914 an American Army-Navy-Marine task force invaded Vera Cruz, Mexico, to close the port to arms shipments intended for the unfriendly Huerta regime.

Then there were larger expeditionary operations involving mainly U.S. Army forces. General John J. Pershing took 7,000 soldiers into Mexico in 1916 to stop raids by the insurgent Pancho Villa. The largest expeditionary force of Americans up to that time went to Europe and fought in France between April 1917 and November 1918. During World War I more than two million Yanks served overseas in the AEF. Afterward, American troops remained in Germany during the occupation period from 1918 to 1923. At the same time a small U.S. Army expeditionary force was in Russian Siberia during 1918 and 1919 for the purpose of meddling in Russia's internal affairs by supporting anti-Bolshevik forces.

A Marine brigade went to China in 1927 to protect American interests, and Leathernecks remained on the China station for the next fourteen years. They were reinforced by additional troops in 1932 and again in 1937.

During the half century before World War II, when American military forces were active almost continuously in contingency expeditions in these varied areas, the impact of military require-ments upon the American people and their economy was relatively slight. Other than the twenty months of World War I, from April 1917 to November 1918, military ventures demanded very little attention or support from the American people. Interventions and expeditions usually consisted of relatively small task forces of regulars dispatched to remote and unfamiliar places. Strange names such as Peitaiho in China, Samar Island in the Philippines, and Bluefields in Nicaragua were mentioned in the papers along with occasional small casualty lists. But in general the details of the actions and the scope of operations were rarely, if ever, well known beyond military and naval circles. Troop movements were at ship's speed, news reporting was by dispatch, and events on the battlefield frequently happened weeks before the American people learned the results. There was no radio or TV which could put the action into every household within hours, no world-wide communications net keeping the President instantaneously abreast of the combat situations, and no Pentagon command post breathing over the shoulder of every commander in the field. Small wars and interventions were pretty much confined within the purview of the Navy and War Departments. They were often typified by romantic and sketchy reports of military adventure in strange places. Interventions were conducted largely to protect the lives and interests of Americans abroad, and other than for the career military and overseas commercial firms involved, there were few people with any direct and vested interest in these military activities.

Isolation and War

In the America of the 1930's isolationism and antimilitarism became a national obsession. The desire to make America immune to foreign quarrels was as old as the earliest settlers in the New World, but it had developed new vigor with the bitter memories of World War I. Americans and West Europeans could find little enthusiasm for collective security measures or organizations to forestall the rising German and Italian dictatorships. Entreaties to resist Fascist aggression sounded too much like the propaganda of World War I. The disillusions from that war had not only strengthened the convictions of the isolationists but also encouraged a pacifist movement that won millions of adherents. Some colleges abolished their ROTC programs, and students organized a burlesque "Veterans of Future Wars."

Hampered as he was by isolationists in Congress, President Franklin D. Roosevelt was restricted to actions in foreign affairs which called for no new commitments abroad during the early years of his administration. The first step toward ending some fifty years of American interventionism south of the border had been taken under Coolidge and Hoover. With the departure of U.S.

Marines from Haiti in 1934, the era of "banana war" interventions in Latin America ended. The United States adopted the Good Neighbor Policy of opposition to armed intervention in the Caribbean area. The policy was not altered until April, 1965, when Marines and U.S. Army troops again returned and intervened in the affairs of the Dominican Republic.

Pre-World War II attitudes about the Far East were a mixture of arrogance toward all Asiatics; missionary benevolence for the benighted Chinese; a fear of the "yellow peril," which included all orientals; and a considerable distrust of the "sneaky" Japanese. The U.S. Navy and Marine Corps were especially concerned about the growing might of Japanese sea power, and those two services were quietly developing plans for war with Japan which many officers were sure was inevitable. However, in spite of a series of provocative incidents and aggression in Manchuria, administration advisers favored no strong measures against Tokyo. American policy remained fundamentally isolationist and was reinforced by the convictions of many citizens that munitions-makers were intriguing to touch off a new arms race. Senator Arthur Vandenburg of Michigan denounced the arms industry as "unutterable" treason and advocated confiscating virtually all individual income in excess of $10,000 in the event of war. Concern about the international arms traffic prompted the Senate to authorize a committee headed by Senator Gerald Nye of North Dakota to investigate the munitions industry.

In the summer of 1936, President Roosevelt appeared completely influenced by the isolationists and pacifists. In an address at Chautauqua, New York, in August, he stated: "We shun political commitments which might entangle us in foreign wars; we avoid connection with the political activities of the League of Nations. . . . I have seen war. I have seen war on land and sea. I have seen blood running from the wounded. . . . I have seen the agony of mothers and wives. I hate war."

By the following year, however, continued Fascist aggression in Europe and the threats of Japanese imperialism caused the President to become increasingly alarmed. He felt obliged to warn the nation in October, 1937, in Chicago, where he spoke of the

"epidemic of world lawlessness" and the need to "quarantine the patients" in order to protect the community. This speech marked the turn of U.S. policy from one of isolationism to one of collective security, and gave advance notice to Tokyo of sanctions against Japan. That date marked the beginning of America's world-wide military involvements.

George Fielding Eliot, the military commentator, wrote in 1938 that it was "absurd" to think that Japan would fight America. He noted that "a Japanese attack upon Hawaii is a strategical impossibility." Nevertheless the President responded to the threat of Fascist and Japanese expansion by steady increases in American rearmament. The Army and National Guard forces were enlarged, and the President asked for the greatest naval construction program since World War I. He explained that the Fascists "respect force and force alone." Isolationists denounced the President as a warmonger who was manufacturing a crisis.

With the invasion of Poland in September, 1939, the Nazis plunged Europe into war. President Roosevelt asked Congress to repeal the arms embargo and stated he regretted the Neutrality Act of 1935. A limited National Emergency was declared. Thus began a series of mighty events and military ventures on a grand scale which created the American military giant, put an end to isolationism, and replaced pacifism with a militaristic culture of growing vigor.

Arsenal of Democracy

Months before the attack on Pearl Harbor, on May 27, 1941, President Roosevelt had proclaimed an "unlimited national emergency," and the United States had already become "the arsenal of democracy." The threat of war was turning the United States and its burgeoning war industries into "the home front" to support the nations fighting Fascist aggression in Europe and the rapidly growing American armed forces. Millions of Americans were taking jobs in war industries and other millions were going into the services. During the subsequent war years there was scarcely a man, woman, or child who was not somehow contributing to the national war objectives. America found the war years ones of tension, anxiety, pride—and for many, the most purposeful of their lives. It was during those years of great military and naval campaigns, glorious victories and widespread sacrifice that the American martial spirit grew to prominence in the nation's character and a new generation was nurtured in a society dominated by military affairs.

For America, World War II, in size, scope, and cost was the single biggest effort the nation had ever made: In all, 16,353,659 men and women served in the armed forces during the war years; 11,260,000 in the U.S. Army, 4,183,466 in the Navy, 669,100 in the Marines, and 241,093 in the Coast Guard. Of these, 292,131 suffered battle deaths, 670,846 were wounded, and casualties from all causes totaled 1,078,162 service men and women.

Almost from a standing start in 1940 the American war machine became in a few years the most powerful the world has ever seen. By 1942 Americans were producing as much war material as Germany, Italy, and Japan together. In 1943, U.S. production was 50 percent greater than that of the Axis powers; the next year it had doubled. Despite the 16 million men and women in the armed forces, civilian war workers increased from 47 to 53 million. By the end of the war the vast American defense-industry team had produced 297,000 military aircraft, 86,000 combat tanks, 6,500 naval vessels, 64,500 naval landing craft, 5,400 cargo ships, 315,000 artillery pieces, 17 million rifles, and 4.2 million tons of artillery shells. The steel industry turned out more iron and steel than the whole world had produced a few years before. Most World War II battles were won by firepower and masses of ships, planes, and guns. The American combination of skilled fighting manpower and the deluge of industrial production overwhelmed the Axis forces.

Federal defense spending soared from $9 billion in 1940 to $95 billion in 1944; in mid-1943 the United States was spending at the rate of almost $8 billion a month. Total outlays in the four war years rose above $320 billion, or twice the total Federal expenditure in all previous history. The national debt rose to $258 billion, almost six times what it was at the time of Pearl Harbor. The war spending brought unprecedented prosperity for millions. Weekly earnings in war manufacturing rose 70 percent, resulting largely from time and a half payment for overtime work. The net cash income of the farmer rose more than 400 percent from 1940 to 1945. Many Americans had never had it so good, and countless fortunes were made under the booming economy of World War II.

The Cold War

Even before Japan was defeated and World War II ended, Americans tried to turn away from militarism and the new responsibilities of power their mighty armed forces had brought to them. Army troops overseas demonstrated for early return and discharges. Pressures came from all sides to demobilize, so between V-J Day and the end of 1945, 3.7 million Army men were returned to civilian life. By the summer of 1946 the Army had been reduced to 1.5 million men and the Navy to 700,000. At the same time, most administration leaders had come to accept the end of America's long-standing preferred policy of isolationism. Senator Arthur Vandenberg of Michigan had proclaimed to the Senate on January 10, 1945, "I do not believe that any nation hereafter can immunize itself by its own exclusive action." The President quickly selected the once isolationist Senator to be a delegate to the forthcoming conference at San Francisco in April, 1945, where the Charter of the United Nations would be created and approved on June 26.

But a world organization for peace was soon found inadequate. Devotion to world cooperation was hardly enough. The United States learned that it had to be willing to mobilize sufficient military force to discourage the Soviet Union from actions that would endanger the peace. The following years of tension between the Soviet bloc and the Free World witnessed repeated Soviet intransigence and real or imagined threats from the Communist world which resulted in a hardening of American policy toward the USSR and an increasing tendency for the United States to rely on military power. At Fulton, Missouri, in March, 1946, Winston Churchill advised his American friends to beware of the Kremlin's "expansive tendencies" and intrigues behind the "iron curtain" of the Communist world. "There is nothing the Russians admired," he said, "so much as strength and there is nothing for which they have less respect than for . . . military weakness." Such talk alarmed some Americans already obsessed with the "unthinkable" prospect of atomic war. Any hard and militant policy leading to an atomic arms race with Russia appeared to many people to be the utmost in folly. The United States, however, had already set up an atomic arms and development program that would lead the nation on the one-way path of atomic war strategy.

The following year President Truman and his new Secretary of State, General George Catlett Marshall, faced a fresh and growing crises in the Eastern Mediterranean. Financial troubles forced Britain to cut off its aid to Greece and Turkey, which were being pressed by Communist insurgents and neighbors. The President requested $400 million in economic and military aid for Greece and Turkey and announced the "Truman Doctrine." "I believe it must be the policy of the United States to support free peoples who are resisting attempted subjugation by armed minorities or by outside pressures," the President declared. Critics of the policy objected to association of the United States with the defense of totalitarian regimes under the guise of resistance to Communist totalitarianism.

The Truman Doctrine was successful, however, in helping to save Greece and Turkey from Communist domination, but continued Soviet initiative in their spheres of interest created frictions and conflicts which come to be recognized as the "Cold War" between the Communist and Free World. In order to develop long-range plans and policies designed to safeguard U.S. and allied interests, a State Department Policy Planning Staff was established under the direction of the experienced George Kennan, an able and well-informed expert on Russia. The subsequent policy relationship between the United States and the Soviets became one of "long-term, patient but firm and vigilant *containment* of Russian expansive tendencies"—by force if necessary. This policy has, with some modification, guided America in its relations toward the USSR up to the present time and is the basis of the Free World alliances, our military aid programs, the nuclear deterrent posture, and the forward deployment strategy of U.S. General Purpose Forces. It has required large military forces, a thriving peacetime defense industry, and American armed presence, ready for combat in the many areas of our interest.

The Marshall Plan for massive economic aid to Europe and all nations which would cooperate was designed to help the war-torn countries move forward and rehabilitate their economies. It became law in April, 1948. The Plan was a resounding success and it passed every production goal, putting Western Europe back on its feet. But the Soviets, who had renounced the Plan, intensified the Cold War against the West. America's foreign-aid goals, which had initially been entirely economic, then took on a largely military character. The Berlin blockade by the Russians in June, 1948, caused some American military reserves to be activated; the armed forces were alerted and deployed. The U.S. Air Force airlift won the battle for Berlin, but the Cold War had been intensified, and the need for a West European military organization became apparent. An alliance to prepare against possible Russian aggression and pledging military aid to any member under attack was deemed necessary by Western leaders. The North Atlantic Treaty (NATO) was signed by the United States and eleven other nations in 1949. Article 5 of the NATO treaty stipulated that "an armed attack against one or more of the signatories in Europe or North America shall be considered as an attack against them all."

Not since the Convention of 1800, when the young United States freed itself from the alliance with France, had the American government agreed in peacetime to a treaty of alliance outside the Western Hemisphere. Nothing so decisively indicated the end of isolationism in the United States, nor put a greater responsibility of missions and readiness upon the peacetime military establishment. The Cold War in effect had divided the world into two armed camps. Every American move in foreign policy was weighed for its military consequences. U.S. military planners and leaders moved henceforth into positions of prominence and influence in the formulation of national security policy and they dominated the new allied commands. America's vastly expanded world role hinged upon military power, but in 1949 that power was limited largely to atomic bombs. Then in September, 1949, the advent of an atomic explosion by Russia some three years ahead of American estimates, altered not only the balance of power but changed forever the kind of world we live in. The threat of nuclear devastation has since influenced the affairs of all nations and the plans of men.

United Nations Defend Korea

Secretary of State Dean Acheson, in a statement on January 12, 1950, amplifying America's foreign policy of containing Communism, outlined a "defensive perimeter" which defined the limits of the area the United States believed vital to its national security. The little-known country of Korea lay outside this perimeter, and he implied that Korea was by no means viewed as vital to America's national interest. Five months later, on June 25, 1950, forces of Communist North Korea invaded the Republic of Korea. The next day the United States put the blatant aggression before the United Nations Security Council and the Council called upon UN members to go to the assistance of the Republic of Korea.

Most Americans approved of U.S. aid and intervention in Korea. General Douglas MacArthur was put in command of all UN troops in the area; and for the first time in the history of nations, a world organization mobilized a military force to halt aggression. To many Americans, however, it seemed to be another American expedition and "small war," as the United States furnished most of the troops. (By the end of the war some 33 percent of the troops were American, 61 percent Korean, and other nations provided less than 6 percent.)

Militarily, Korea caught America less well prepared for war than had Pearl Harbor. Secretary of Defense Louis A. Johnson's economy efforts had reduced the Army to 591,487 and the Leathernecks to 29,415. MacArthur had four undertrained, poorly equipped occupation divisions in Japan. The Marines had a well-trained but understrength brigade in California. All the services, however, had ample cadres of war-experienced officers and non-commissioned officers, and their reserve units consisted largely of trained and professional veterans of World War II.

The initial battles in July and August found the American forces barely holding their own in the Pusan perimeter, but the bold Marine amphibious landing at Inchon in September, 1950, deep in the enemy rear, reversed the tide and the Eighth Army swept across the 38th parallel into North Korea. Despite the risk that China might enter the war, and blinded by the success of the UN counteroffensive which was destroying the North Korean forces, the Joint Chiefs of Staff abandoned the policy of containment and ordered MacArthur to continue his advance to within a few miles of the Chinese border. The leaders of the armed forces and President Truman desired a decisive military victory over the aggressors, and MacArthur predicted the end of enemy resistance by Thanksgiving. But intelligence was faulty and estimates of Chinese reaction were wrong. A massive Communist Chinese Force of 300,000 "volunteers" poured south from Manchuria and drove the UN allies reeling back into South Korea. General MacArthur rebelled against the Presidential and Joint Chiefs' policy of limited war, stating, "There is no substitute for victory." Although many proud and militant citizens agreed with the distinguished general, he was properly relieved from duty by his civilian superior and Commander in Chief. General Omar Bradley, Chairman of the Joint Chiefs of Staff, observed that an atomic war with China "would involve us in the wrong war at the wrong place at the wrong time and with the wrong enemy."

In early 1951 the UN forces counterattacked back up to the 38th parallel and the Communist forces accepted an offer of negotiation. A "limited war" of bloody attrition continued, however, until the summer of 1953. Truman continued to resist some advice to push for an all-out war and military victory, and many Americans remained impatient with the concept of limited war. For the first time they found themselves in a war which they could not truly win and from which they could not withdraw. The alternatives of limited war or atomic disaster has been a traumatic experience for all. In the words of Senator J. W. Fulbright, "It is this knowledge which constitutes the revolution of our time. . . . that at any moment our civilization may be all but annihilated." It hangs over the world—and sensitivity to its meaning separates the generations.[3]

The Emergent Military

It was during these early post-World War II years that distinguished wartime military leaders shifted to influential policy-making and leadership positions throughout the government, diplomatic, and business sectors. The victorious American generals and admirals enjoyed world-wide respect, their countrymen were deeply proud of their accomplishments, and they were widely recognized as leaders, planners, and managers. Because of accelerated wartime promotions some were retiring from military careers at an early age. Many were available for further useful service and were sought out by government and industry. The extent of military penetration into the civilian hierarchy after World War II was without precedent in American history. In 1948, it was estimated that one hundred and fifty military men occupied important policy-making posts in civilian government.[4]

Generals Eisenhower, Marshall, and MacArthur were preeminent among the galaxy of wartime military men who continued to exert considerable influence during the period: General of the Army Dwight D. Eisenhower was Chief of Staff of the Army, 1945–1948; President of Columbia University, 1948–1950; Supreme Allied Commander Europe (NATO), 1950–1952; and elected thirty-fourth President of the United States, 1957–1961. General of the Army George C. Marshall was Special Representative to China in 1946, Secretary of State during 1947–1949 and Secretary of Defense in 1950–1951. General of the Army Douglas MacArthur was Supreme Commander Allied Forces Japan during 1945–1951, Commander of the United Nations Forces in Korea during 1950–1951, and retired to Chairman of the Board of Remington Rand.

Some other prominent military men who filled influential positions in government and industry during postwar decades are: Lt. Gen. Walter Bedell Smith, Ambassador to the USSR, Undersecretary of State, and then American Machine and Foundry; Rear Admiral John W. Bays, Chief, Division of Foreign Service Administration; Major General Thomas Holcomb (USMC), Minister to South Africa; Lt. Gen. Albert C. Wedemeyer, Special Representative to China and Korea; Admiral Alan G. Kirk, Ambassador to Belgium; Admiral Raymond A. Spruance, Ambassador to the Philippines; Maj. Gen. Kenneth D. Nichols, General Manager of the A.E.C.; General Omar N. Bradley, Veterans Administration Director and an officer of Bulova Watch Co.; General Alfred M. Gruenther (Commander in Chief of SHAPE), Chairman of American Red Cross; General James M. Gavin, Ambassador to France and Chairman of Arthur D. Little, Inc., General Maxwell D. Taylor (Chairman of the Joint Chiefs of Staff), Ambassador to South Vietnam, special adviser to two Presidents, and head of the Institute of Defense Analysis; General Lauris Norstad (Supreme Allied Commander in Europe), President of Owens-Corning Fiberglas Corporation; Vice Admiral William Raborn, director of the Central Intelligence Agency, Vice President of Aerojet-General Corporation; General Paul Freeman (Commanding General of the Continental Army Command), Vice President of the Mellonics Systems, Development Division of Litton Industries. There are others equally noteworthy.

Many of the most significant positions in government were at one time or another held by these and other distinguished officers. The wartime leaders were not only popular heroes but respected opinion-makers. The Cold War period was a time of international readjustment. The military minds offered the benefit of firm views and problem-solving experience to the management of the nation's affairs. Some of the appointments of military men to high civilian posts during the Truman years also reflected a desire to use the political popularity of the top war commanders. For the first time in American history numerous professional career officers not only became popular public figures but also became deeply involved in domestic politics.[5]

While the distinguished military leaders were exerting the influence of their personalities, beliefs, and methods upon the government, diplomatic and business worlds, many aspects of military doctrine learned by war veterans were being disseminated and adopted throughout American culture and organizational life. The military and naval staff procedures, their organizational and their problem-solving methods had been developed and refined in service schools during the years before the war, and were taken back by the war veterans and into civilian society. Military systems and doctrine have had considerable impact on a wide range of civilian organizations and management developments. To name a few: the general staff system and the staff and line organizational concept; staff studies and operations orders; the military style of briefings and oral-visual presentation; estimates of the situation; leadership and management training; task forces; planning and programming; operations evaluations; systems analysis; program management; the doctrine of chain of command; and tables of organization and equipment.

Simultaneously and ever since, military vernacular has also become a part of Americans' everyday language. The special vocabulary of veteran soldiers, sailors, and airmen has spread over the years among Americans in all walks of life, adding not only color but an unconscious militaristic flavor to the American idiom. Some of the more common expressions now a part of everyday language are: "blitz," "clobber," "boondocks," "top brass," "check points," "objectives," "task force," "G.I.," "gung ho," "square away," "knock off," "preventive maintenance," "logistics," "Roger-Wilco," "concept of operations," "G-2," "main thrust," "target area," "zero in," "interface," "Snafu," "pass the word," "scuttlebutt," "phase lines," "chow," "VIP," "shook up," and "dope off."

Atomic Deterrence and Limited War

After the Korean War, American foreign policy and military strategy planners became obsessed with the power and prospects of atomic war. Secretary of State John Foster Dulles placed no faith in the concept of limited war. He proceeded to announce in January, 1954, that henceforth America would depend less on local area defense and more upon the deterrent of massive atomic retaliatory power. The concept presented the prospect of every diplomatic dispute becoming a war of nuclear annihilation.

The policy of massive retaliation placed the burden of credibility and execution upon the U.S. Air Force and the Strategic Air Command, which began to prosper in both budget allocations and prestige. The other services sought desperately for roles and missions in atomic war that would justify not only respectable size but their very existence. The Navy developed new concepts of atomic weapons delivery culminating in the missile submarines. The Army and Marines conceived new organizations and tactics for the atomic battlefield which eventually reached tactical absurdity as they prepared to employ hundreds of tactical nuclear weapons on the battlefield. They intended to defend the Free World by destroying our allies' countrysides.

In August, 1953, the Russians detonated a hydrogen bomb, and in 1954 the United States exploded a bomb one hundred times as destructive as any previous man-made explosive. Atomic war became even more unthinkable for rational men—but the arms race proceeded at full speed. The armed forces had insatiable requirements for more and varied atomic munitions, and the Atomic Energy bureaucracy had gained endless momentum. The Russian Sputnik in September, 1957, also launched the intercontinental ballistic missile race. Initially the USSR was deemed ahead of America in rocketry, but in following years the United States closed the "missile gap" and put 1,000 ICBM's with atomic war heads underground aimed at targets throughout the Communist world and ready to fire in one indiscriminate salvo.

Foreign policy during this period was concerned largely with efforts to win the support of the small nations of the world. President Eisenhower asked Congress in January, 1958, for authority to use troops "to secure and protect the territorial integrity and political independence" of countries requesting aid against "overt armed aggression from any nation controlled by international Communism." Recognizing that the Communists had not abandoned their ambitions, the United States Government under President Eisenhower took steps to secure the situation by further alliances. Bilateral treaties were concluded with the Republic of Korea and the Republic of China on Formosa. In July, 1958, the President dispatched 9,000 U.S. Marines and Army troops to Lebanon to protect the existing government from pro-Nasser elements. At the same time a crisis developed at Quemoy held by Nationalist China off the coast of Red China. The U.S. Seventh Fleet gathered vessels to support Formosa and Quemoy and made a shocking revelation: the Fleet's capabilities were limited largely to the delivery of atomic bombs. Stocks of conventional shells and bombs were low, and conventional tactics were rusty and neglected. With this rude awakening the Joint Chiefs of Staff began a slow turn away from their infatuation with atomic war and saw the need for more flexible capabilities. The long-neglected U.S. Army, under the dynamic guidance of its Chief of Staff, General Maxwell D. Taylor, led the Marines and Navy to shy away from the doctrines of massive retaliation and atomic war as the single strategic concept. The possibility of non-nuclear limited wars gained acceptance and the armed forces redesigned their doctrines.

Beginning in 1961, civilian defense leaders under President Kennedy evolved two additional doctrines which have radically altered the nation's defense planning. One is known as "flexible response" and the other is called "gradualism." Both doctrines de-emphasize our atomic strength and the principle of massed combat power; military forces are leashed and controlled within political and geographic limits determined by the civilians. However, the primary strategy in support of U.S. national security continues to be based on the threats of nuclear destruction and the "strategic deterrent" of atomic weapons. These strategic policies were employed successfully in the Cuban missile crisis of November, 1962, largely because Cuba was remote from the USSR and not really worth Russia's risk of atomic war. By the same token the strategies have failed in Vietnam because it too is remote from any true interests of the United States, has certainly not proved to be worth its great cost—and there is nothing of value there that can be obtained by nuclear war. Nevertheless the strategy of graduated response and limited war theories were the basis of the largely civilian concepts and decisions which led the United States into the Vietnam entanglement and intervention in the winter of 1964–1965.

In order to give support to the nations of Southeast Asia, the United States took the lead in 1954 with the creation of an alliance included in a treaty and reinforced by a collective-security system known as SEATO—the Southeast Asia Treaty Organization. In this alliance, the United States joined with Great Britain, France, Australia, New Zealand, Thailand, Pakistan, and the Philippines to guarantee the security not only of the member nations but also to come to the aid of certain protocol states and territories, if so requested. Vietnam was included in the SEATO protocol and the U.S. leaders have from the outset felt a fundamental obligation to that troubled country which has guided our actions in Vietnam. The SEATO treaty provides that "each party recognizes that aggression by means of armed attack would endanger its own peace and safety, and agrees that it will in the event act to meet the common danger in accordance with its constitutional processes." The only other members who responded to the aggression in Vietnam, however, have been Australia, New Zealand, Thailand, and the Philippines, each of whom has contributed small token forces.

The U.S. official interpretation of the treaty has been that determination of aggressive attack is a unilateral responsibility and does not require collective decisions on action to be taken to meet the danger. The commitment we have undertaken to protect South Vietnam was necessary, in the view of Secretary of State Dean Rusk and other Johnson administration planners, as a result of a series of expanding assurances made to the government in Saigon by Presidents Eisenhower and Kennedy between 1954 and 1961. These administrations, it has been claimed, considered the defense of South Vietnam a part of protecting our own "peace and security." With the resistance of U.S. combat forces to the enemy's "aggression by means of armed attack," in the wilderness and hamlets of the small remote nation, we were led to believe that we were defending the United States!

Despite Secretary of State Rusk's repeated claims that the involvement of U.S. combat forces in Vietnam was the only honorable way to safeguard the nation from Communist aggression in furtherance of policies initiated by the Eisenhower and Kennedy administrations, in fact the policies and plans of those two Presidents did *not* indicate any intention to become deeply involved in Southeast Asia. Their basic stand was that the United States should help the South Vietnamese help themselves, but not to take over the war from them.

During the Korean War period Eisenhower had said, "If there must be a war there, let it be Asians against Asians." In 1954, during the Indochina war, Eisenhower warned against getting into an Asian land war, and later, in a letter to former President Ngo Dinh Diem of South Vietnam, he carefully said the U.S. help would be limited to economic aid, and even that was conditioned on domestic reform. Shortly before his death in 1963, President Kennedy reaffirmed this policy. He said, "We can help them [the Vietnamese], we can give them equipment, we can send our men out there as advisers, but they have to win it . . . In the final analysis, it is their war." Also during the years prior to 1964 the Joint Chiefs of Staff resisted any temptations or recommendations to get involved in a land war in Southeast Asia. They believed such action both unnecessary and unwise.

Actually our armed intervention in Vietnam was not a continuation of Eisenhower-Kennedy policies so much as it was the result of new aggressive and militaristic policies evolved by President Johnson's civilian advisers who desired to be generals and military strategists, and to the urge among Pentagon careerists who were tempted to test their theories of counterinsurgency, and to try out new organizations and equipment in a "limited" war against "Communist aggression."

Perhaps the most conclusive indication of the administration's miscalculations in 1964–1965 and the changes in strategic policy which have evolved as a result of the Vietnam war is the fact that, in the hindsight of costly experience, it can be safely said that if we had the opportunity we would not repeat the same decisions which put our combat forces into Vietnam. Knowing what we now know about limited wars of counterinsurgency in the Southeast Asia environment, none of the past four Presidents would be likely to again become so committed, regardless of pertinent treaties or the nature of the aggression.

The limits of conventional firepower as well as atomic weapons power became increasingly apparent in Vietnam following the Tet offensive in early 1968. If the limited war stalemate of Korea had been traumatic for Americans, the failures in Vietnam came as an even greater shock and were the beginning of a profound shift in America's approach to the rest of the world. The high-water mark of confidence, arrogance, and pride in the power to influence the world with American money and arms had been reached. The 1969 cutback of military strength and the withdrawal of forces from Vietnam—a limited war which had failed in most of its goals— presaged a reduced American presence in Asia. Vietnam taught us that going it alone on a military venture is the one policy we wish to avoid in Asia. There has been a concurrent and growing urge to also draw down U.S. troop strength in Europe and other forward areas. America, twenty-five years after the glories and victories of World War II, is making a historic and limited withdrawal from its policies of involvement and military intervention in the world's problems. The strategy of containment of Communist aggression would itself become, it is hoped, less aggressive and provocative.

So American militarism evolved during the years following World War II as a product of Cold War tensions, resultant policies of containment and deterrence based upon military force, and as a result of the requirements for large and powerful armed forces which made the policies credible. The American people had come to accept, with no little pride prior to Vietnam, the idea of being responsible for the "freedom" of all nations requesting aid and have created the military power needed to help provide the benefits of the American system to the less privileged—and to provide an American solution to every world problem.

Professor Gordon Allport of Harvard said some years ago that "wars begin in the minds of men." "The indispensable condition," he stated, "is that people must expect war and must prepafe for war, before under war minded leadership they make war." The ultimate source of war and militarism, then, lies in human nature and the ideologies of men.

The Roots of Militarism

The basis of America's modern militarism has been a hallowed trinity of ideals or creeds; *patriotism, national defense,* and *anti-Communism.* These terms mean different things to different people and each can be employed to motivate and justify actions, to attack opposing ideas, and as a refuge for the chauvinist. Their pure and simple meanings are not in themselves a basis for militarism but they are frequently used and distorted by militarists for many purposes. Like "motherhood," "hot dogs," and the "Fourth of July" these terms are all-American, sacrosanct, and usually held above criticism. American militarism is founded upon this trinity of ideological beliefs which are the source of the national military policy—but American militarism is *motivated* by much less well recognized factors; defense-establishment careerism, defense-industry profits, fascination with military technology and weapons of destruction—and a national pride and competitive spirit. It is also prompted by the many alliances and commitments we have assumed to safeguard the "Free World."

At the base of America's expanding militarism is the defense establishment consisting of its uniformed members, its civil servants, and its appointed civilian leaders. These groups all have vested interests in their respective functions and careers. Supporting the defense establishment is the vast permanent complex of industries which provide defense supplies and equipment. These industries are essentially profit-motivated and represent the vested interests of stockholders, their employees, the local communities, local businesses which depend upon defense payrolls, and the Congressional representatives of special-area interests. All of these groups thrive upon a large and busy defense establishment.

Modern American militarism is also motivated by the constantly burgeoning production of new weapons and equipment for war. Defense research and developments reflect the acme of America's advanced technology and production skills. The money and talent concentrated in equipment development and new, ever more destructive weapons creates a dynamism and momentum of its own. The fascination and technical challenges presented by new systems and military projects provide purposes frequently independent of any valid defense requirements.

Then there are the numerous alliances and foreign commitments the United States has undertaken since World War II in the "areas of U.S. interest" which have provided the basis of America's

defense policy and national military strategies.[6] The missions resulting from the national commitments have created the vast requirements for men, money, and equipment which the defense
establishment considers necessary in order to properly perform its
assigned functions. Thus the increasing tendency of recent administrations to subordinate other national plans and programs to
those of the military. Military domination of all other government
interests, as reflected in the annual Federal budget, is unquestion-
able evidence of the extent of militarism in the United States.

Also a basic cause of militarism is war itself, and as long as we
have the one we will be menaced by the other. The perceptive
French observer of early America, Alexis de Tocqueville, expressed it:

"War does not always give democratic societies over to military
government, but it must invariably and immeasurably increase the
powers of civil government; it must almost automatically concentrate the direction of all men and the control of all things in the
hands of the government. If that does not lead to despotism by
sudden violence, it leads men gently in that direction by their
habits."

The American settlers and immigrants of the eighteenth and
nineteenth centuries came to this country to avoid the wars and
militarism that dominated so much of life in Europe. As a tradition
and ideal, militarism has never been a popular concept in America.
Now, however, the scale and scope of military and defense matters
have become major factors of existence. American militarism is a
many-faceted culture trend which reflects the times we live in, the
proud and competitive nature of Americans, and the mission to
defend the Free World as we define it.

"Militarism," in the words of Woodrow Wilson at West Point
in 1916 when describing the threat of Imperial Germany, "does
not consist of any army, nor even in the existence of a very great
army. Militarism is a spirit. It is a point of view. It is a purpose.
The purpose of militarism is to use armies for aggression." Militarism is also described as a policy or principle supporting the
maintenance of a large military establishment. In its extreme form
it is defined as the tendency to regard military efficiency as the

supreme ideal of the state, and *it subordinates all other interests to those of the military.* This book is an attempt to describe the nature and extent of militarism in America today.

Footnotes

[1] Walter Lippmann, *United States Foreign Policy: Shield of the Republic,* Boston: Little, Brown & Co., 1943, p. xi.

[2] Samuel P. Huntington, *The Soldier and the State,* Cambridge, Mass. 1964.

[3] J. W. Fulbright, Owens-Corning lecture Denison University, Granville, Ohio, April, 1969.

[4] Richard C. Snyder and H. Hubert Wilson, *The Roots of Political Behavior,* New York, 1949.

[5] Samuel P. Huntington, *The Soldier and the State,* Cambridge, Mass. 1964.

[6] The U.S. has 8 formal alliances to defend 43 countries, plus military defense agreements with 21 additional countries. *US News & World Report,* July 21, 1969.

Chapter II

A NATION OF VETERANS

"There are no greater patriots than those good men who have been maimed in the service of their country."

Napoleon

They drifted in and out of the drab hotel in steaming Atlanta. They talked about old comrades, campaigns, and combat jumps. The veterans of the famous 82nd Airborne Division were gathered for their twenty-third annual convention. They mingled quietly, with their beer and memories, and listened to talk of fallen friends and the current war. The past and present members of the elite fighting outfit sat with their wives at the memorial luncheon and heard a chaplain ask them to remember "our brothers in arms." They rejuvinated their martial spirits and contemplated the troubled world.

The 82nd was the first of America's proud Airborne divisions. It fought with great distinction in Sicily, Normandy, and Central Europe in World War II. It participated in the Dominican Republic intervention in 1965. Elements of the division were sent to Vietnam following the enemy Tet offensive of 1968. Many of the Army's most distinguished leaders received their airborne training and indoctrination in the 82nd. The veterans of the famous division are proud professionals, America's "Guard of Honor," and the three hundred and fifty old and new soldiers gathered in convention were still "Airborne—all the way." The local news report reflected attitudes typical of the American military experience:

"Brig. Gen. Alexander A. Bolling took over the podium to remind the group of 'moral courage and intestinal fortitude.' Bolling led the division's third brigade to Vietnam during the Tet offensive in February 1968. The brigade was the division's first unit to enter combat since World War II.

"Bolling said that not one of the soldiers of the 82nd killed in action 'died unhappy.'

" 'There is a pride that builds up when we lose our men. They die happily for their country,' he asserted.

"Bolling told of a scene in Chicago recently that explained how his men in Vietnam feel about the war. "There was a girl on a corner at a demonstration with long, straight hair—and that's all right. Next to her was a boy with long, curly hair—and that's not all right,' Bolling said. The conventioners cheered and laughed.

" 'The girl asked a soldier who was there why he had gone to Vietnam. He turned to her and said, 'So people like you can stand on a street corner and shoot off your fat mouths.'

" 'Being with a group like this makes me realize that we still have the moral courage, the intestinal fortitude to carry on in Vietnam.' " [1]

World War II was a long war that touched upon the lives of most Americans. The millions of American men who served received training and experiences in the greatest drama of our times. Men matured, were educated, gained rank, and acquired stature during their years in uniform. Despite their earlier attitudes many returned to civilian life as indoctrinated, combat-experienced military professionals, and for better or worse would never be the same again. America will never be the same either. We are now a nation of veteran military and naval professionals. To the 14.9 million veterans of World War II, Korea added another 5.7 million five years later, and ever since the large military establishment has been training and releasing draftees, enlistees, and short-term reservists by the hundreds of thousands each year. In 1969 the total living veterans of U.S. military service numbered over 26.3 million. The total U.S. population twenty-one years of age or more is 116 million, and about half are males. So approximately 45 percent of the nation's adult males are now veteran military men. In 1968 their average age was 44.2 years.[2]

There are some 14,000 veterans who are eighty-five years or older and more than 30,000 under twenty years of age. Of the total number of U.S. veterans, 23,519,000 (over 80 percent) qualify for wartime benefits, the Veterans Administration has reported.

In 1967, there were 112,353 totally disabled veterans and 1,886,926 partially disabled veterans receiving compensation for service-connected disabilities. These numbers were rising steadily in 1969 as a result of the Vietnam war. The average annual Federal payment rate to veterans in 1967 was $985.[3] The Veterans Administration budget for Veterans Benefits and Services in 1969 amounted to 7.3 billion or 3.9 percent of the expenditures for defense. There were 3,182,141 living veterans on the rolls and receiving compensation and pension benefits in 1967.

Today most middle-aged men, most business, government, civic, and professional leaders have served time in uniform. Whether they liked it or not, their military training and experience has affected them, for the creeds, the ideologies, and the experience of military service are impressive and long-lasting. For many veterans the military's efforts to train and indoctrinate them may well be the most impressive and influential experience they have ever had. For the young and the less educated their military experience probably represents the summit of their learning.

Veterans' Groups

Veterans' organizations are varied and plentiful. Foremost in size is the American Legion with a 1969 membership consisting of 2,381,339 veterans of military service. (The American Legion Women's Auxiliary had 910,204 wives of these veterans.) The Veterans of Foreign Wars (VFW) is the other largest veterans' group (1,800,000 members). Then there are other similar groups: American Veterans of World War II (AMVETS, 200,000); Vet-

erans of World War I (228,551); Disabled American Veterans
(245,000); Catholic War Veterans (50,000); American Veterans
Committee (10,000); The Military Order of Foreign Wars of the
U.S. (2,000); Military Order of the World Wars (12,300); and
there are the Blinded Veterans Association (1,200); the Korean
War Veterans; the Jewish War Veterans; and the Military Order
of the Purple Heart (15,200).

Besides these, there are several large associations of veterans of
military service not primarily related to wartime service: The Retired Officers Association (94,000); the Reserve Officers Association (56,000); the Non Commissioned Officers Association of the
U.S.A. (30,000); the Womens Army Corps Veterans Association
(2,000); the Army and Navy Union of the U.S.A. (50,000);
Fleet Reserve Association (68,000); the Marine Corps League
(12,000); Military Chaplains Association (2,300); Military Engineers Society of America (26,000); Military Surgeons of the U.S.
(5,600); the National Guard Association of the U.S. (45,500); the
Naval Reserve Association and Marine Corps Reserve Officers
Association.

The veterans' organizations constitute important military-oriented lobbying and opinion groups. Most of the veterans' organizations tend to support a large ˙defense establishment and the
weapons and policy programs being fostered by the Pentagon. The
top military leaders long ago learned how to use the veterans'
groups as sounding boards and supporters for their most militaristic speeches and programs. Very few career military men are
active in veterans' groups—or even belong to them—but the
regular officers are pleased to cultivate the backing of the veterans'
organizations.

The VFW's top priority legislative goal for 1969, for example,
was world-wide deployment of U.S. armed forces—"as convincing
demonstration of U.S. support for our allies." Other goals were: an
enlarged and modernized merchant marine; continued ROTC programs; construction of critically needed troop, family, and bachelor
housing; establishment of standing veterans' affairs committee in
the Senate; and last but not least, continued gains in veterans'

rights and benefits. The Pentagon could not have drafted a platform more pleasing to the military.

The 1969 annual meeting of the Reserve Officers Association,
another influential veterans' organization, resolved to support continuation of Selective Service, maintenance of active forces at adequate strength and provided with the most modern weapons,
increasing and equipping reserve forces to meet full mobilization
requirements, and building public support of the concept that every
citizen should participate in the defense program.

Secretary of Defense Melvin R. Laird used the 1969 Annual
American Legion convention as the sympathetic audience for his
rebuttal to criticism of the defense establishment and his deceptive
warning of the dire perils and the multitude of dangers posed by
pending Congressional budget cuts of defense programs. He told
of the "risks to which the American people are exposed," and
". . . further major cuts for the present fiscal year would involve
even greater risks and further disruptions." He didn't spell out the
nature of the risks and disruptions but implied their fearful nature.

Legion National Commander William C. Doyle, a general in the
National Guard, responded with the expectation that the convention would produce a "strongly worded resolution" from its National Security Committee condemning the cuts in defense spending.
The Legion is always a dependable supporter of Defense Department programs, and defense leaders know they can count on a
standing ovation from the Legionnaires for their pet platitudes and
patriotic appeals.

While these veterans' groups usually proffer loyal support to
the current war venture of the military and promote strong national security programs, over the years they tend to concentrate on
programs of direct benefit to their members in the form of cash
payments, bonuses, tax benefits, and other services.

Other veterans' associations more oriented to comradeship and
memories than to any special group interests or benefits are the
many division and unit associations. All the World War II Marine
divisions and many wartime Army divisions formed associations
after the war. Their purpose was initially to compile and produce

unit history books and perpetuate their war friendships, exploits, and records. Many warship crews, air wings, squadrons, and separate units also formed associations of wartime comrades. For many of these men their best years were spent in uniform and their happiest and most exciting days were those experienced while serving their country. If they continue to be militaristic in their attitudes and beliefs, it is because their formative and impressive years were experienced while under the influence of military ideology, training, and indoctrination during both World Wars and subsequent limited wars.

The Military Experience

Within the modern armed forces the inculcation of ideals is considered the most vital of all instruction—this is in contrast to the reduced emphasis on ideology in almost all other contemporary institutions. Because of the essentially unregimented nature of Americans, the military establishment has found it necessary to develop an all-compelling unity of beliefs and purposes which will inspire men to action, when under pressure and danger, for higher goals than material comforts or personal welfare. Military ideology is directed toward the individual's belief in service, defense of the national survival, and preparation for violence and battle. Training for combat is completely irrelevant to normal conduct, self-interest, or civic ethics. The indoctrination with military codes and creeds experienced by the millions of men and women who move in and out of the services has a continuing prolonged and even regenerative effect upon the ideas, attitudes, and martial fiber of the nation as a whole.[4]

Another purpose of military ideology is to minimize the brutal and degrading aspects of warfare by creating a higher morality of purpose to justify the killing. The "defense of freedom," opposition to "Communist aggression," "assistance of nations under attack from outside aggression," the "honor of national commitments and alliances," the "defense of the Free World," and the "preservation of world peace" typify recent objectives for which military ideals are directed. So it is out of the impact of ideals and the firmness of his beliefs that the military man develops the strength to face situations which it would otherwise be normal to avoid. American military ideology is the product of what are probably the most effective training establishments in the world.

The American armed forces since World War II have attained such a high degree of competence in training young recruits and new officers that they produce not amateur citizen-soldiers but highly qualified professional military, naval, and air men. It takes only a matter of months for each of the services to remold the average young American and turn him into a skilled, indoctrinated, and motivated member of the armed forces.

"Professionalism" typified the American soldiers' attitudes for the first time in a major war in Korea. The common soldier fought solely and simply because he was ordered to fight and not because he felt any identification with the political goals of the war. Indifferent to the aims of the war, he was motivated largely by unit *esprit,* and concerned mainly with rotation home. General Westmoreland and other U.S. commanders in Vietnam have frequently expressed their high regard for the "professionalism" and devotion to high military ideals demonstrated by the fine young American men serving there, another limited war with motivations similar to the Korean War.

The degree of success attained by the training systems of course varies with individuals. Some men suffer military training and organization with reluctance and cynicism, others are converted into chauvinists. They find in the military codes and routines a way of life which provides them with firm ideological beliefs and a self-confidence gained from the organizational unity and purpose. Most young Americans, however, adapt to military training and service with a moderate and open-minded attitude based upon a readiness to accept the system and to perform their obligation of serving the nation. All they ask is to be well and sensibly trained and to be managed and led by officers who are reasonably considerate and know their jobs.

As a result of the frequent expansions and emergency build-ups since World War II, the military services have evolved recruit-training procedures, specialist schools, and officer-training methods of great efficiency. In fact, the military training and school processes

and techniques have in many respects advanced considerably
beyond civilian teaching methods. Although military training is
concerned mostly with teaching technical skills, military codes,
doctrines and procedures, rather than logic, reasoning, or creative
thinking, it has become very effective in achieving its purposes.
Even the training and orientation of military instructors in the
basic methods and principles of effective teaching is superior to
many civilian approaches. The military can take the average officer
or NCO and in a matter of two or three weeks turn him into a very
capable teacher with more effective skills in speaking, platform
manner, use of training aids, and understanding of how to organize
instruction than are found in many college classrooms.

The unique aspects of the military training experience are stress
of the value and importance of discipline and conformity, organization traditions, unit *esprit* and loyalty to service, and the military
mission. Each of the armed services teaches somewhat different
skills and doctrines related to their specific functions, but all of the
military have in common the codes of discipline, veneration of
traditions, and the demands of *esprit de corps.*

Military discipline simply requires that the man in uniform obey
all proper orders and conform to the clearly specified regulations
for the organization. Most men have no problems living with military discipline; many are even happy to have their lives regulated
and their daily routine and needs provided for them by the system.
Life can be simple and orderly for the man who complies with the
rules. This is why many veterans can look back upon their time
in service as some of the most carefree days of their lives. The
organization provided a secure and orderly nest, free from the
competition and commercialism of the outside, and the only worries
and efforts were related to planning personal pleasures and passes
into the civilian world. At the same time, under military systems of
organization and discipline, the individuals' goals, standards, and
interests are completely subordinated to the group's purpose. Some
men who have been in service do not see any merits in regimenta-
tion or organizational and individual discipline as a means to attain
group efficiency and better self-management, but many veterans

who have experienced military discipline maintain attitudes sympathetic to the methods and purposes of the military system.

Very few civilian organizations stress and perpetuate the large body of traditions which are so conscientiously cultivated by the military services. Certain school fraternities, fraternal lodges, and old schools or colleges foster their traditions and history with some success. In recent years, however, a more sophisticated generation has been less impressed by the "old school spirit" and has found even less satisfaction in other archaic traditions. The Greek-letter fraternities as sanctums of social traditions are losing ground on many campuses. In the armed forces, however, traditionalism is not only very much alive and an important part of military life, but is constantly being nurtured by new campaigns, battles, and heroic exploits.

Each service has its gallery of heroes, its history of combat glories and sacrifice, its symbols, ribbons, and tokens, and its lexicon of slogans and mottoes. These elements are constantly combined and displayed in military rituals and ceremonies designed to remind the troops of their heritage and to inspire them to live and perform in the traditional manner. Traditions are the warp and woof of military character; they provide the color and flavor to military life, and the lore and myths of past glories that inspire men to deeds of bravery. The pride and traditions experienced in military service remain with most men all their lives. "Once a Marine, always a Marine," is more than a slogan; it is a fact of life for Marines.

If discipline fosters conformity to the military system and tradition establishes sentimental ties, it is *esprit de corps* which inculcates in the military man a sense of union and common interests—and responsibilities toward his service, his organization, and his comrades. It is this well-developed loyalty which lingers on for years and influences the veteran's attitudes toward the military establishment and to his particular branch of the armed forces. Service *esprit* usually is so highly developed that most individuals have mixed feelings of guilt or disloyalty if they even criticize their own service to outsiders. At the same time, few veterans hesitate to belittle the other services—for to do so is considered to be a form of loyalty and pride in the individual's own branch. This is a carry-over from the attitudes developed while on active duty when competition and comparison with the other armed forces was obvious evidence of *esprit de corps* and group loyalty. In fact, the development of *esprit de corps* and an enthusiastic loyalty to unit and service have been so successful in the armed forces during the past decades that it is probably one of the chief causes of inter-service rivalry, overlapping and duplication of functions, and waste of resources that have plagued the military services and resulted in much of the recent rash of criticism of the defense establishment.

In its extreme form among some professionals, service loyalty has tended to supersede the national policy and interests. Some ambitious officers have been prone to equate the nation's good with what is good for their particular service, or special doctrine, or choice weapons system. Careers have been enhanced by single-minded loyalty to a service or to a specialty such as submarines, strategic bombing, or other operational functions. In recent years, a reputation of strong advocacy of the service "party line" and de-fense of its roles and missions is almost a requisite for promotion to high rank.

Submarine crews, fighter squadrons, destroyers, bomber crews, marines, airborne units and special forces teams are the type of military organizations which especially foster *esprit de corps* and are able to develop a high degree of pride and devotion to unit and service. Each of the armed services recognizes the advantages gained in martial spirit from such loyalty and identification, thus the special uniform symbols of green berets, shoulder patches, insignia, and other items of dress or equipment emblems which set the organization apart as unique. The Marine Corps has always considered itself to be an entirely combat-oriented, combat-ready, and homogeneous organization needing only one emblem, the Globe and Anchor, so it resists any need for official recognition of its other identifying unit symbols and patches. All the services, however, work at the various means of indoctrination and propa-ganda that stimulate *esprit de corps* and develop the strong loyalty that sets the armed forces apart from all other large American organizations.

Only the gladiators on the college athletic fields approach the physical courage expected of the fighting man in a unit of high *esprit*. And no civilian organizations ever get the devotion, bravery, and sacrifice that have repeatedly been displayed by average young American military men in our recent wars. These young men perform beyond the call of duty mainly because they do not want to let their units down. This is at once the glory and the tragedy of our modern armed forces; the control, and not the waste of such *esprit* and valor is the great obligation of the military leaders. "Gallant" and costly victories over worthless "Hamburger Hills" are evidence of superb unit *esprit,* which may provide considerable satisfaction to career militarists, but in the long run such sacrifice and waste only erodes the military character and the leadership upon which *esprit de corps* must be based.

It is this combination of discipline, tradition, and *esprit* which makes up so much that is different about the military experience and sets the veteran apart. Because the emotions and demands and loyalties of military service are unique and impressive, military training and experience affect all men. The lives, the attitudes, and the beliefs of America's war veterans have been influenced by their military service; and because they represent such a large share of the adult male population their degree of militarism creates a strong imprint on the national character.

Codes and Creeds

Other than the Church, the Boy Scouts, and certain secret fraternal societies, no organization in American life spells out such an extensive code of conduct and creeds of honor, duty, courage, and loyalty to the country as do the armed forces. The veteran of military training and service has been exposed to some of the best-organized and well-propagated ideologies and patterns of doctrinal belief to be found on the American scene.

Foremost in the military catalogue of ideals and creeds is the sense of honor. Honor is the basis of the military belief system. A man is considered honorable if he holds himself to a course of conduct because of a conviction that it is in the general interest, even though he is well aware that it may lead to inconvenience, personal loss, humiliation, or grave physical risk. Military honor is not upheld in order to receive esteem and recognition, but to give service by strong character and faultless conduct. It includes integrity and interest in the good of the service beyond personal pride, and it includes the performance of duty to the fullest degree of ability at all times. Military honor is both a means and an end. When military honor is effective, its power and influence is considerable, because it is directed at a single purpose; to prepare the trained military man to fight.[5]

The armed forces of the United States originated in a revolutionary political movement—in an anticolonial struggle. Yet the military code of honor stems from the aristocratic forms against which the colonies struggled. The military and naval systems of honor were transferred from the Old to the New World because the key officers of the Revolutionary forces had earlier experience and contact with the existing British military institutions. It is this Old World cultural heritage that has perhaps lingered longer in American life among the military institutions than in any other organizations. It is why the American military professionals tend to favor and emulate the aristocratic customs and traditions of the British, French, and German armed forces—and even favor some of the militaristic dictatorships of Latin America and elsewhere. Among the essential elements of the American code of military honor derived from British and European traditions are: the ideals that officers are gentlemen; loyalty to commanders is a personal obligation; professional military men are members of a cohesive brotherhood with its own standards and self-regulation; and professional fighting men must preserve and enhance the traditions of combat glory.[6]

Honor is intended to be binding upon the entire military profession, yet it is in constant strain with the varied and contrary values of contemporary civilian society. Even within the armed services and among the career professionals the evaluation of standards of military honor and integrity have been included in recent examinations of the performance and purposes of the military establishment. In a democracy it has not been completely appropriate for honor to be the dominant value of the military professional. It has to be combined with public prestige and popular recognition. The recent "crisis" of criticism of the military has rekindled the military's concern for its self-image and self-esteem as much as it has the concern for its organization and purpose. The matter of military honor, which is fundamental to the self-image of the professional leaders of the American armed forces, has been under considerable strain. The military needs to receive sufficient prestige and respect to insure a degree of self-esteem. Under public attack and criticism, the profession tends to lose confidence in its self-image, it suffers pains of schizophrenia in deciding whether it is to behave as a fighting force or mainly as a well-managed organization. The simple-minded general who claims that the purpose of his professional forces is "to kill the Viet Cong" is an anachronism. Most career officers do not want the military to be viewed as aggressors and professional killers, but as patriotic public servants running a well-managed establishment in defense of the country.[7]

Closely related to the code of military honor is the requirement for a deep sense of duty to perform well. All military men are taught that it is their duty to obey all orders and to carry out all assigned tasks according to directions and regulations. The careless omission of a maintenance assignment on a military aircraft or the faulty setting of an artillery gunsight can result in disaster. It is every man's duty to perform his job as well as he knows how. Nothing less is acceptable. General Robert E. Lee advised his men, "Do your duty in all things. You cannot do more. You should never wish to do less." Duty is also considered to be a matter of serving the country and the military organization in the performance of its functions. The extent and nature of this duty is a matter which has become a subject of considerable debate. Military training also stresses the fundamental obligation to serve the nation loyally and without question to carry out the policies and orders of the President, who is Commander in Chief, and the orders of his appointed officers. Loyalty is considered to be a cardinal

military virtue. This obligation is set forth in the enlistment oath
and in the commission of all officers. Each of the armed forces
also expects a high degree of loyalty to the service, to unit of assignment, and to unit leaders.

Loyalty has never ranked high in a country where the supreme
virtue has been individualism, for loyalty implies the subordination
of the individual to a goal or standard outside of and superior to
himself, and it emphasizes collective loyalty to group.[8] Although
loyalty has never been typical of American civilian moral philosophy, it has been an important aspect of military indoctrination
since World War I. In fact, group loyalty and the team *esprit,*
mentioned earlier, are cultivated much more assiduously and
vocally than is any overt patriotic expression of loyalty to country
and cause. As a result, most veterans become much more oriented
to "battalion," "ship" or "squadron" in expressions of loyalty than
to any other large national or patriotic purpose. Newspapermen
continually query the troops about why they fight, or for their views
on defense policy; in most military organizations of high morale the
men usually reply that they are satisfied to devote their loyalty and
efforts to the outfit. It is only after leaving the service that the
veteran begins to rationalize his patriotic motives and loyalties to
the nation.

With the exception of a few other hazardous professions, the
ideal of courage in the face of danger is peculiar to the military experience. But no other profession poses the considerable
physical dangers of the battlefield. Courage in battle is the most
ancient of military ideals. In earlier times when men went armed
and warfare was a way of life the demonstration of manly courage
was frequently an end in itself. Such a purpose is still a tantalizing
challenge to many men, and a surprising number of professional
militarists today continue to be fascinated by the tests of courage
posed by modern warfare. Americans admire the display of courage. In the words of John F. Kennedy, "The greenest garlands are
for those who possess it." [9]

Few challenges during most men's lives compare to the individual
test of courage and leadership which some face in battle. Those
who survive the test and know in their hearts that they have per-

formed their duty well and unselfishly gain a moral ascendency over other men that no amount of money, prestige, or public honor can displace. The man who knows his own degree of courage and strength need defer to no one. In the words of Voltaire, "Whoever serves his country well has no need of ancestors."

Because we are a nation of military veterans having a history of war and violence, heroism in battle is widely recognized and venerated in all walks of American life. Inasmuch as most of the top-ranking military leaders are officers with distinguished careers, including frequent awards for heroic conduct in battle, they tend to receive considerable respect and high prestige in the halls of Congress and in public life. America has always been attracted to heroes, cultivating them wherever found, and the military is prolific source of demonstrated courage.

The risks and dangers of military service are many and multiform. They tend to bind the veterans together with bonds of experiences not shared by women and civilians. Although many honorable military veterans have never seen a live enemy or heard the crack of an unfriendly shell, or even been on a field of battle, there are many other inherent dangers in the trade of soldiering. Life at sea is always fraught with danger. Military flying is a relatively high risk occupation. Weapons training, gunfire, handling explosives, life in the field facing all kinds of weather, and the real threat of enemy action—these make the military profession different, exciting, and fascinating. Such dangers have always challenged men of vigor and courage. To some, the experience of combat and the test of war is the ultimate proof of manhood. In peace as well as war the military is a hazardous profession, and it is for this reason that the country provides generous medical, retirement, and other benefits to its service men.

The friendships experienced in the military service are usually the most unreserved and lasting ever found by most men. The relationship of comrades or "buddies" is peculiar to military life. Men in business or industry rarely have the same trusting and unselfish feeling toward their colleagues as do the fighting men of the armed forces. The young men in the junior ranks are bonded together by common experiences, by the demands of the military systems—and by dangers shared. In no other profession do men literally die for each other as so often happens in combat situations. It is only among the older officers and senior ranks that competition with peer groups, similar to civilian business, begins to erode the selfless relationship between old friends and classmates. Because the military promotion system entails ever increasing attrition in the senior ranks, colonels and generals find that they advance only over the dead careers of their comrades. Among the veterans, however, as well as the career military, old wartime comrades, men who have experienced campaigns, battles, and hardships of expeditionary service together, there are usually lasting friendships based upon mutual respect and sentiment. They help to bind the veterans and the active military establishment with bonds of common experiences, interests and unity of purpose.

The armed forces provide earlier experience in leadership of other men and give a larger amount of responsibility to young officers and enlisted men than do most other professions. The techniques of leadership and the characteristics of effective leaders are repeatedly taught to all ranks. Men in their late teens and early twenties are prepared to command and lead squads, gun sections, aircraft crews, and to take the helm of a ship. Responsibility for extremely expensive equipment and the lives of other men is routine for young soldiers, sailors, and airmen. The challenges of leadership provide some of the most satisfying experiences of military duty, and leadership is perhaps the single most beneficial aspect of service training that veterans take back into civilian life. Countless able men have matured and found their potential as leaders while serving in uniform.

Additional creeds, codes, and training peculiar to the military experience are found in the customs, courtesies, and ceremonial rituals typical of each of the services. The formality and protocol, the standards of dress, grooming, and posture—even the language and vernacular of the separate services—all add up to a total indoctrination and manner of living which influence and impress the individual. The experience is certain to affect every veteran of uniformed service. These ideals and codes of the military, separately and altogether, foster virtues and beliefs meant to develop and motivate men of high principle. Most men have need of some standards and codes as well as higher purposes upon which to focus their efforts. For millions of men the only such guidance they ever get is from military service. It is for this reason that the many veterans of service in the U.S. armed forces are generally oriented sympathetically toward militaristic ideals and policies.

Footnotes

[1] Albert Scardino, "82nd Honors Its Dead," *Atlanta Constitution,* August 9, 1969. Reprinted by permission.

[2] *Statistical Abstract of the U.S. 1968,* Dept. of Commerce, Washington, D.C., 1968.

[3] *Ibid.*

[4] Department of Defense, *The Armed Forces Officer,* Washington, D.C., 1950.

[5] Morris Janowitz. *The Professional Soldier.* Free Press, New York, 1960.

[6] *Ibid.*

[7] *Ibid.*

[8] Samuel P. Huntington. *The Soldier and the State,* Cambridge, Mass., Harvard University Press, 1964.

[9] John F. Kennedy, *Notes for Profiles in Courage.* 1955.

Chapter III

THE WEAPONS MERCHANTS

*"Modern war is a death grapple between peoples and
economic systems, rather than a conflict between armies
alone."*

Bernard M. Baruch, 1870–1965.

The Defense-Industry Team

The American people are caught in the current of defense spending for the merchandise of war. Yet dangerous as the arms race
may be, it is also immensely profitable to those at work within the
defense-industry complex. In addition to satisfying the Strangeloves
of military technology and the Pentagon careerists, it offers a livelihood to millions of Americans, in and out of uniform, whose
primary concern is merely to earn a living for their families. The
industries and businesses which fill military orders have become the
largest single producer of goods and services in the United States
and the armed services the largest single consumer organization.

Defense industry pours some $45 billion a year into over five
thousand communities where more than eight million Americans,
including members of the armed forces and all their families, and
comprising 10 percent of the labor force, earn their living from
defense spending. War has become the nation's leading industry.
The $79 billion now being spent on defense exceeds the profits of
all American business—or to make another comparison, is almost
as much as the total spending of Federal, state, and local govern-
ments for health, education, old age and retirement benefits, housing, and agriculture. The Federal defense budget has become a

dominant "growth industry." It is defense expenditures and not welfare programs that have so greatly enlarged the Federal government's role in the economy.[1]

The Federal budget for fiscal year 1969 totaled $186,062,000,-000. Of this amount $79,788,000,000 or 42.9 percent was expended for national defense. This was between 9 and 10 percent of the Gross National Product, a percentage which has remained fairly constant for the past ten years. The Department of Defense spent most of the $79+ billion in fiscal year 1969 for several major categories, programs or agencies:

Military personnel (active, reserve and retired)	$22,996,000,000
Operation and maintenance of all forces	$22,516,000,000
Procurement of supplies and equipment	$24,455,000,000
Research and development	$ 7,647,000,000
Military construction	$ 1,332,000,000

In addition there were other programs such as military assistance, supplemental Vietnam war costs, atomic energy, stockpiling strategic and critical raw materials, and the Selective Service System.

The Department of Defense's annual procurement contracts for military weapons, ammunition, equipment, supplies and services provide the fuel for the thriving defense industries. The following indicates the growth of military orders for goods and services in recent years:

1963—	$28,100,000,000
1964—	27,500,000,000
1965—	26,600,000,000
1966—	35,700,000,000
1967—	41,800,000,000
1968—	41,200,000,000
1969—	42,300,000,000 (Est.)

Procurement of weapons, equipment and supplies annually accounts for almost 45 percent of defense costs. Defense procurement includes products ranging from aircraft ($7 billion), ammunition ($2.9 billion), and ships ($898 million) to furniture ($20.2

million) and musical instruments ($1.6 million). The funds flow
into every state in the Union and at least 363 of the nation's 435
Congressional districts. Whole towns and communities are completely dependent upon military spending. Collecting more than half
of 1969 expenditures were ten states—in order: California, Texas,
New York, Connecticut, Pennsylvania, Ohio, Massachusetts, Missouri, New Jersey, and Indiana.

The impact of the military-industrial combine goes well beyond
huge employment and massive spending. Arthur F. Burns, econo-
mist and presidential counselor, stated, "The defense establishment
has left its mark on both the structure and functioning of the economy. The effects are all around us. Some defense oriented industries
—notably the aerospace group, electronics and communications—
have become a major factor in the economy, and their development
has favored many communities—for example, Los Angeles, San
Diego, Seattle and Baltimore." These defense industries have tended
to retard growth in other sectors, Mr. Burns said, and drain away
skilled workers engaged in civilian production because of the good
pay and advanced technologies found in military production.

In a 1967 speech, former Defense Secretary Robert S.
McNamara discussed the dynamics of the size and scope of the
defense and industry combination. "There is a kind of mad momentum intrinsic to the development of all new [nuclear] weaponry," Mr. McNamara said. "If a weapon system works—and
works well—there is a strong pressure from many directions to
procure and deploy the weapon out of all proportion to the prudent
level required." New developments such as the proposed ABM
system can create entirely new requirements for military organizations, industrial plants, and supporting communities. To understand
how defense business can dominate our economy it is necessary for
the citizen to have some idea of the nature and magnitude of our
permanent defense industry and its military market.

Vested Interests

The defense-industry team is a combine of many people with
vested interests in national defense. It is a conjunction of the immense defense establishment and the vast permanent arms industry.

There is an additional complex of related interests which include military reserves, veterans, scientists, university research centers, Congressional representatives, local businesses, labor, professional publications, and even news media which depend upon the special interest groups for circulation and advertising.

This so-called complex of military and industry is not an evil conspiracy of power-hungry men determined to dominate the nation. Nor is it a monolithic organization which seeks wars to justify its existence. It is rather an evolutionary development resulting from the many military, political, and social factors discussed in this book. It is motivated largely by self-interest—as well as by "patriotism" and "national defense." It has been brought about by the extensive and varied missions imposed upon the armed forces.

Militarists in Congress, such as L. Mendel Rivers, Democrat Representative from South Carolina and chairman of the powerful House Armed Services Committee, exemplify the effects of the multitude of interests and motives which influence the national militarism. Representative Rivers claims he was never fortunate enough to serve in the military but he has managed to be captivated by the military leaders and serves them with undaunted loyalty. He has done more than most generals to advance the interests of the nation's military. In the process of championing the armed services, Mr. Rivers has also brought solid economic benefits to his constituency, the Charleston area in South Carolina.

During Mr. Rivers' tenure in Congress the Charleston district has gathered an impressive collection of military installations and defense plants. The installations demonstrate the vast political capital that can be amassed through close cooperation with the defense establishment. A thriving naval shipyard, a Polaris submarine base, a Naval weapons station, a Naval supply center, an Air Force base, Parris Island Marine Corps Recruit Depot, a Marine Corps Air Station, an Army supply depot, and two Naval hospitals—are all in the vicinity of the old seaport city. Big defense contractors have also flocked to the district. During the four years since Mr. Rivers became chairman of the Armed Services Committee, defense plants have been built in the district by Avco Corp., J. P. Stevens & Co.,

General Electric Co., McDonnell-Douglas Corp, and Lockheed
Aircraft Corp. United Aircraft Corp. plans a new helicopter plant in
Charleston in the near future.

The local Chamber of Commerce estimates that defense-related
activities account for 55 percent of the area's payrolls. The military
installations alone pump $317 million a year into the Charleston-
area economy. Mr. Rivers is credited with the influence responsible
for most of these defense installations and his success is due largely
to his well-recognized closeness to the military establishment. The
military services cooperate with Mr. Rivers because he gives them
what they request and defends them and their interests against
Congressional critics. The military are smart enough to exploit a
political advantage.

Many members of Congress are also active reservists. There are
thirty-two Senators and 107 Representatives with Reserve commissions. Many others are well-indoctrinated and sentimental
veterans. Each of the services goes to great lengths to cultivate the
support and curry the favor of its alumni in Congress. Between
representing constituencies dependent on weapons manufacturing
and the payrolls from military installations—or having personal
ties with one of the services, there are few Congressmen free of
vested interests in the military-industrial team.

Another striking example of vested interests is the defense establishment's impact upon the state of Georgia which doesn't even
rank in the first ten of the states in total funds received from the
Department of Defense. Georgia has thirteen major military installations headed by the vast reservation at Ft. Benning, home of some
53,000 Army troops. The giant Lockheed-Georgia plant outside
of Atlanta builds the C-5A Galaxy as well as the C-130 and C-141
military transports. It pours a $6 million weekly payroll into the
local economy; Lockheed and other Georgia-based defense firms
received $964 million in prime military contracts during 1968. In
addition military personnel in Georgia received $650 million in pay
and allowances while 45,400 civilian employees at military installations received $337 million in salaries during 1968. Georgia also
has 500,000 veterans receiving $280 million in benefits. If such
defense-related activities as NASA, the Atomic Energy Commis-

sion, and the Corps of Engineers' projects working in Georgia during 1968 are added, total defense-related money going into the state annually amounts to about $2.3 billion.[2]

In 1967, 10.3 percent of the total public and private U.S. labor force of 72,255,000 people were employed in defense related industry. The defense workers totaled some 7,428,000 men and women. Of this number, 2,022,000 were involved in private industry manufacturing materials for the Department of Defense. The others were employed in mining, agriculture construction and service functions. Their annual payroll was approximately $8 billion.[3]

Profits and Losses

The top five defense contractors of the nation in 1968 were General Dynamics (the F-111 fighter-bomber, Polaris submarines—$2.2 billion in defense sales); Lockheed (the C-141 transport aircraft, Polaris missile—$1.9 billion); General Electric (jet engines, electronics—$1.5 billion); United Aircraft (jet engines, helicopters—$1.3 billion), and McDonnell-Douglas (Phantom F-4 fighter-bomber, Douglas A-4 bomber—$1.1 billion). A study of these and other large defense firms by the Logistic Management Institute showed that their profit on each dollar of defense sales was 4.2 cents as against an average for all U.S. industry of 8.7 cents. In addition, the companies' annual earnings on each dollar of invested capital slipped steadily over the past decade, averaging 7.3 cents as against 10.1 cents a year for industry as a whole. (Senator Proxmire's subcommittee on government economy refuses to accept the findings of this study and suggests that the General Accounting Office make a new study of defense profits. The subcommittee believes defense profits are very similar to those of nonmilitary durable goods makers.) A Department of Defense study of defense industry profits concluded that firms with the poorest performance in designing highly technical electronic systems—which frequently fail—have regularly received the highest profits. Defense profits, as a percentage of sales may not be as high as many people suspect, but even 4.2 cents per dollar on $2.2 billion is substantial.

Many people have made fortunes as merchants for defense—and as investors in a prolonged growth industry.

In a speech in Philadelphia, June, 1969, Admiral Thomas H. Moorer, Chief of Naval Operations, replied to some of the criticism of defense spending. He noted that defense's share of national spending is 4 percent less in 1969 than it was in 1960. The $79 billion budget for fiscal year 1969 represents 43 percent of the total Federal expenditures. Ten years previously, the arms budget was $43 billion or 47 percent of the total government spending. Increased costs must be related to the Vietnam war which in 1969 was costing $30 billion annually and the extra expense was "coming out of the hide" of the defense forces, the admiral said. (What other purposes these forces had he didn't explain.) The cost of national defense has only been about 9 percent of the Gross National Product or about what an average man allocates from his income for his personal insurance needs, he said. The admiral agreed that the defense establishment was big and expensive, but in light of potential enemy capabilities he indicated that he wasn't at all sure it was big enough or too costly.

Despite such rationales there are ample reasons to question the costs. Not only is defense spending huge in totals of dollars, but of growing concern to citizens is the frequent evidence of sheer waste and loss. In recent years some $9 billion worth of projects have been canceled, some after the new weapons were well along in their development. These include the B-70 super-bomber (a loss of $1.5 billion), the nuclear-powered plane ($512 million, spent), the Snark robot bomber ($720 million, lost), the Navaho missile ($680 million, gone), the Dyna-Soar space plane ($405 million, wasted), and the Skybolt air-to-ground missile ($440 million, down the drain). There have also been the recent cost overruns of such well-publicized and expensive programs as the C-5A, the F-111, the M-551 Sheridan armored vehicle, and the M-70 Main Battle Tank, to mention a few—as well as cancellation of the Cheyenne armed helicopter and the Manned Orbiting Laboratory programs.

The admiral's own service has contributed an impressive array of program cancellations and operational losses which have not improved public confidence in either military economy or management. In addition to cancellation of its version of the F-111 fighter-bomber in 1968 at a cost of $571,000,000, the Navy has experienced cost overruns on new ship construction and spent $45 million for only six months' active use of the battleship *New Jersey*. Collisions at sea, ship fires, the loss of the *Pueblo,* submarine sinkings (including one $50 million unfinished sub scuttled at dockside) and other costly accidents have all contributed to the Navy's generally fouled-up image.[4]

The C-5A's $1.5 billion and Minuteman's (ICBM) $478 million overruns disclosed to Congress earlier in 1969 were dwarfed by the two larger items: $4.46 billion for the F-111 swing wing jet bomber and $3.2 billion for an MK 48 Torpedo program that has been accumulating overruns since it started in 1964. Other weapons programs exceeding $1 billion in overruns are $1.66 billion for an Air Force F-15 jet fighter, $1.2 billion for the submarine-fired Poseidon missile, and $1.5 billion for the Short-Range Attack Missile, an air-to-ground missile.

By late in 1969, the mammoth total of all these overruns reached $16.2 billion in the military's 34 major weapons programs, as reported to Congress by Secretary of Defense Melvin R. Laird.

It's Only Relative

The defense budget figure of close to $80 billion for 1968 is not, however, the complete picture of defense costs. There are other defense-related expenditures which don't appear in the official defense budget: in 1968, international programs including military aid totaled $4.4 billion; space research and technology, including military space systems, totaled $4.5 billion; and the ever-growing veterans' benefits amounted to $7.1 billion. So total costs related to defense actually come to over $96 billion. Seeing these expenditures in relationship to other current Federal programs gives a clear picture of the degree of militarization of our society: Federal health programs amount to $10 billion; welfare and aid to states total only about $3 billion. Any true perspective of the vast defense-industry team has to be viewed largely in these quantitative terms of millions of people and billions of dollars and should not be distorted by the details and complexities of the thousands of programs.

Merely understanding the meaning of *$1,000,000,000* is strain
enough for most of us.

The chairman of the Senate Armed Services Committee, Richard
Russell, once remarked: "There is something about preparing for
destruction that causes men to be more careless in spending money
than they would if they were building for constructive purposes.
Why is this, I do not know; but I have observed over a period of
almost thirty years in the Senate that there is something about buy-
ing arms with which to kill, to destroy, to wipe out cities, and to
obliterate great transportation systems which causes men not to
reckon the dollar cost as close as they do when they think about
proper housing and the care of the health of human beings."

The Military Market

It is the mating of the Department of Defense and big business
that is the true center of the complex of the military and industry,
and it is the area that most affects the national and local economies.
So it is also important to comprehend the size and nature of the
defense establishment or Department of Defense side of the military-industry team in order to fully appreciate the magnitude of
this aspect of our militaristic society. The Department of Defense
(DoD) includes civil servants as well as the uniformed members
of the armed forces.

In 1969, 6.3 million people, civilians and military, were employed by defense and related agencies. This consisted of 3.4 million military and 2.9 million civilian personnel. Civilians working
directly for the Department of Defense totaled 1.3 million, and the
remaining 1.6 million people are employed by other defense-related
agencies and activities.

The 1969 strength of the active armed forces reached a figure of
some 3,477,500 men and women to meet the Vietnam war and
other defense needs. This total was made up of Army, 1,508,395;
Navy, 794,550; Marines, 306,435; and Air Force, 868,141. There
were approximately 422,065 regular and Reserve commissioned
officers on duty. Generals and admirals totaled 1,322, and reserve
junior officers on temporary active duty accounted for about 220,-

000 of all officers. (For a detailed breakdown of military personnel by service, officers and enlisted, see Appendix 1.) Base pay plus allowances for the active armed forces came to approximately $19.6 billion in 1969.

To get a perspective of such statistics, consider: the Defense Department employs roughly as many civilians as live in New Hampshire, Vermont, and Maine combined. There are about as many Americans in uniform as work on American farms or in construction jobs or in the combined fields of finance, insurance, and real estate. For a detailed summary of major military forces by types of units such as divisions, brigades, warships, and air wings and operating aircraft, see Appendix 2.

A substantial element of the military establishment is made up of the various categories of National Guard and Reserve forces of the four services. There were 2,758,000 men and women serving in these reserve forces as of June 1967. Of these, 983,000 were on paid drill status undergoing periodic training sessions in selected high priority and "ready" type units. Reserve forces pay in 1969 cost $905 million. For a detailed summary of Military Reserve Personnel Not on Active Duty, see Appendix 3.

Another infrequently mentioned measure of the magnitude of the defense establishment is the amount of property owned by the Department of Defense. In 1967 the DoD owned a grand total of $195.5 billion worth of property. Of this, $146 billion worth was in the United States or its possessions and $48 billion of property belonging to the Department was in foreign countries or afloat.[5]

For example, by the last official count we maintained forty-eight "major military installations" in Japan—thirty for the Army, eleven for the Navy, and seven for the Air Force. We have a dozen installations in the Philippines including the huge Clarke Field AF Base.

There are 146 U.S. military installations in West Germany, fifty-five in Korea, eighteen in Okinawa, nine in Italy, eight in Spain, seven in Thailand, and three each in Turkey, Greece and Taiwan. There are also American bases in Ethiopia, the Azores, Iceland, and Pakistan. The major U.S. bases on foreign soil number over 343; minor bases numbered 1,927 in August, 1969.

Manning these overseas installations, the U.S. military, U.S.

civilian employees, foreign nationals, and American dependents—
total over 1,704,800 people on the payroll of Uncle Sam.[6]

Over the years, the real purposes of many of these overseas bases
has changed from tactical and strategic locations of military value
to elaborate American housing and logistic installations away from
home. They provide locations and facilities for some units that
would have no reason for existence if based in the United States,
and they furnish justification for interesting and attractive overseas
travel and adventure for the troops and their families. A large
amount of the foreign deployment of American forces has become
a customary and programmed requirement rather than the product
of current strategic needs. Much of it represents a large investment
in long-standing overseas establishments at locations no longer of
direct value or importance to national security.

Soldiers in Business

The critical conjunction between the military establishment and
defense industries is lubricated by the numbers of retired officers
who have moved from active service by lateral entry into the executive levels of industry. In 1960 there were but 691 retired generals,
admirals, naval captains and colonels employed by the ten largest
defense contractors. There were 186 senior officers employed at
General Dynamics alone. A study made by Senator Proxmire revealed that in 1969 the number had increased to 2,072 senior
officers employed by major defense firms. There were 210 with
Lockheed, 169 with Boeing, 169 at McDonnell-Douglas, and 104
at North American Rockwell—all are heavily specialized in defense
business. These do not include the additional hundreds of commanders, lieutenant colonels, and majors who have also found
lucrative spots as program specialists in defense industry.

These officers represent an excellent source of trained, experienced, and mature executive manpower of considerable value to
defense businesses. They know the military systems, they are
familiar with the professional language, they probably helped develop the defense material requirements—and they frequently
know the right people in the services sponsoring the procurement
programs. Despite restrictive conflict-of-interest regulations and

normal professional ethics, it is only natural that retired officers working for industry strive to foster their particular programs or weapons systems. Most retired officers maintain contact with their friends on active duty, they have similar backgrounds of indoctrination and beliefs, and a common interest in more and better armaments.

Defense industry is a natural field of endeavor for many of these hardware- and systems-oriented officers. It offers them respectable work and needed income; few retired officers can get along on their retired pay alone. At the same time, the industry can get top-notch talent for less cost than demanded by civilians with comparable skills. There is certainly no military-industry conspiracy involved in this situation and probably very little actual conflict of interest. If there is any matter for concern about retired officers in defense industry it is because military experience doesn't train them to be cost-conscious in the areas of development and procurement, and their doctrinary views on military systems and requirements contribute too great a unity of interest and philosophy within both the military establishment and defense industry.

Defense-Industry Associations

If retired officers provide a lubricant between the armed forces and the weapons merchants, the many military service–defense industry associations provide the ties that bind. The relationship between defense industry and the military establishment is closer than many people realize. They combine to form a powerful public opinion and political pressure lobby. The several military service associations provide both a forum and a meeting ground for the military and its industries. The associations also furnish each of the armed services with the means of fostering their respective roles, objectives, and propaganda. Together they promote larger, more expensive defense programs.

The armed forces post-graduate professional educational system, created by the Army and the Navy during the years between the Civil War and World War I, was supplemented by creation of a variety of military and naval associations and their professional journals. In their early years these associations and publications were designed essentially for the enhancement of the professional and scientific knowledge of their members and as media for the expression of ideas concerning the military trades. In the period since World War II these associations and their publications have changed. The associations are now largely concerned with lobbying for their special group interests, and the magazines have become so dependent upon advertising for their financial welfare that they are strong competitors for the support of defense industry. Also in recent years career officers have found it increasingly hazardous to express their independent views in the professional journals unless they conformed to service doctrines and positions. Critical, intellectual, and creative writing by officers on military matters appears only rarely in the modern association journals.

Each of the four services has an association, generally similar but varied in size and influence. The Air Force Association and the Association of the U.S. Army are the largest, best organized, and most effective. The Navy League, typical of the "silent service" traditions, is not as well coordinated in its public relations efforts, and the Marine Corps Association is not even in the same arena with the other contenders, the Marine Association's main activity being the publication of its semi-official monthly magazine. Actually, their respective magazines are the major operations and the primary media serving the several associations' purposes.

Air Force and Space Digest, for example, is the organ of the Air Force Association and the unofficial mouthpiece of U.S. Air Force doctrine, "party line," and propaganda. It frequently promotes Air Force policy that has been officially frustrated or suppressed within the Department of Defense. It continually beats the tub for strength through aerospace power; interprets diplomatic, strategic, and tactical problems in terms of air power; stresses the requirements for quantities of every type of aircraft; and perpetuates the frequently exaggerated myths of the effectiveness of bombing. This is well coordinated with and supported by the multi-billion-dollar aerospace industry which thrives upon the boundless desires of the Air Force. They reciprocate with lavish and expensive ads in every issue of *Air Force.*

All 100,000 members of the Air Force Association receive the magazine. Members include active, reserve, retired, and veterans of the U.S. Air Force. Additional thousands of copies go to defense industry. The heavy mixture of advertising, propaganda, and Air Force doctrine continuously repeated in this publication provides its readers and writers a form of intellectual hypnosis. They begin to believe their own propaganda because they read it in *Air Force*.

The Air Force Association holds at least one national convention a year, attended by thousands of members and the representatives of aerospace industry (on fat expense accounts) who "cultivate" and entertain their Air Force friends. The Association conducts meetings, forums, luncheons, and banquets. The theme of all these events is the need, value, importance, and progress of the U.S. Air Force and its doctrine of aerospace power. At its 1968 meeting in Atlanta the Association pronounced typical policy resolutions: "There is no alternative, in our judgment, to a heavy increase in America's military effort," the Association declared in discussing the possible failure of the Vietnam peace talks. The increased military effort, it said, should include "an end to sanctuaries in North Vietnam, denial of seaborne imports to North Vietnam by . . . air and naval power, and coordination of the above with a sustained ground offensive." "There can be no neutral solution in Vietnam. One side must win and the other must lose." The Association spokesman went on to declare, "We must stay, we must prevail. The level of effort must be raised. The tempo must be quickened." And, "A military victory will provide the only sound basis for a satisfactory political solution." Such jingoist talk may well have delighted Air Force staff planners in the Pentagon and echoed the private views of frustrated bomber pilots, but it certainly didn't reflect the judgment of responsible government officials and most intelligent citizens. President Johnson eventually got the message and halted the bombing of North Vietnam eight months after the Air Force Association had made its declarations on the omnipotence of aerospace power.

The Association of the U.S. Army conforms to a similar pattern. Its propaganda organ is *Army* magazine. Every one of the 96,345 Association members—[7] active, reserve, ROTC, retired, or just plain veteran—receives the excellent *Army* magazine. The Association and its magazine are unofficial in that they have no active Army personnel assigned to the management or staff. However, the Association is run by retired or reserve Army people who work hand-in-glove with the Department of the Army. The goals and objectives, the roles and missions, the doctrines and policies of the U.S. Army provide the annual stated objectives of the Association.

The Army Association holds a well-organized and influential meeting each year at a large hotel in Washington, D.C. Army people from all over attend, including those from the many Association chapters and reserve components. Again, meetings, speeches, forums, luncheons, and banquets review Army problems, accomplishments, and objectives. Army Association leaders are reoriented and reindoctrinated in the major Army positions and objectives. The press and other media are given every assistance in getting the Association's (and the Army's) views on all topics of interest. For example, the Association's concentration upon limited-war theories and the need for modernization of the Army's equipment and airlift for the Strategic Army Corps during the 1957–1963 period bore much fruit in subsequent years. The Army Association and its magazine are well supported by the sustaining membership fees and advertising paid for by the many industrial firms which sell to the Army. Dozens of these companies have elaborate exhibits and demonstrations of their hardware in the halls of the host hotel. Presentations and hospitality rooms for Army guests are provided by the Washington representatives of these companies. Top company executives and their marketing staffs are in attendance. Many of these men have Army duty backgrounds and are delighted to entertain old comrades and high-ranking Army officers at their companies' expense. The annual meetings of the Association of the U.S. Army are impressive demonstrations of "togetherness" on the defense-industry team.

The Navy League follows a somewhat similar drill except on a smaller scale. The League has only about 41,885 members, and the annual meetings held around the country are neither as elaborate nor as well organized as those of the Army and Air Force. Navy veterans, prominent civilian sympathizers, and Reserves attend, but industry is less evident in the form of exhibits because

Naval material is too complex, secret, or ponderous to be displayed. In addition, the League has no effective publication. Its *Navy, the Magazine of Sea Power* (circulation 50,000) is not strong in the active Navy and attracts relatively little advertising. The Navy League claims to be the civilian voice and the civilian arm of the Navy. Its policies "urge that our country maintain world leadership in scientific research and development" and "support industrial preparedness, planning and production." The League also watches closely for any incursion upon the roles and missions of the Navy and Marine Corps by the other services or by the Department of Defense civilians. The popular professional publication of the Navy, however, is the *Naval Institute Proceedings,* a slick monthly which is subscribed to by most regular Naval officers (65,000 circulation) and, while it promotes sea power, Naval traditions, and Naval doctrine, it also preserves a relatively academic approach to the Naval profession.

The *Marine Corps Gazette* of the Marine Corps Association is that organization's main activity. The Association, with about 22,500 members, has no meetings, no program other than cheap group life insurance, and does not constitute an important public opinion, pressure, or propaganda force.

Another relatively new association, which combines and fosters the military-industrial team's interests, is the Armed Forces Management Association. It has a few chapters at military logistic bases and in large cities with the main purpose of improving military management of defense research and development, procurement, and relationships with industry. However, the main related venture of the association is the civilian-owned monthly, *Armed Forces Management* magazine, one of Ziff-Davis' stable of magazines. It has cleverly cashed in on McNamara's unified approach to defense establishment logistics research and development, and supply management. *Armed Forces Management* covers all of the services editorially, circulates about 35,000 free copies throughout defense industry, the military staffs, and headquarters, and attracts a wide variety of defense material advertisers. It also broadens the views of the military readers beyond the more parochial and doctrinaire interests of the single service association publications. *AFM* very effectively helps to cement military and industry relations.

In addition to the service associations there are numerous other influential military-industry oriented organizations for special defense functions. The most prominent are: The American Ordnance Association (43,152),* Armed Forces Communication and Electronics Association (12,177), National Defense Transportation Association (12,276), Society of American Military Engineers (22,896), Army Aviation Association of America, Inc. (11,153), The American Society of Naval Engineers (3,954), The National Security Industrial Association (over 600 firms), The Aerospace Industries Association of America (88 major aerospace firms), The Council of Defense and Space Industries Association, and the Joint Civilian Orientation Conference Association. (The last-named is a Department of Defense-sponsored activity which annually takes groups of prominent men from industry and civic life for extravagantly staged visits to military activities and installations. It is an official DoD Public Affairs effort to orient and to "sell" the armed forces to civilian leaders.)

Most of these associations publish slick monthly magazines which are circulated to all members.

Even the Secretary of Defense has a publication to help sell the military's views to industry. *The Defense Industry Bulletin* is an official Department of Defense free publication circulated widely throughout industry to inform manufacturers about Pentagon policies. It is published monthly by the Office of the Assistant Secretary of Defense for Public Affairs at taxpayers' expense. It serves as a means of communication between DoD, defense contractors and other business interests and helps to guide the defense-industry team.

All of these associations and their publications, which live largely on defense advertising revenue, not only preach service doctrine, but, within the confines of their individual objectives, further the special interests of the military and their defense contractors. In

---

* Numbers in parentheses refer to membership. Source: Standard Rate and Data Service, Business Publications, Skokie, Ill., June 24, 1969.

general the industries represented by these associations support, for economic reasons, the same military policies which the officers support for professional reasons. The associations openly campaign on behalf of the active services and the objectives of their leaders. They are usually in favor of expanding military forces and bigger and better weapons. Their attitudes and beliefs are militaristic and belligerently "anti-communist," in keeping with the national military philosophy. The associations have considerable influence in shaping, refreshing, and firming the opinions of their members. As a result of this informational self-persuasion the military-defense industry groups share many common views on matters of national defense and further stimulate the nation's militarism.

The Purpose and the Price

Millions of Americans have acquired a vested interest in the lavish weapons systems that provide their livelihood, and in the foreign policies which have plunged the United States into a spiraling arms race with the Soviet Union. Our containment policy has made us the world's leading salesman of armaments and committed us to defense of "freedom" in almost fifty countries—some with regimes of dubious worthiness.[8] Generated by these global military involvements, the vast military-industrial "team" has become a powerful force for its own growth and for the perpetuation of those involvements. Huge military machines designed for the defense of peace have historically sought things to do.

So the American economy is hooked on the stimulants of defense expenditures and defense employment. Any efforts to reduce major defense programs, to cut defense costs, or to reduce the size of the armed forces will have widespread economic, social, and political effects. The withdrawal symptoms will be much more painful than those caused by the pullout of troops from Vietnam, which gives mostly pains of pride. Reduction of defense expenditures will cause economic aches to many, but in the long run should give relief to the taxpayers in general. The alternative to "kicking the habit" of swollen defense costs may well be a disastrous trip on an inflated war-economy escalator.

Some Defense Department authorities, of course, see no alternatives to a large defense-industrial combine needed to supply the arms and equipment required by the military forces in order to carry out their missions. To forget about trying to defend the United States, stopping arms production, and trusting the peaceful intentions of the Communist powers is not an acceptable solution, they maintain—nor is a program to put defense production in the hands of the Federal government historically attractive. Conversion to a vast bureaucracy of government plants and arsenals would create a monster worse than that of the Pentagon.

Prudence indicates the wisdom of maintaining a widely dispersed industrial base ready to provide modern weapons and supplies when needed. The production capabilities of American private industry are superior to any in the world and are the foundation of U.S. military power. The recent concern about the defense establishment is not so much due to the symptomatic costs and waste as it is the purposes and powers at work.

The Air Force Association Statement of Policy pronounced at Houston, Texas in 1969, spells out a general concern:

> Above all, the American people must be told the truth
> about the price and the purpose of our military political
> commitments. . . . Only thus can both the common
> defense and domestic tranquillity best be served.

To this we add our Amen.

Footnotes

[1] Julius Duscha, *Arms, Money and Politics,* Ives Washburn Inc., New York, 1965, p. 62.
[2] Bill Winn, "Marching Through Georgia," *Atlanta Magazine,* March, 1969.
[3] *Statistical Abstract of the United States, 1968,* Department of Commerce.
[4] "Esquire's Official Court of Inquiry into the Present State of the U.S. Navy," *Esquire,* July, 1969.

[5] *Statistical Abstract,* Department of Commerce, Washington, D.C., 1968.
[6] "Around the World: Quiet Cutback by U.S." *U.S. News & World Report,* August 4, 1969.
[7] Standard Rate and Data Service, Business Publications, June 24, 1969.
[8] J. W. Fulbright, Owen-Corning lecture, Denison University, Granville, Ohio, April 18, 1969.

Chapter IV

CAREERISM

"War is an art, to attain perfection in which, much time
and experience, particularly for the officers, are necessary."
John C. Calhoun, 1782–1850

In an address to the graduating cadets of the U.S. Military
Academy on June 4, 1969, General William C. Westmoreland,
Chief of Staff of the U.S. Army, stated the standards of leadership
and character required of the modern career officer:

> You must possess unquestioned personal integrity
> and the highest of morals.
>
> You must be fair, consistent and dignified.
>
> You must be able to face the dangers that every man
> in uniform has faced since time immemorial.
>
> You must be able to undergo the physical hardship
> that not every man is willing to endure.
>
> You must readily accept discipline—but what is more
> difficult, you must be the disciplinarian.
>
> You must accept periodic criticism of the military
> as inevitable, some of which may be unfair and irre-
> sponsible. However, you should not be a slave to this
> criticism, but take solace in the knowledge that you are
> defending a civilian society that permits free expression.
>
> You must willingly accept and adjust to family sep-
> arations whenever national interest demands.
>
> And in a period when material things are becoming
> more and more the incentive for the individual, you

must take pride in a job 'well done' rather than material remuneration.

In short, you must display those attributes that you expect—even demand—from those whom you will lead.

The general then stated, "These standards prescribe a man of unusual motivation, a man of dedication, of dedication to serve our nation for the gratification that only service to one's country can give."

The Elite Cadre

There are about 422,000 commissioned male officers on active duty in the four armed services. Of these well over half are junior ranking reserve officers on temporary active duty. Only about 63,000 regular career officers are in the elite cadre of senior ranks —the commanders, lieutenant colonels, colonels, Navy captains, admirals, and generals, but they constitute the nuclei of professionalism in the military establishment. In spite of civilian controls and the national urge toward peace, this small group of men exerts a considerable martial influence upon the government and the American people. The professional officer corps is at the fountainhead of America's new militarism. These men are the career professionals who have survived the attrition of frequent selection and have learned their trade in fifteen or more years of schooling, demanding service, and combat experience. They are the commanders, staff planners, managers, and decision-makers who determine the policies, doctrines, and direction of the armed forces.

Membership in the military elite comes only after many years of professional education, training, and experience. Military career patterns are highly standardized, and it is possible to identify the highlights and events that were crucial to the average officer's career. Until the very recent past, education at a service academy was the first and foremost requirement for a career Army or Navy officer. The hard core of high-ranking military leaders has been mostly academy graduates, and as a group the graduates of West Point and Annapolis still dominate the upper ranks of the Army and Navy.

The Navy top leadership has always been largely academy trained, and Professor Janowitz noted in 1950 that 96.6 percent of the admirals were graduates of the Naval Academy.[1] As of January, 1969, 252 or 82 percent of the Navy's total of 307 admirals were Annapolis graduates. In the lowest flag rank of Rear Admiral there were 54 non-Naval Academy officers out of a total of 262, indicating the emergence of NROTC products in the top naval ranks.

Although Academy dominance of senior naval ranks is slowly changing with the advancement of ROTC civilian college men who have made careers in the Navy since World War II, Academy men will probably continue to see that their fellow alumni get a large share of the top ranks. Of thirty-one captains selected for flag rank in 1964, for example, only three were from civilian colleges; the rest were USNA. The group typified the other military services' patterns of qualifications for promotion to star rank. All but three wore personal combat decorations for bravery, ten were recipients of the Navy Cross, eleven of them had a total of seventeen Silver Stars, and twelve had the Bronze Star Medal. Seven of them had Legion of Merit award for important service, and there were fifteen Distinguished Flying Crosses in the group. All but one had been to advanced senior-level schools and seven held masters' degrees. They averaged 49.5 years of age and ranged from forty-seven to fifty-three years old. There were twelve aviators, nine submariners, seven surface officers, and three engineering specialists.[2]

The more extensive and varied officer requirements of the Army have not permitted West Point to monopolize the Army to the same degree as Naval Academy graduates in the Navy. In 1898, West Pointers made up 80 percent of the Army's officer corps. In World War II almost all top Army commands were held by Academy-trained officers, but by 1950 the West Pointers made up only 58.4 percent of the Army general ranks.[3]

By July of 1969 the Army's 519 general officers were divided almost equally between West Pointers and non-Academy graduates. Although the senior ranks of general and lieutenant general were

87 percent West Point graduates, the newest generals in the rank of brigadier were 64 percent non-Academy officers, indicating a trend toward more ROTC and OCS trained officers in the top Army ranks.

Major General Samuel W. Koster, USA, Superintendent of West Point, has reiterated that "West Point graduates set the tone for the Army's officer corps. They are recognized and emulated wherever they serve." Nevertheless, the image and prestige of the Academy has reportedly been slipping, and it has even experienced some recruiting problems. In past years the Academy annually turned away scores of highly qualified applicants; now it has trouble filling its expanding corps of cadets in the face of civilian college competition and the more recent antimilitary sentiments of American youth. West Point's influence within the Army has also weakened in recent years. There is some question as to the relative merits of West Point officers and ROTC products of civilian schools. As in the other services, the ROTC and OCS products have proved to be as capable officers as most of the Academy graduates.

In the past few years the exodus of service Academy graduates from the military profession has increased to a point where, five years after graduation, between 20 and 25 percent have resigned. In 1957 the ROTC program was providing more young officers for the Regular Army than West Point, and the Army has been striving since World War II to retain more ROTC graduates as career officers. Now, as ROTC and OCS trained officers integrate into the regular establishment, there should be a rising percentage of non-Academy graduates in the senior ranks of both the Army and the Navy.*

Of all the armed forces, the Air Force bears the greatest resemblance to the skill base of civilian society because of the complexity of its technology. Also, as the newest service, stemming from the Army Air Corps, its relative expansion in response to World War II demands was the most extensive. Being the youngest serv-

* The high qualities of leadership, skill, and dedication of service Academy graduates in peace as well as war have been exemplified by America's astronauts, a large percentage of whom are products of West Point or Annapolis.

ice, it does not have a traditional career pattern as an entrenched element of its organizational identity to the extent that it exists in the Army and Navy.

The officers holding the rank of brigadier general or higher in 1951 were for the most part recruited into the officer corps of the U.S. Army Air Corps. The infusion of large numbers of non-Academy men during World War II produced many officers whose distinguished-combat records qualified them for rapid promotion in the new and expanding Air Force, so there was a relatively small cadre of Academy graduates in the U.S. Air Force when it became a separate service. As graduates of the Air Force Academy become available for high ranks and command, they will get a good share of the top ranks, but most likely they will not receive the disproportionate promotions to general officer rank and the high commands as have been typical for Army and Navy graduates of the service academies. The proportion of Academy-trained officers between 1951 and 1964 declined at all top Air Force levels except that of lieutenant general. The percentage of Academy graduates in the Air Force's generals' ranks in 1964 were: general, 69 percent; lieutenant general, 67 percent; major general, 49 percent; brigadier general, 23 percent.[4] In January, 1969, 104 of the Air Force's 443 general officers were West Pointers.

The U.S. Marine Corps is probably the most tradition-bound of the American armed services, owing primarily to the fact that its technological base has not changed as extensively as those of the other services. Having retained its fundamental character as a ground combat organization, it has not been inclined to be dominated by its small percentage of Naval Academy graduates. In fact, it has had only six Academy graduates serve as Commandant since 1911. A distinguished combat and command record has generally typified the desirable qualifications for Commandant of the Corps, and source of origin has not been an important factor.

In 1964, under the regime of Naval Academy graduate, Commandant Wallace M. Green, the Marine Corps had more Academy graduates in top slots than in any previous period. Two of five lieutenant generals were Annapolis men, twelve of twenty-three major generals were USNA graduates, but only three of thirty-one brigadier generals were Academy men. Since 1967 the trend in the Marine Corps has again been toward a reduction in totals of Academy graduates in general rank. Twelve of the Marines' seventy-seven generals were Academy graduates as of January, 1969.

The Marine Corps not having a strong tradition of Academy graduates in its senior ranks has been able to develop a relatively strong career motivation among the bulk of its officers obtained from ROTC, Platoon Leaders Class, and officer candidate school sources. The Corps has also maintained a healthy leavening of officers selected from the ranks—and all Marine officers, regardless of source, assume the special *esprit de corps* which gives them an organizational identity and status not so typical of the larger services.

Actually the influence and importance of the Military and Naval Academy graduate have not been based so much upon their numbers but rather upon their ideologies, their attitudes, and their values which have always dominated the ethics and set the standards and goals for the American military establishment. The Academy graduates have traditionally established the professional tone —as well as created the militaristic philosophies of the armed forces. Since the academies have necessarily stressed service loyalty rather than identification with the national military establishment, the endless interservice rivalries of the American military profession have also been fostered to a large degree by Academy educations.[5] However, achieving high and influential rank in the armed forces also hinges upon other important criteria of achievement than the source of education.

Professional Schools

Not many institutions, industries, or civilian branches of government have the resources, techniques, or doctrine for training leaders such as are now employed by the armed forces in their excellent graduate-school systems. Military leaders are taught to command large organizations, to plan complicated operations, and to wield influence. Frequent attendance at schools is important to officer career development.

The military career pattern falls generally into three levels:

tactical officers, middle-level commanders, and senior ranks of generals and admirals. The sequence of professional education fits this pattern. First a college-level education, civilian or academy, followed by specialized service training such as artillery, flight, or armor instruction. Specialized schools are attended within the first five to ten years after commissioning and are designed to train the officer for the initial responsibilities of tactical leadership. Next at the command and general-staff-level school, after ten to fifteen years service, the career officer is prepared for the duties of middle- and higher-level command and staff responsibilities. Then finally, in preparation for general or flag rank, the curriculum of the services' war colleges is oriented to strategic doctrines. At the very pinnacle of the military school system the national-level joint schools, such as the Industrial College of the Armed Forces and the National War College, prepare selected colonels and Navy captains for war industrial planning and the integration of national security strategy and national policies at the highest levels of government and industry.

In addition, the requirements for more skills and specialization in the career development of officers have resulted in the practice of sending selected officers to civilian schools for advanced degrees in subjects of value to the armed forces. More than 40 percent of recent West Point classes have attended civilian graduate schools within twelve years after leaving the Academy. The Air Force has a similar high percentage.

Attendance and distinguished performance at these postgraduate military and civilian schools are important to the career advancement of the regular officers. The skills on which a reputation at a war college are built are considered relative to the officer's potential as a manager and planner. Friendships made at the schools among peer groups also provide new alliances important to career development and promotion.[6]

Military school instruction is concerned largely with doctrines, professional codes, weapons systems, tactics, and techniques. It produces technicians and disciples, not thinkers. Many school-trained officers are highly intelligent and capable operators but their profession doesn't encourage them to be intellectual. However, among the professions, there are none that compare to the military in their organized and large-scale ability to re-inform and stimulate their executives to conform to the principles and methods of the trade.

So not the least of the effects of the military and naval post-graduate schooling is the reindoctrination and refreshment of the service codes and values, the renewal of service doctrinal beliefs, and the military point of view. They rarely, for example, produce officers inclined to speak out against any service doctrines or national military policies—or militaristic ventures such as Vietnam.[7]

Making Numbers

For most of their careers the professionals are exposed to constant competition for selection and promotion. Attrition is high, and only the most capable survive to attain the elite senior ranks. Few other professions have such rigorous selection systems; as a result the top military leaders are high-caliber men who have been carefully chosen.

Promotion to the senior ranks depends upon a pattern of career qualifications which are generally similar in each of the services. Promotion by selection systems with selection boards made up of senior officers is also uniform in the services. Furthermore, the boards tend to select officers in their own image and thus perpetuate a somewhat stereotyped individual who fits the ideals of each of the services. Not being business organizations, where profits are clear evidence of successful performance, the measure of officers considered qualified for higher rank and command have some criteria not found in civilian life, and unlike civilian careers, most military men are retired at the beginning of their most productive years. At the same time there remains much similarity between advancement in the hierarchy of a large corporation and promotion in the armed forces.

Career success in the military frequently hinges upon being in the right spot at the right time. Changing assignments every two or three years enables the officer to move suddenly from an obscure job to one of considerable career potential. A good command or staff billet can afford an opportunity to perform in a combat situa-

tion or to serve a prominent commander and earn a valuable com-
mendation. Therefore ambitious officers seek command assignments and request duty where the action is.

In times of war and emergency, career officers are well aware
of the benefits to be derived from a tour in the field or at sea with
a combat command. No professional officer ever desires to create
the impression that he is anything but eager and ready for a combat-
zone assignment. In spite of the recently increased acceptance of
the value of the military manager, the traditional American military
goal is to serve with distinction as a leader in battle.

For many career officers war is an exciting adventure, a competitive game, and an escape from the dull routines of peacetime.
The possibilities of combat and expeditionary service also provide
opportunities for distinction which continually inspire and challenge
the professional. The code of professional honor has had to be
self-generating by drawing upon its own historical achievement,
and although the pursuit of glory in combat is not a dominant
ideal of the modern American military man, the ideals of toughness, aggressiveness, sentiment and courage blend into a typically
heroic mold.

The heroic image still typifies the American military ideal, and
as a general practice each of the services selects officers for higher
ranks who have served heroically in combat or who have demonstrated a desire to gain glory and distinction for themselves and
their service. Furthermore, this special awareness of combat service
and career distinction is openly displayed by all ranks in the form
of campaign ribbons and decorations. The knowledgeable observer
can quickly "read" the high points of a military man's career by
the ribbons he wears. For this reason, within the profession, ribbons and decorations are status symbols of great importance and
quickly help to define the professional pecking order and qualifications of each individual. Considerable sacrifice and effort are made
in order to earn prestigious awards and ribbons which become
blue-chip assets in promotion opportunities.

Since the Korean War, the professionals have joked about the
merits of small wars. "It's not much of a war—but better than
none at all"; or, "It's the only war we've got." The mature military

man, however, has normally mixed feelings of eagerness and reservation about going off to war.

First, he has his overriding sense of sworn duty as a professional fighting man. If the President, his Commander in Chief, deems it necessary to commit U.S. forces anywhere for any reason, the professional is obliged to go without question and as a loyal member of his service. If the issues of national defense and popular support are clear and certain, the individual's problem is made simpler.

However, Cold War contingency deployments and limited war expeditionary service have not been so simple. Many career professionals have spent years of their lives since 1945 at bases overseas, on duty at sea or cruising the skies, and patrolling the borders of the Free World. Frequent and prolonged family separations with the related financial strains, burdens put upon lonely wives, disruptive household moves and fatherless children—all tend to dampen the professional's enthusiasm for foreign duty and military ventures. The older the fighting man becomes, the less excitement and satisfaction he finds in each new emergency deployment, unless he sees promises of career opportunity and benefit which override the possible dangers and inconveniences.

Few good military men, and especially officers, will deny that the challenges of command and leadership presented by combat are both tempting and attractive. For the highly trained ambitious and conscientious officer, "the battle is the pay-off." It's what the business of soldiering, flying, or naval gunnery and seamanship is all about. The real professional may have no great devotion to the cause for which the President has committed him, he probably has no personal hatred for the designated enemy—and he is certainly not usually happy to leave the safety and comfort of his home and loved ones. But if he's a man of pride, if he's a true professional, he will quickly fall in step with his comrades. He will want to "march to the sound of the guns." He will ask to go, he will seek a command, and he will hope for some personal share of the glory. This has been the nature of fighting men for ages. The American armed forces have attained such a high degree of professionalism since 1945 that it is now expected that all hands are "ready" for battle—and it is well understood that combat duty provides the surest path to distinction and promotion in each of the fighting services.

The caution with which new developments in the science of war is accepted by the military tends to develop within the professional officer a conservative but realistic view of himself and his profession. The career officer has traditionally been accused of regarding with suspicion those aspects of civilian politics and diplomacy which affect his work. Actually, he is not suspicious of civilian society, but is only puzzled occasionally at what he deems a lack of realism with which civilian affairs are often conducted. The military man considers himself a realist in matters of military power, enemy capabilities, and threats to the nation. His mission is to defend his country and his specialties are weapons, combat power, logistics, and planning. National insurance is too serious, he believes, to be based upon idealism, chivalry, or wishful thinking. Although basically he claims to detest war—he regards it as the inevitable arbiter of human affairs. The military profession thus suspects treaties and alliances and prefers to express its distaste for war in the form of strong military preparedness.[8]

The extent to which the military profession abhors war has always been debatable. In 1835 Alexis de Tocqueville wrote in *Democracy in America* that since "an officer has no property but his pay, and no distinction but that of military honors," the military professional desires war "because war makes vacancies."

The purpose of the modern U.S. defense establishment is to prevent wars, yet in this mission it has not been notably successful. At the same time there is no avoiding the fact that individuals in the profession have found wars to be a means for advancement and both a motivation and justification for all the planning and training.

The Staff "Indians"

The men who rise to the top of the military hierarchy have usually demonstrated their effectiveness as leaders, planners, and organization managers. They may also have performed heroically in combat, but most of all they must have demonstrated their loyalty as proponents of their own service's doctrine and their dedication to the defense establishment and its policies. The over-riding sense of duty to follow orders is the basis of the military professional's effective performance in the arena of defense policy planning. The military planners have their guiding doctrinal beliefs, their organizational loyalties, their discipline, and their ambitions. The civilians in the Office of the Secretary of Defense and in the Department of State can rarely play the defense policy planning game with the same advantages. The military are organized for planning, they work harder, and they concentrate on being instantly ready to solve the problem with military action, insuring at the same time that their respective service receives its proper mission, role, and recognition in the operation.

Little known outside of the profession and carefully guarded in their "secret" offices, the services' *planners* are a most influential group in the military establishment. These largely nameless and obscure officers are predominantly eager, hard-working, and ambitious young lieutenant colonels, Navy commanders, colonels, and captains who have been carefully selected for duty on the top staffs. They are qualified by attendance and distinguished performance at the service and joint schools. They are capable staff-paper writers, articulate briefing officers, and professionally well informed. They have demonstrated their loyalty to their services' "party line." The planners are the key schemers and military doctrinaires. Their duty and purpose is to analyze defense problems and missions, prepare position papers, formulate policy drafts, organize plans and programs, and to put all of these ideas into words and briefs for their staff chiefs and for the generals and admirals.

The most select and senior planners are assigned to the Joint Staff and serve the Joint Chiefs of Staff in the Pentagon. They work on the national level JCS plans and problems which become the basis of the national strategic policies and the directives to the unified commands. Theoretically they are divorced from their service loyalties and biases while serving on the Joint Staff. But each officer understands that his parent service keeps an eye on his performance and expects him to faithfully represent his service's doctrine and to protect its functions, roles, and missions in all phases of joint planning.

At each of the four services' headquarters in Washington "joint action" officers in the general staff sections do the detail planning and prepare the position papers for their respective chiefs of service —the Army Chief of Staff, Chief of the Air Staff, Chief of Naval Operations, and the Marine Commandant. These officers analyze every item on the Joint Chiefs' weekly agenda of problems which is of concern to the service and prepare briefings of the problem and the recommended service position for their chiefs. They conduct word-by-word analysis of the study or plan under consideration to insure that their respective service position, doctrine and interests are protected and reflected in the paper before it gets JCS approval. They prepare "talking papers" for their chiefs to use at the JCS meetings and they provide him with addendum or corrigendum memos that he can submit to the JCS in order to make the paper acceptable to his service before it is approved or forwarded to the Secretary of Defense.

There is nothing outside of Congress' legislative bill production which compares to the paper ritual of the Joint Chiefs and the service staffs in the creation of national-level defense plans, programs, and policies. In this process the top generals and the various civilian appointees in the Office of the Secretary of Defense tend to become captives of these "Indians"—the planners—who do the research, write the papers, learn the details, and have the answers. The vast number of projects and problems which occupy the efforts of the top military staffs are frequently so complex, technical, or extensive that they have to be reduced to simplified briefings in order to be digested and even understood by the busy service chiefs and the Pentagon civilians. In the process, opinions tend to become facts, and what commences as objective analysis crystalizes into policies and positions. The recommendations of middle-level staff officers go forward to the highest echelons of the defense establishment because the top leaders either don't fully understand the problem or have no other ideas and information.

It is in this arena of staff planners on the joint staffs where the results of careerism, parochialism, and interservice rivalry become dominant factors affecting the ideological values of the military profession, the purposes of many defense programs, the aggressive nature of contingency planning—and the militarism of the defense establishment. Officers in staff planning assignments have only a few years to make their marks as high-level staff officers. They work hard to satisfy their chiefs to foster their service's doctrines and to establish a reputation as loyal defenders of their respective organizations. In the process they also put out the finest staff work in the Federal departments.

The Dangerous Years

If the ranks of lieutenant colonel (Navy commander) and colonel (captain) are the most satisfying and challenging of a normal military career, they are also the most hazardous. The normal rate of attrition for selection and promotion from lieutenant colonel to colonel is about 50 percent in each of the services. From colonel to brigadier general, the attrition or pass-over rate runs between 80 and 90 percent of the eligible officers. These are the big promotion hurdles for the career officer who hopes to complete thirty or more years of service and to retire in a star rank. The promotion perils faced at this stage of their careers probably contribute more than any other factor to the stresses, the zealotry, and the parochialism of the professional leaders and to the course of militarism which has helped lead the military establishment into its recent troubles.

The ranks of lieutenant colonel, colonel, or Navy captain find the average officer in middle age and in mid-career. He has given his best years to military or naval service; he is usually a family man, a home owner, with a sizable equity in his military retirement benefits. He is trapped by his career and has numerous reasons to stick with it and strive to move ahead. It takes a courageous and confident officer to voluntarily leave the system at this stage of life. It's easier to work hard, conform, and attempt to fulfill the criteria for promotion.

The average lieutenant colonel or commander has twenty-four years of commissioned service and is about forty-six years old. The average colonel or captain coming up for selection to brigadier general or rear admiral has about twenty-seven years' service and is forty-nine years old. These officers have teen-age children and

pending expenses of schooling. Their age puts them in a group that
has relatively less appeal on the civilian job market. Their active
duty pay and allowances place them in a respectable and secure
upper-middle income bracket. (A lieutenant colonel with twenty-
four years' service has an annual income of over $17,500; a colonel
with over twenty-six years' service, about $20,950. The rank of
brigadier general will pay $23,400 annually, which compares
respectably with civilian executive compensation rates.)[9] So these
senior officers have strong motives to win promotion. They have
many personal reasons to follow the pattern of successful career
officers and to conform to the military professional's stereotype.
The ideologies and ethics of the profession which motivated the
officer in his youth, like the ideals of the young liberal college
student, become qualified by the hard realities of family responsibility, job status, and retirement security. The middle-aged career
officer has about the same self-interests as any other professional,
despite his creeds of service and sacrifice.

The Old School Spirit

They may not field the biggest and best football teams, but for
sheer spirit, color, and competition the annual meeting of the Army
and Navy academies is a contest hard to match. Every game has
been a sell-out for many years. The traditional event is usually held
at Philadelphia, and for hours before game time the highways
leading into the city are jammed with fans from up and down the
Eastern seaboard, and their automobiles are bedecked with "Beat
Army" or "Sink Navy" streamers. Not all the fans are alumni of
the service academies; some are merely loyal veterans of the Army
or Navy, and many are families of cadets and midshipmen. But the
roads and railroads from Washington, D.C., command post of the
armed services, are loaded with career officers and academy graduates. Nothing so rejuvenates the enthusiasm and *esprit* of a jaded
and frustrated Pentagon colonel or Navy bureau captain as does
the sight and sound of the corps of cadets and regiment of midshipmen—or the direct confrontation on the gridiron of the Army
and the Navy. As the old proverb has it, "There's no love lost be-

tween soldiers and sailors." To the casual observer, surrounded by graying and distinguished officers, the noisy, competitive spirit and some spleen expressed by the partisans and the comments about the merits or antecedents of the other side come as somewhat of a surprise to anyone accustomed to the less vehement sophistication of most Eastern college football fans. The regiments of midshipmen and cadets are unique cheering sections. They stand, shout, and cheer constantly throughout the game. The alumni have been through the same drill as undergraduates and express a similar spirit year after year. The Army-Navy football games are serious contests for the fans, undergraduates, and alumni. The games are frequently vivid, emotional experiences, and do much to establish attitudes of interservice rivalry which persist for a lifetime.

The Army-Navy (and now Air Force Academy) rivalry on the gridiron extends into all their other sports. No American college competes in as many sports as do the service academies. Most of the graduates of these fine schools become so imbued with school spirit that it remains with them throughout their careers and often reappears in the secret machinations of Pentagon planners and joint staff officers. Interservice rivalry is as American, normal, and intense as a football game. In the military it is perhaps a somewhat juvenile carry-over from school days, but many officers mature late in life—for them much of their career is an Army-Navy game.

Competition and rivalry are of course typical of American organizational experience. The armed forces professionals are basically no different from civilian organization men. Military career officers also seek success, recognition, and some security. They work for the organization and for rank and status in it. There is competition between individuals within the services, there is rivalry between the services, there are frequent contests between the Defense Department and other departments and Federal agencies—and then there is the most important rivalry, that between the military establishment and the many threatening and potential enemies it has identified throughout the world. Professional military men focus their energies on one or more of these rivals throughout most of their careers.

Military men are strong competitors in all of these arenas because as a group they are an especially vigorous, healthy, and athletic type and there is no doubt that a certain amount of rivalry has stimulated and benefited the armed forces. Most armed forces officers who rise to influential ranks are physically above average and have been active in competitive sports. In the modern U.S. services physical fitness has become somewhat of a fetish, and each of the services fosters exercise programs and athletic competition among its leaders. Most career officers want to be fit and skilled competitors and they take satisfaction in being best—in winning. Such success to a degree substitutes for personal financial profits and the accumulation of material wealth which motivates the ambitious civilian. Unlike corporation executives who can transfer their loyalties from one business organization to another, the military officer is committed to the service of his choice. If he wants to move up in the organization, he must become known as a faithful disciple of his service. In order to promote the organization and its success, he has to compete for goals other than dollar profits, within the fields of operational doctrines, service doctrines, roles and missions, defense appropriations, new weapons programs, and service prestige.

He also competes for recognition by the media and the public so that he can be proud of his service and maintain self-esteem. Each of the armed forces seeks favorable publicity and credit for its achievements as well as for its leaders and heroes. It provides nourishment and fulfillment to the organization to have its image enhanced by distinguished performances. The objectives of publicity and public relations are to improve the pride and morale of the men in the services, to encourage loyalty and understanding on the part of relatives, to attract volunteer recruits, and to gain the support of the news media, civic officials, and Congress. These are the publics upon which the strength and status of each service ultimately depend.

Among the well-indoctrinated military professionals, there is frequently only a fine line between zeal and zealotry in these matters. Professor Morris Janowitz, in his study of the professional soldier, said that military careerists were usually dedicated men—"not too different from the priesthood and ministry in serving a cause." [10]

Footnotes

[1] Morris Janowitz, *The Professional Soldier,* Free Press, New York, 1960.
[2] Lt. (jg) C. E. Erbsen, USNR, "Fiscal Year 1965 Flag Officers," *Navy Magazine,* September 1964.
[3] *Ibid.*
[4] *Air Force Register,* Office of the Air Adjutant, 1964.
[5] Janowitz, *The Professional Soldier, op. cit.*
[6] *Ibid.*
[7] John T. Hayward, Adm. USN-Ret. "The Second-Class Military Adviser: His Cause and Cure," *Armed Forces Management,* November, 1968.
[8] Carl M. Guelzo, Major, USA. "Chore or Challenge, A Professional Ethic for the Nuclear Age." *U.S. Naval Institute Proceedings,* May, 1964.
[9] Armed services pay scale effective 1 July 1969.
[10] Janowitz, *The Professional Soldier, op. cit.*

Chapter V

READINESS

"Rapid and effective counteraction is the single most important operational capability for limited war."
Army Information Digest, *June 1958*

The Pearl Harbor Syndrome

The successful surprise attacks by the armed forces of Imperial Japan initiated on December 7, 1941, had a traumatic effect upon the American military establishment from which it has not yet recovered. The heavy losses on Oahu, Hawaii, at Pearl Harbor, and the subsequent defeats suffered by the U.S. Army, Navy, and Marines throughout the Pacific area in the early months of 1942 were shocking experiences which not only united the nation in its determination to fight back but convinced the American military forces that readiness for war was the most important responsibility of the defense establishment.

For some seventy years prior to Pearl Harbor, the most usual theme of American military literature was the need for *stronger* military forces. It was the military's answer to the problems of war and peace. Military power in being, not merely potential national resources, would determine the outcome of future war, the military leaders maintained.[1]

By mid-1941, spurred by the Nazis' aggression and war in Europe, as well as the growing threat posed by Japan, all elements of the U.S. military establishment were undergoing expansion and modernization. The Army had reached a strength of 1,500,000 with almost twenty-eight divisions in service. A two-ocean Navy was being rapidly fitted out, and naval personnel strength had increased from 126,400 in September, 1939, to 325,000 in December, 1941. The Marine Corps consisted of 25,000 Leathernecks on December 7. A state of unlimited national emergency had been declared on May 27, 1941. Yet, when war came in the Pacific in December, 1941, American military forces were caught by surprise and were defeated by the Japanese in almost every engagement.

For sheer audacity the Japanese raid on Pearl Harbor is probably without parallel in naval warfare. It entailed moving a carrier task force undetected across 3,500 miles of open sea to within striking range of America's most powerful Pacific base. For the attack to succeed, the Americans had to remain uninformed and unprepared, the fleet in the harbor, and their aircraft on the ground until the attack was upon them. Incredible though it was, that is exactly what happened. However, the U.S. armed forces in the Pacific in December, 1941, were by no means small or weak—they were simply not ready. The emphasis was still on training not on defense. They had not yet learned the hard lessons of war and defeat. The lessons came swiftly and without mercy during the following weeks.

In less than six months the Japanese army and navy completed a remarkable series of advances throughout the South and Central Pacific, carving out a gigantic empire which took the allies more than three years to recapture. American forces went down in defeat and into captivity wherever the Japanese attacked: Wake Island; Guam; Tientsin, China; Bataan; and Corregidor. The *USS Houston* was sunk, the carrier *Saratoga* torpedoed. Only at Midway Island in June, 1942, were the Japanese amphibious forces denied a landing and their supporting forces defeated in a great naval victory that stemmed the tide.

The disastrous events of those early months of World War II resulted in two major additions to American military doctrine. To the earlier policies of preparedness to meet any possible threat with *sufficient and modern forces in being,* the armed forces each evolved rejuvenated doctrines of *combat readiness,* and the new Joint Chiefs of Staff added the doctrine of *unity of command* as a major lesson learned from the debacle at Pearl Harbor. The services embraced the ideas of combat readiness enthusiastically. Unity of command has sometimes been a less palatable doctrine.

Fleet Readiness

The principles of *readiness* for combat have been dominant in U.S. Naval and Marine Corps doctrine since long before the Japanese attacks plunged America into World War II. By their very nature, naval forces have an inherent and organic state of combat readiness. A fully manned warship, underway at sea, is essentially a fighting machine ready for combat at all hours. It has mobility, firepower, and a crew that can man battle stations within minutes. In peacetime, warships are normally fully provisioned with ammunition and combat supplies. Their daily training drills include "general quarters" and battle stations. The entire ship responds rapidly to the commands of the captain and is capable of exerting its complete range of combat powers. Only when a modern fleet is in port with anchors down and crews ashore does a naval force lose some of its readiness, and even then, sophisticated intelligence, surveillance, and dispersion procedures reduce vulnerability. Japanese success at Pearl Harbor resulted from deficiencies in each of these procedures on December 7, 1941.

Peacetime sea duty in the Navy is closer to wartime routine than the peacetime duty of any other service. Long periods at sea, watch standing, drills, and practice gunnery are typical of fleet operations, in war or peace. Thus, naval men literally sleep with their guns, and readiness for battle is a way of life. For this reason the Navy has traditionally been the most belligerent of the services and still considers itself the "front line of defense," the initial instrument of national military power.

The Marine Corps long ago staked out its claim as *the* military "force in readiness." Marines have always considered themselves as the appropriate and initial instrument of national military power for the simple reason that historically it has been their role to land wherever and whenever American lives and property are in danger. The United States, before the air age, was essentially a maritime power and the naval forces were the forward line of defense and the first on the scene of overseas crises. The Marine landing forces went ashore to conduct a wide variety of peace-keeping, security, or limited combat operations—and "such other duties as the President might direct"—without a declaration of war. The U.S. Army was not normally employed so readily, as it required some degree of mobilization and slow movement to embarkation ports, as well as a declaration of emergency or war.

The Leathernecks, on the other hand, were trained and indoctrinated for rapid embarkation and movement overseas. Traditionally Marine expeditionary forces had been quickly assembled and dispatched to disorderly areas in the Caribbean and in Asia which were in the sphere of U.S. interests. "Combat readiness" became a central theme of the amphibious doctrines developed by Marines in the years prior to World War II and continues to be Marine Corps gospel. The information handbook, published by the Headquarters of Fleet Marine Forces in the Pacific in 1965, specifies that the Marines' mission is "to be prepared, on the shortest notice, to advance our country's interests by action varying from a silent show of force to a full-scale amphibious attack." "Readiness . . . is a Marine watchword." "The most important readiness factor of all, however, is the individual Marine's traditional state of mental readiness—his eagerness to get moving, to be the first on the scene of action to be the FIRST TO FIGHT!"

Air Alert

It was the Air Force's Strategic Air Command (SAC), however, which established new standards of readiness for battle in the Cold War years following the Korean War. The strategy of massive atomic retaliation enunciated by Secretary Dulles hinged upon the deterrent effects of the Strategic Air Command's giant bombers' abilities to survive an enemy first strike, become airborne, penetrate Russian air defenses, and deliver a crushing atomic blow upon dozens of key targets in the USSR.

To make such a capability a credible fact, the aggressive bomber commander of World War II, General Curtis E. LeMay, put together one of the most complex, highly trained, and dedicated military apparatuses ever assembled. SAC became not only the most powerful military force in the world but the key element of

America's basic national military strategy for prevention of Russian aggression and the preservation of peace. All military plans and policies revolved around atomic warfare concepts, called the "New Look," and limited, conventional warfare capabilities were given relatively low priorities. During the years between 1952 and 1960 the U.S. Air Force and SAC enjoyed the status and prestige of being "number one" in the hearts and minds of civilian defense leaders, and Congress allocated a large share of the annual defense budget for Air Force bombers as evidence of their infatuation with atomic firepower.

The well-publicized capabilities of SAC stressed constant readiness for combat. The bombers were kept in various phases of ready condition prepared to take off on short notice. The aircraft were fueled, armed with atomic bombs, and a percentage of each wing's crews at the many dispersed air bases were on duty around the clock, ready to take off within fifteen minutes. "SAC alerts" were the new and demanding training drills conducted frequently by SAC headquarters. Bombers were launched on realistic "Fail Safe" training missions where the flight crew learned it was only a drill some hours after take-off.

During the 1962 Cuban missile crisis, SAC went one step further toward war readiness by having a percentage of SAC bombers airborne, armed with atomic bombs, and prepared to head for assigned targets at all times. This practice existed from 1962 until some time during the Vietnam war when it was dropped in favor of the earlier and less expensive and less provocative readiness stance. The demise of this drill was also hastened by the accidental loss of several atomic bombs from airborne alert bombers off the coast of Spain and on Greenland.

Then, of course, the latest addition to SAC's deterrent forces, the Strategic Missile wings, are probably the ultimate in readiness. Squadrons of the Intercontinental Ballistic Missiles (ICBM) totaling over 1,000 atomic missiles sit in underground silos awaiting only the turn of keys in the hands of a few dozen young officers to launch death and destruction upon millions of people half a world away. The readiness for this calamity is now only a matter of minutes and a few short messages.

Other Air Force commands have also maintained a high state of readiness over the years. The North American Air Defense Command has maintained fighter-interceptors on strip alert around the clock at key locations.

During the swing away from a single national strategy based upon massive atomic retaliation, which began with the administration of President John F. Kennedy, the Air Force, like the other services, sought logical roles and missions in limited and conventional wars. With this new interest, and under the prompting of the U.S. Army, the Tactical Air Command experienced a renaissance and aspired to a high degree of readiness for strategic mobility, rapid world-wide deployment, and a capability to provide close air support for the U.S. Army. The war in Vietnam has provided an extensive test of the Tactical Air Command's readiness to conduct limited and counterinsurgency operations. The test of readiness to deploy massive tactical air power to a combat zone 10,000 miles away was successfully passed in 1965 and 1966. The effectiveness of tactical air power in a war of counterinsurgency remains debatable.

The Army Fire Brigade

In the latter 1950's the U.S. Army found itself desperately searching for roles and missions in a defense establishment which was dominated by the strategy of massive retaliation (the missions of the U.S. Air Force and naval air) and the theories of atomic warfare. The Army's role in a strategy of nuclear war was a relatively minor one. Ground forces were not considered to be the arm of decision—or even to constitute a deterrent force in the atomic war. So under the talented leadership of General Maxwell Taylor and other airborne indoctrinated officers, the Army reoriented its concepts toward the limited war role. This was also in reaction to its increasingly obsolete function as a mobilization base for a general war build-up in the pattern of World Wars I and II.

The Army planners determined that the forces required to wage a limited war and the priority of tasks would be significantly different from forces and tasks for an unlimited war. They believed that an important element in preparedness for limited war was to have a well-defined doctrine for limited war. By mid-1958 the Army had spelled out its proposed doctrine for limited war which it considered to be feasible in the atomic age.[2]

Among other principles, the new doctrine stressed that limited war is fought for limited objectives and that limitations would be placed upon area of conflict, targets subject to attack, and weapons employed. The Army also emphasized that *rapid* and effective counteraction is the single most important operational capability for limited war, that is, the ability to intervene quickly. Army leaders maintained that the Army's ability to react swiftly and decisively in case of a local war served as an ever-present preventive to general war.

With this new concept of the Army's role, the Army developed a doctrine of mobility and readiness comparable to that of the other three services. The Army maintained that readiness for combat was everybody's business. To make such a doctrine feasible, the Army designed the Strategic Army Corps (STRAC) around its airborne divisions and their popular techniques of airborne mobility. The STRAC was intended to apply measured or graduated force as an instrument of national policy in dealing with limited war. (It was the persistent and well-rationalized Army concepts of limited war and graduated retaliation or "flexible response" which were subsequently published in General Taylor's influential book, *The Uncertain Trumpet,* in 1959, and which became an important part of the defense policies of the Kennedy and Johnson administrations. They also provided the basic theories of "gradualism" for the McNamara team of civilian strategists and analysists in the 1961–1968 period.)[3]

Initially the Strategic Army Corps consisted of three combat-ready divisions based in the United States (the 82nd Airborne Division, 101st Airborne Division, and the 4th Infantry Division) and miscellaneous other support units. Total strength in 1959 was about 114,500 troops. This was the Army's new "Fire Brigade." The selected units were kept up to strength and received priority issue of new equipment. To put STRAC in the readiness business, units were maintained in a high state of alert, patterned after SAC. The

101st A/B Division kept one rifle company on fifteen-minute "alert duty" at all times. The men remained in the barracks area, gear was packed, trucks were loaded and ready to roll to the airfield where troop carrier aircraft were kept standing by. An entire battle group was kept on a three-hour alert duty status for two-week periods. All training was oriented toward readiness for airborne movement as the "spearhead" force for limited war. Army publicity touted STRAC as the "brush fire" force, "skilled, tough, ready around the clock" to fly to any spot in the world and apply measured force to stamp out trouble before it started.

The critical feature of the STRAC limited-war concept was its dependence upon strategic mobility in order to be a feasible doctrine. Although the Army leaders gave lip service to sealift mobility, the Army airborne officers were really interested mainly in airlift. Rapid reaction at air speed was the single most important requirement.

At the inception of the Army STRAC concept the other services resisted the whole idea at the national and joint planning level. The Air Force had no great interest in diverting funds to either new troop carrier aircraft or joint mobility airlift exercises with the Army. The Navy saw the airlift concept as a form of direct competition with the Navy's historic function of protecting and moving troops overseas by ship, as well as an Army attempt to usurp the Navy's role as the initial instrument of national policy in limited contingencies. The Marines viewed the Army plan with considerable suspicion as a scheme to steal the Marines' traditional role as the ready force which is always "first to fight." The Marines also customarily moved by amphibious shipping, and could see in the Army airlift plans the beginning of an Army-Air Force combine which could directly threaten the requirement for the Navy-Marine amphibious team.

Nevertheless, despite the interservice intrigue which boiled within the Pentagon and served to frustrate the Army's ambitions, until the appearance of Secretary McNamara, Army leaders pushed ahead. With the help of the Association of the U.S. Army pressures, effective publicity, and the logic of General Maxwell Taylor, the Army doctrine for limited war and the related need for increased airlift was approved by the administration of President John F. Kennedy. The single strategy of massive nuclear retaliation was modified by an "agonizing reappraisal" of U.S. policy, the possibility of limited war was recognized, and the U.S. Army revived in stature and importance. The Army began a modernization program. New conventional war weapons programs were initiated. A large increase in strategic air transports was approved. The Air Force teamed up with the Army and planned extravagant air mobility exercises.

The Strategic Army Corps was then expanded into a new joint unified command called "Strike Command," located at McDill Air Force Base, Florida. This is now essentially an Army-Air Force command and in many ways it served to crystallize the rivalry between the Army-Air Force team and the Navy-Marine Corps team in the constant search for missions and the competition for command and dominance in contingency plans.

Strike Command was organized in October, 1961, to include not only the Army STRAC but most other U.S. based combat and combat-support-type units of the Army and the Air Force's Tactical Air Command that were not already assigned to any of the unified area type of commands. Strike Command reports directly to the Joint Chiefs of Staff and the Secretary of Defense. The Strike Command is intended to provide an integrated, mobile, highly combat-ready force trained as a unit and instantly available for use as in augmenting existing theater forces under the unified commanders, or as the primary force for use in remote areas such as Central Africa or the Middle East.[4]

The new command established the readiness posture of U.S.-based Army forces on a par with the other services. Prior to the depletion of Strike's forces by unit deployment to Vietnam, the command conducted regular joint field tests and mobility exercises which culminated in the speedy invasion of the Dominican Republic and the rapid build-up of forces in Vietnam in 1965.

Airlift-Sealift

While airlift has been considered by the Army-Air Force team as the primary means of strategic mobility in quick reaction crisis,

under the guidance of Secretary of Defense McNamara the concept
of a balanced airlift-sealift strategy was evolved. Part of the lift
requirement "should be met by modern, fast and efficient sealift
responsive to Department of Defense direction," he stated. This
role would be filled by a Fast Deployment Logistics ship (FDL)
with high-speed roll-on, roll-off characteristics. These ships, geared
to a 20-knot speed, would carry, without disassembly, heavy
wheeled and tracked vehicles and even Army helicopters. They
would also serve as mobile forward area vehicle depots.

The proposed FDL ships have been considered by the Navy to
be deterrents analogous to the strategic retaliatory bomber and mis-
sile-weapons systems. These ships are conceived to act in concert
with the policy of land-based pre-positioning of Army material and
airlift of critical Army equipment by C-5A aircraft. Army personnel
moving in other commercial and military jet aircraft then act "as a
deterrent to hostile military adventures in any region of the globe."
The FDL's provide a flexible means for stationing combat equipment and supplies for land forces near any area of potential trouble
"for prompt use if needed," according to a Navy pamphlet explaining the concept. General Donn R. Pepke, Deputy Director for
Strategic Plans and Policy, in the Office of the Deputy Chief of
Staff for Military Operations, called the rapid deployment concepts
for the 1970's which provide for the marriage of airlifted personnel
with land- or sea-based pre-positioned material "a new advance in
warfare." This timely deployment of men and equipment to a
troubled area is expected to deter aggression and limit the spread of
conflict, once it starts, with lower commitments of forces and fewer
casualties to U.S. forces and less destruction to the country being
supported.[5] (For some reason this concept did not seem to work in
Vietnam.)

Despite the merits of the airlift-sealift concept, in 1967, 1968,
and 1969 Congress repeatedly scuttled the FDL ship program in
what many on the military-industry team considered was a deliberate attempt to undermine the military capability to support U.S.
foreign policy and world-wide commitments. Inasmuch as the FDL
ship-construction program called for thirty ships at a unit price
of $46.8 million, economy, as well as some doubts about the ag-

gressive policies it would support, probably also had a bearing upon the Congressional actions.

America's existing (1969) doctrines of readiness and rapid reaction depend upon the strategic mobility of both ships and aircraft which are designed to provide the capability to move the required forces rapidly. The current airlift and sealift programs comprise: the Military Airlift Command's strategic airlift aircraft (C-133, C-141, C-124, and forthcoming C-5A) and the troop ships, cargo ships, tankers, and "Forward Floating Depot" ships operated by the Military Sea Transportation Service. These forces, when augmented with the resources of commercial air and sealift in emergencies, combine to provide the total lift considered desirable to meet defense requirements. The Fiscal Year 1970–1974 Defense Program and the Fiscal Year 1970 Defense Budget again requested Congress to approve at least fifteen of the FDL ships which would provide an improved strategic lift capability in future years.

In his statement for the proposed Fiscal Year 1967 Defense Budget, Secretary McNamara indicated how far the defense establishment hoped to go down "readiness road." He stated, "We have each year consistently raised our goals both with regard to airlift and the sealift. We are now proposing an expanded airlift program which will provide by FY 1973 an equivalent thirty-day lift capability from West Coast airfields to Southeast Asia more than ten times greater than that available in FY 1961, and nearly double the goal I talked about last year."

This kind of vision undoubtedly thrilled the Pentagon's rapid-response planners—but in retrospect of the Vietnam experience it is unlikely that many citizens find a tenfold improvement in our ability to move American troops to Southeast Asia an attractive accomplishment.

The C-5A—Not How Much, But Why?

The concept of the highly ready quick-reaction force located in the United States, prepared for movement overseas by modern means of strategic airlift and sealift, has been largely based upon the C-5A aircraft program which became the center of interest and controversy in the spring of 1969.

The Lockheed C-5A Galaxy, super cargo aircraft, is an example of the Defense Department's tendency to become infatuated with new technology and equipment capabilities which can then be employed to justify new operational concepts and national strategies. The defense planners are so enthralled with the new capability that their concepts become the creatures of the weaponry and equipment, rather than merely means to accomplish the defense objectives deemed necessary by the American people and their government. Moreover, the military and the equipment manufacturers go to some lengths to sell the new strategic concepts and the related requirements for the new equipment. The new hardware is described as necessary for "national defense" and as a means to "halt communist aggression." New organizations to operate the equipment also open up command and career opportunities for the managing service. Additional generals, more staffs, and new supporting bases and facilities are also frequently deemed necessary.

The unique capabilities and unprogrammed costs of the C-5A cargo aircraft have been fully described in the press. Since the U.S. Air Force announced in May, 1969, that the aircraft might overrun their initially estimated cost by $2 billion or more, Congress and the media have strongly criticized the Air Force and Lockheed for what are considered to be highly irregular and questionable contracting and procurement procedures. Senator William Proxmire dubbed the repricing formula contained in the Lockheed contract as "one of the most blatant reverse incentives ever encountered" by the Economy in Government Subcommittee of the Joint Economic Committee.

A result of the furor over the inflated costs is that one very important aspect of the C-5A program has been neglected by the critics. It is the strategic concept for the operational usage of the giant transport upon which the requirement was based in the first place. Aside from the technical accomplishment of building the largest military cargo aircraft in the world, a plane which promises to far exceed its performance specifications, as well as its planned cost, there still remains the question of who needs it and for what purpose? Its size and performance are certainly not its primary justification.

The C-5A is the result of the Army's long-standing aspirations for air transported strategic mobility which would put the Army into the readiness business on the same basis as the other three services. In the years following the 1957 General Maxwell Taylor-Army "Strategic Mobility for Army Forces" studies, the Army pushed for an airlift capability to move strategic forces at air speeds from the United States to forward bases in the unified commands or to foreign combat zones. The objective was to lift division-size forces overseas and to support them for the initial thirty-day period by airlifted supply. The concept includes a capability to move Army units and their equipment to any spot on the globe (such as other Vietnams) at jet speed, and includes lifting the heavy combat vehicles and equipment at the same speed as the troops. The C-5A is designed to lift up to 100 tons of equipment and to operate from unimproved and restricted airfields in forward combat zones and undeveloped areas.

With such a capability Secretary McNamara felt he could make a case for a smaller U.S. Army strategically based in the United States rather than at forward bases on foreign soil. This concept was eventually adopted and spelled out in the 1966 annual Secretary of Defense posture statement which described the FY 1967 Budget and the strategies it was designed to support. McNamara stated that a central reserve of mobile General Purpose Forces in the United States, ready for *immediate* deployment, provides considerably more operational flexibility and does not require as big an overseas military establishment as does a strategy which relies on such geographically dispersed forces. However, rapid deployment from a central reserve requires very large strategic airlift and sealift forces in being and readily available at all times, he said. Also, part of the concept is that a heavy airlift capability will reduce the requirement of pre-stocking equipment, which is now kept available overseas, for troops airlifted from home stations.

The alternative to Army strategic mobility using airlift and the pre-stocking of forward supply depots is the old procedure of movement to ports of embarkation, loading ships (MSTS or civilian charter, which are not always readily available) and spending weeks and even months at sea, sailing to distant objective areas. The result is considerable passage of time from movement order to eventual deployment in the combat zone. Sealift poses time restrictions upon Army "readiness" in relation to the other three services. Such a policy would also prevent the Army from being quickly on the scene "anywhere, anytime around the clock" as a ready "brush-fire force."

During the Kennedy years and then the Johnson administration, the Air Force's airlift capabilities were modernized and increased well over 200 percent. In the period 1961–1967 over 470 C-130 Tactical Air Command (TAC) troop transports were procured and 208 C-141 jets were added to Military Airlift Command (MAC). In addition, during the same period hundreds of new civilian jets came into the airlines and were available to the Civil Reserve Air Fleet and for charter use by the military services. As a result, the Vietnam buildup and its subsequent logistic support have seen the largest, most successful and effective military airlift in history. There has been a constant stream of giant C-141 and commercial jets supplying troops and critical cargo and evacuating wounded Americans speedily back and forth across the Pacific. In-country movement of men and supplies has also been largely by TAC air transports in South Vietnam. Our military forces world-wide are now supported by the greatest national airlift capacity ever assembled. But this apparently is not enough. The C-5A requirement is based upon the concept and desire (not a proven need) to move the heaviest items of Army ground equipment, such as 50-ton tanks, by air at jet speed.

So, in 1965, the C-5A program began—designed to further increase the strategic airlift for movement and support of U.S. armed forces in overseas areas. The huge transport when available in 1970 will not only carry more heavy combat gear than any previous aircraft, but will do so at a reduced ton-mile cost of only 2.9 cents and at a speed of up to 611 miles per hour. It represents a quantum step forward in U.S. strategic mobility capabilities. The 115 planned C-5A's could carry as many as 69,000 troops in the air at one time—or 11,500 tons of heavy equipment in the air headed overseas at once. This represents the ability to lift several

Army divisions and their essential combat supplies and equipment halfway around the world at 600 miles per hour. It is a technical accomplishment and a strategic capability to be proud of—and also might well justify one to ponder the implications. It will enable the United States to move major combat forces into action in hours rather than days or weeks. It will permit the execution of contingency military plans at jet speeds—actually before Congress and diplomats are capable of analyzing, discussing, and formulating measures or alternatives to military action. The military will be able to affect policy faster than normal legislative or executive reactions can be expected.

In recent years Defense officials (military and civilian) have maintained that the Fast Deployment Logistic ships (FDL) and the C-5A combination would be almost essential to the nation's ability to respond effectively with brigade-size forces or larger in the initial thirty to sixty days following an executive decision to act in a crisis. They have felt that the combined FDL ships and C-5A rapid deployment capability could mean the difference between the United States maintaining its influence in a given area or not. Without the rapid-response capability, the United States would face the choice of not responding at all—or possibly becoming involved in a larger conflict because of the slower response and shorter time it would allow for executive deliberations.

This concept and requirement is based upon the assumption that national policy will continue to consider *all areas of the world as possible combat theaters* and that there may be a need to dispatch troops and equipment to those areas where the United States does not already maintain forces or pre-positioned equipment, or where the mobile and balanced fleets—including Marine landing forces, are not already available at the scene. (Naval forces enjoying the freedom of the seas have usually been the flexible and adequate type of forces needed for limited interventions.) Such concepts and assumptions, when considered in terms of specific geographic areas, become even less impressive and convincing.

There is no real requirement for such an extensive strategic mobility capability in the Western Hemisphere. We already have sufficient air- and sealift to meet any possible needs in the Central or South American and Caribbean areas.

There is already a substantial and tested capability to move forces to Europe in support of our NATO commitments. We now maintain pre-stocked depots of supplies for at least two divisions which can be flown in C-141 and commercial jets to that theater. If there is an atomic war in Europe, pre-stocked supply depots, airfields, and large aircraft will be early casualties. It is difficult to visualize C-5A's operating in an atomic battle area. The policy decisions which determine the extent of need for C-5A's and related FDL ships then appear to hinge largely upon the desire to be able to move substantial forces rapidly to such places as Africa, India, Southeast Asia, Indonesia, and Japan-Korea.

So unless the planners can build a truly convincing requirement which appears more logical and promising than our recent experience with a limited land war in Vietnam, it is doubtful that there will actually be a valid case for very large numbers of C-5A's and FDL ships to support our basic national defense policy requirements. Nevertheless, the present defense program as proposed in the FY 1970 Budget and related posture statement prescribes the strategic airlift forces currently deemed necessary. The rapid response capability needed, according to defense leaders, can best be provided by at least six C-5A squadrons (96 aircraft)* and 14 C-141 squadrons (164 aircraft). In order to get maximum utilization of these aircraft they will each have two or more flight crews and "associated" reserve unit crews available for emergency back-up. It is not clear what economical and practical work these numbers of aircraft can be put to during peacetime. Like other such vast systems they will tend to seek missions. There will be a normal urge to test their capabilities in moving troops and equipment on expensive intercontinental strategic mobility exercises. Will such usage be a form of provocation, or will it be viewed by the world as "in the interests of U.S. defenses"? Is there a real

* The remaining 17 C-5A's would be spare and special-purpose aircraft. (On November 14, 1969 the U.S. Air Force announced that due to the rising costs of the C-5A it would procure only 81 of the giant aircraft.)

need for such an extensive capability of moving large Army forces
to remote areas at jet speed?

Yankees, Stay Home

The extent to which readiness and mobility can become ends in
themselves was clearly revealed in the massive and rapid intervention in the Dominican Republic in April, 1965, when the contingency plans and interservice mobility rivalry apparently super-
seded diplomacy. Before most people realized what was happening,
the momentum and velocity of rapid-reaction plans projected almost
23,000 U.S. soldiers and Marines into the small troubled republic
in an impressive race to test the mobility of these forces, and to
attain overall command of "U.S. Forces Dom. Rep." Only a frac-
tion of the force deployed was needed or justified. A small 1935-
model Marine landing force could probably have handled the mission—essentially the safeguarding and evacuation of some 1,400
American nationals—which was accomplished within twenty-four
hours. But the Army airlifted much of the 82nd Airborne Division
to the scene, along with a lieutenant general, and took charge of
the "critical" situation, a "communist-led revolt" which endangered
American lives—particularly the life of the American ambassador
who, according to President Johnson, was inclined to plead for U.S.
troops while talking to the White House from beneath his desk! [6]
Some intervention troops remained on in the Dominican Republic
until early 1966, long after the Americans had been evacuated.

Subsequent information and opinion indicated that, although the
landings in the Dominican Republic may have been successful
military drills, they were for dubious objectives and not only
violated America's long-standing Good Neighbor Policy of avoiding
armed intervention in Latin America—and rekindled old concerns
among Caribbean nations about "Yankee Imperialism"—but, according to *Christian Science Monitor* correspondent James Good-
sell, the revolt in the Dominican Republic was not led by Communists. The rebel cause actually was based upon some well-
founded grievances, he reported. Also, Senator J. William Fulbright
in a speech on the situation in the Dominican Republic, September
15, 1965, stated, "U.S. policy in the Dominican crisis was charac-

terized initially by over-timidity and subsequently by overreaction.
. . . The United States assumed almost from the beginning that
the revolution was communist dominated, or would certainly become so." However, American intelligence sources compiled a list
of only seventy-seven suspected Communists active in the Dominican revolution. This was the alleged basis of President Johnson's
massive military intervention and strong action designed to prevent
a government controlled or heavily infiltrated by international communism from taking power in the Dominican Republic.[7]

The Dominican ex-president, Juan Bosch, who was deposed in
1963 by a military coup, pointed out that when the Dominican
rebels attempted to overthrow the military dictators and their
"pentagonized" army (created by U.S. military aid), it was replaced
by American forces which in a few days landed far more men than
the Dominican armed forces had had before the revolt.[8]

Perhaps the most relevant opinion was that of Professor Wolf-
gang Friedman, who stated, "Intervention in the affairs of another
country, the occupation of its territory, the invasion of its sover-
eignty is illegal, as indeed is patently clear from the language of
both the United Nations Charter and the OAS Charter, unless there
is evidence of aggression by a third party. And such evidence is not
simply the advent of a left wing government that may or may not
have Communist elements. . . ."[9]

Despite the possible justifications of the U.S. intervention in the
Dominican Republic, from the point of view of the Norfolk-based
Atlantic Unified Command and the Army and Marine troops involved, it was a successful mobility exercise. The healthy interservice rivalry was best expressed by the "U.S. Forces Dom. Rep."
commander, Lieutenant General Bruce Palmer, Jr. (Commanding
General XVIII Airborne Corps, U.S.A.) when he reported to the
annual Association of the U.S. Army convention in Washington,
D.C., October 11, 1966:

> I believe that the major conclusions and lessons of the
> Dominican stability operations have become apparent to
> you during this brief discussion. As I see it, the U.S.
> clearly demonstrated the rapid reaction capability of our

strategic reserve forces of all services. For U.S. ground soldiers, it brought home the truism that stability operations are essentially the business of soldiers—a task for land forces. [In contrast to Marines, the general meant. *Author*.]

Moreover, this type of mission calls for the best of troops. We had just that with the U.S. Army and U.S. Marine Corps. Speaking parochially, however, as XVIII Airborne Corps Commander, I must show my partiality for our paratroopers. As light infantry, they come no better. Furthermore, in my opinion, the Airborne Division is the ideal formation for such operations. Their organization, arms, and equipment are well suited and can be readily adjusted to most any terrain or environment.

Ten thousand miles away, in Southeast Asia, another mobility exercise and test of each service's state of readiness was also well underway in the spring of 1965.

Ready, Willing, and "Underway"

As time passes, a growing body of evidence reveals that in the months preceding February, 1965, when the United States armed forces commenced bombing the north and deploying combat troops into South Vietnam, there were many moves by the military and civilian defense leaders to involve America more actively in the war. All the services and the White House advisers participated in what may not have been exactly a conspiracy but was at least a well-organized readiness—indeed, an inclination—to get into the war. During the period of late 1964 and early 1965 many armed forces officers believed it was then necessary and proper that U.S. combat forces be employed not only to protect the rapidly growing U.S. investment in aid to South Vietnam but to also stop the Viet Cong Communist insurgents on the battlefield before the ARVN was disintegrated and before the "dominoes" of Southeast Asia commenced to tumble. Each of the American services also had its own special interests and objectives at the time.

By the end of 1964 the U.S. Army had some 23,000 military advisory people already on duty in South Vietnam. This was an increase from a strength of 16,000 in December, 1963. In addition to the "green beret" Special Forces, there were "nation-building" Special Action Forces which included units of engineers, military police, psychological warfare, helicopters, civil affairs and logistic service-support-type personnel who were attempting to shore up the shaky forces of the several Saigon regimes. As the numbers of Americans grew they naturally were increasingly exposed to the attacks of the Viet Cong guerrillas throughout the combat zone and they frequently suffered casualties. So there appeared to be an expanding need for American combat units to provide for area defense and local security. The Army high command desired more troops, but President Johnson had been campaigning in 1964 as a man of peace and had stated that a land war in Southeast Asia was no place for American boys. Nevertheless, many Army combat units in the United States were pointed at the Pacific and were making ready; Army schools and training stressed counterinsurgency tactics and techniques; all ranks studied the tactics of guerrilla warfare; the Special Forces was expanded; concepts of helicopter-borne air mobility and fire support were studied and tested. The momentum of Army planning was moving the Army toward land combat operations in Vietnam.

The Viet Cong attack on the Army Special Forces Camp at Pleiku on February 7, 1965, finally pulled the trigger which launched the largest expeditionary force in American "peacetime" history into the quagmire of Vietnam and the type of Asiatic land war which the Army Chief of Staff, General Matthew B. Ridgeway, had warned against in 1956 and the Joint Chiefs of Staff had avoided up until 1964. The 173rd Airborne Brigade, stationed on Okinawa, landed in South Vietnam on May 5, 1965, in what was the beginning of the Army ground combat forces buildup which eventually reached a total of over 530,000 American troops.

Okinawa, the "keystone" bastion of forward-deployed American forces in the Western Pacific, served its purpose as the launching pad for the initial deployments into Vietnam, for Okinawa was also the home base in 1965 of the 3rd Marine Division of Fleet Marine

Forces Pacific. Some 15,000 U.S. Marines, two thirds of a reinforced division, were stationed there. During 1963 and 1964 the
division had stepped up its practice of sending numbers of young
company-grade officers and selected staff NCO's to South Vietnam
for short periods of "on-the-job" training with the small but elite
Vietnam Marine Corps which was constantly engaged in counterinsurgency (and political security) operations. At the same time,
other division officers went to South Vietnam and made aerial
reconnaissance flights for "terrain familiarization" purposes over
possible beachheads and areas of tactical operations. The division
also kept a battalion Special Landing Force afloat with the 7th
Fleet's Amphibious Force. "Assault" landing exercises were made
along friendly areas on the coast of South Vietnam by these battalions during their tour with the Fleet.

On several occasions during the years prior to 1965, the 3rd
Marine Division formed provisional brigade task forces with contingency plans for combat amphibious assault landings in Vietnam.
On at least one alert period, the brigade embarked for action.
Plans for amphibious intervention in South Vietnam were continually updated and presented in briefings to high-ranking visitors
from Pearl Harbor and Washington, whose chief concern then was
the reaction of Communist China "when" Marines were eventually
deployed to Vietnam.

The Viet Cong attack on Pleiku took place on February 7. On
February 9 the Marines' 1st Light Antiaircraft Missile Battalion,
which had been airlifted into DaNang, became operational. To
move this type of heavily equipped unit took weeks of planning.
One month later, in March, initial Marine ground combat units,
the 9th Marine Expeditionary Brigade from Okinawa, landed near
DaNang. In fact, they landed on the same DaNang beaches Marines had been studying for five years since 1961, when the
Marine Corps Schools in a training demonstration called OPERA-
TION CORMORANT had chosen the site for a map exercise and
hypothetical amphibious invasion.

The Marine landing was the introduction of U.S. ground combat
troops into South Vietnam. Once again, the Leathernecks were the
"First to Fight" and had demonstrated their readiness in relation

to the slower-moving U.S. Army. The entire Pacific naval establishment found much satisfaction in this accomplishment. Prior to the commitment, some senior officers and many eager junior officers had expressed a growing concern because the Corps was not actively involved in the Vietnam combat. It was a condition contrary to all Marine Corps traditions. The Army Special Action Forces were engaged in counterinsurgency operations and few Marines were seeing action. The Marines had no special counter-insurgency-type units such as the Army's Special Forces, so the only Leatherneck solution was to commit Fleet Marine Force combat units on a substantial scale. Eventually the Marines deployed an air and ground force of 83,000 troops in the III Marine Amphibious Force which became responsible for the defense of the northern provinces of I Corps and the Demilitarized Zone (DMZ).

At the beginning of 1965 the U.S. Air Forces in Vietnam were almost fully occupied with training and developing the Vietnamese Air Force. A few Air Force tactical jet squadrons had been on hand at the DaNang and Bien Hoa air bases since August, 1964, when the Tonkin Gulf incidents "prompted" the deployment of certain U.S. air units to Thailand and South Vietnam; however, these aircraft were kept on the ground in a state of instant readiness. At the same time a small number of prop-driven old A-1E's, flown by Air Force pilots, had logged 764 strike sorties against the Viet Cong in support of the ARVN and U.S. Army Special Forces camps during 1964. By early 1965 the Air Force was quietly moving in strength into South Vietnam and neighboring Thailand where bases and supplies were being established, but offensive air operations had to await another provocative incident.

So the enemy attack on Pleiku also served to launch U.S. air power into the Vietnam war on a large scale. Along with Navy and VNAF pilots, the Air Force retaliated for the Pleiku attack when Air Force jet pilots struck targets in the north for the first time on February 7 and hit targets in South Vietnam on February 18. By the end of 1965, the USAF had flown almost 50,000 strike sorties in support of the Republic of South Vietnam and U.S. ground forces. About 10,570 of these were strikes over North Vietnam. The Air Forces dropped over 80,290 tons of bombs including 23,610 tons upon North Vietnam in 1965. This magnitude of air effort in a period of less than eleven months indicated the high state of readiness of the Air Force to undertake limited-war air operations. The Air Force was also confident that it had the means to turn the tide in Vietnam and to defeat insurgency and Communist aggression if it were permitted to use what it deemed appropriate power. *Air Force* magazine of March, 1966, summarized the Air Force's view of its initial impact upon the war effort:

> Tactical airpower, US Air Force style, had its first chance to prove itself in a guerrilla war during 1965 in South Vietnam. The results were extremely impressive. So impressive, in fact, that not even the most ardent airpower advocate could fully appreciate the degree of success unless he had been in the right spots in Vietnam and had actually witnessed the results.
> The record clearly shows that tactical airpower was the decisive element which turned what at the beginning of 1965 was a near-hopeless situation in South Vietnam into a decidedly more hopeful one in the early weeks of 1966.
> . . . the war is far from over, but the future is much brighter and the record shows that it was tactical airpower, US Air Force style, that gave our ground troops the edge they needed to break up the VC drive and turn the tide of battle in our favor. . . .

Three years later, in the spring of 1969, the Air Force was making more sorties and dropping more bombs per month than at any period of the war. Air power was still "turning the tide of battle."

The U.S. Navy was not standing idly by either during the months prior to America's joining the Vietnam war in February, 1965. As early as February, 1964, the U.S. Navy advisers assisted the South Vietnam maritime forces' plan and execute OPLAN 34-A, a program of commando-type raids along the coast of North Vietnam.

There followed a series of actions which led up to the Tonkin Gulf incident and the subsequent U.S. force buildup.

In July, 1964, the destroyer *U.S.S. Maddox* began to patrol in Tonkin Gulf waters. These were not routine patrols; the ship was on electronic espionage missions.

(On July 27 the Defense Department announced that another 5,000 U.S. military assistance Special Action-type troops were going to South Vietnam.)

On July 31 the South Vietnamese Navy raiding force, under OPLAN 34-A, conducted the first bombardment of the offshore islands of Hon Me and Hon Ngu in North Vietnam with vessels recently supplied by the U.S. Navy.

On August 2 the *Maddox* was patrolling off North Vietnam. It had been instructed to approach no closer than eight nautical miles of the mainland and no closer than four nautical miles of any offshore islands. (North Vietnam considered this to be well within their territorial waters.) It was only the third occasion since 1962 on which an American naval vessel had approached this close to the North Vietnamese coast. The *Maddox* was allegedly "attacked" on the night of August 2 by one or more North Vietnam "torpedo" boats. No damage was done to the *Maddox,* and subsequent reports by a *Maddox* crew member indicate there is some reason to question whether the *Maddox* was in fact attacked or merely being investigated by the patrol boats.[10]

On August 3, President Johnson warned of "serious consequences" if the attack were repeated and announced that he was sending the *Maddox* and a second destroyer back into the same area. Also on the night of August 3–4 there was a second coastal bombardment of installations in North Vietnam by South Vietnam naval forces. Secretary of Defense McNamara later testified that he was not aware of this operation at the time.[11] It was known, however, to local U.S. Navy task force commanders and presumably was planned by the joint South Vietnamese and MACV headquarters in Saigon. This attack alerted the North Vietnamese and probably provoked their alleged second attack upon U.S. destroyers in the area twenty-four hours later.

On August 4 the *Maddox,* now accompanied by the *U.S.S.*

Turner Joy, returned to the same Tonkin Gulf waters on orders of the President, who was reportedly deeply chagrined that the *Maddox* had failed to hit any enemy boats with its gunfire on August 2. Again North Vietnam torpedo-patrol boats reportedly intercepted the destroyers. The boats were fired upon by the warships and two were reported sunk. Actually, enemy patrol-boat contacts reported by the two destroyers on the night of August 4, and the alleged torpedo attacks, were largely the products of radar contacts and sonar reports by inexperienced and excited seamen on a pitch-black night in rough seas. Subsequent investigations revealed that there is considerable reason to doubt that an attack upon the *Maddox* and the *Turner Joy* did, in fact, take place.

However, the vivid messages from the two ships during the night of August 4 provided all the reasons needed by the eager militarists at CINCPAC Headquarters in Pearl Harbor and the belligerent White House and Pentagon planners in Washington. Retaliation plans and decisions began to fall into place, but at the very top, President Johnson and Secretary McNamara persisted in efforts to get a full account of the reported attack before the President announced to the nation that he had launched reprisal bombings on North Vietnam. At the same time, the top Navy commanders in the Pacific had made up their minds that an attack had actually taken place. Admiral Ulysses Grant Sharp, Jr., Commander in Chief Pacific (CINCPAC), and Admiral Thomas H. Moorer, Pacific Fleet Commander, were clearing the decks for action.

Nevertheless, at McNamara's insistence, Admiral Sharp was directed to seek verification and additional details of the attack from Captain John J. Herrick USN, commanding the two destroyers making up the Tonkin Gulf patrol. Herrick's report eventually reached McNamara's Pentagon command post some twelve hours later, on August 5. It stated that the naval air support did not locate any enemy targets; that *Maddox* scored no known hits and never positively identified an enemy boat as such . . . Weather was overcast with limited visibility . . . There were no stars or moon, resulting in almost total darkness throughout action . . . No known damage or personnel casualties to either ship . . .

Turner Joy claims sinking one boat and damaging another . . . The first boat to close *Maddox* probably fired a torpedo at *Maddox* which was heard but not seen. All subsequent *Maddox* torpedo reports were doubtful in that it is supposed that the sonar man was hearing ship's own propeller beat.

Nineteen minutes before Captain Herrick's uncertain message was received in the Pentagon on August 5, the first attack aircraft began launching from the *USS Ticonderoga* and the first retaliatory air strike was soon made by sixty-four naval carrier bombers which hit the torpedo boats' base at Quang Khe in North Vietnam. They also attacked patrol boats and oil installations in the vicinity. The ready Navy had jumped the gun and started the U.S. war on North Vietnam.[12]

On August 6, the Secretary of Defense announced that designated Army and Marine forces (in addition to the 5,000 announced ten days earlier) were alerted and readying for movement. Also he stated that "certain military deployments to the area are now underway," and that there was a "movement of fighter bomber aircraft to Thailand." The aircraft units' moves had been authorized by the Secretary of Defense on August 4, so movement plans must have preceded execution by some days or weeks.[13]

Under the pressures and concerns caused by the alleged attacks on the U.S. destroyers, the Tonkin Gulf resolution was passed by Congress on August 7, 1964, giving the President and his advisers a free hand to take additional "precautionary measures in South Vietnam," and to "repel armed attack." Escalation of the American armed forces' participation in the struggle of Vietnam gained velocity from then on.

The question remains as to who was responsible for these highly provocative naval operations. Did the Secretary of Defense and the President actually know what was being planned and done by the U.S. and South Vietnam naval forces at this tense period? Or were these well-calculated measures being taken by the military and the administration leaders to expand the war into North Vietnam and to support secretly prearranged decisions? Were the series of events in the Tonkin Gulf in August, 1964, used to cover and to authorize the deployments for a wider war, for the bombing of the

North and the commitment of combat troops in the South? Or was the powerful U.S. Fleet really the innocent victim of, in the words of McNamara, "unprovoked and deliberate attacks in international waters?" [14]

At any rate, the military's deployment plans and movement schedules began to take over from the diplomats and civilians. And apparently, as in the Dominican Republic invasion, the momentum of military plans and movements became virtually impossible to halt. By June 8, 1965, General Westmoreland was authorized to commit his troops in direct combat against the Viet Cong. President Johnson announced on July 28, 1965, that American troops in Vietnam would be increased immediately to 125,000. "Additional forces will be needed later," he said. Only seven months before, in January, Secretary of State Dean Rusk had announced that the United States would *not* "expand the war."

In his early 1966 "defense posture statement," Secretary Robert S. McNamara expressed his pride in the readiness of U.S. forces: "The rapid deployment and support in combat of a force of over one quarter of a million men to an area 10,000 miles from our shores clearly demonstrates that our logistics system has that capability. Never before has this country been able to field and support in combat so large a force in so short a time over so great a distance." McNamara, like many of his colleagues, was so enraptured by the logistic capabilities and the military operations that the purpose and objectives of the "great deployment" probably became obscured. By now perhaps the mistakes, the tragedy, and the costs of Vietnam have revealed that the readiness and rapid-response exercises of 1965 were somewhat less than admirable.

Footnotes

[1] Samuel P. Huntington, *Soldiers and the State*. Harvard University Press, Cambridge, Mass., 1964.

[2] *Army Information Digest,* Department of the Army, Washington, D.C., June, 1958.

[3] Maxwell D. Taylor. *The Uncertain Trumpet,* Harper and Bros., New York. 1959.

[4] Brig. Gen. C. V. Wilson, U.S.A. "Weapon at the Ready" *Ordnance,* March–April, 1965.

[5] James L. Trainor, "Navy's Fast Deployment Ships Designed for U.S. Military, Economic Needs," *Armed Forces Management,* February, 1967.

[6] "March of the News," *U.S. News & World Report,* June 14, 1965.

[7] *Dominican Action—1965,* the Center for Strategic Studies, Georgetown Univ., Washington, D.C., 1966, p. 65.

[8] Juan Bosch, *Pentagonism, A Substitute for Imperialism,* Crane Press, New York, 1968.

[9] "The Dominican Republic Crisis 1965," *The Hammarskjold Forums,* New York, May 1966.

[10] *I. F. Stone's Weekly,* Washington, D.C., March 4, 1968.

[11] The Gulf of Tonkin, the 1964 Incidents, Hearing Before the Committee on Foreign Relations, United States Senate, Ninetieth Congress, Second Session with the Honorable Robert S. McNamara Secretary of Defense, on February 20, 1968.

[12] Joseph C. Goulden, *Truth Is the First Casualty,* Rand McNally & Co., New York, 1969, p. 156.

[13] *Ibid.,* p. 236.

[14] Merlo J. Pusey, *The Way We Go to War,* Houghton Mifflin Co., Boston, Mass., 1969, pp. 116–147.

Chapter VI

MILITARISM AT THE TOP

"A national war machine . . . the most exhilarating of all vehicles to drive."

Correlli Barnett: The Swordbearers

Background of the Joint Chiefs of Staff

During the World War II years of stress and national purpose the long-standing alienation of the conservative military and the liberal intellectuals was minimized, and the military profession came into an unprecedented level of power and prestige. Between 1940 and 1968, the military view that human nature does not change, that armed forces do not make wars, and that military strength is the only source of security and peace became the dominating philosophy. The world of real wars, cold wars, and Communist threats justified the military virtues of duty, discipline, and loyalty—and the use of force to resolve human problems. In the eyes of most liberals, however, such creeds have been a sorry reflection on the human intellect and have disqualified the militarists from the intellectual community. Nevertheless, from the beginnings of World War II up until the recent public disenchantments with militarism's failures in Vietnam, the professional military leaders and their philosophies have enjoyed considerable, albeit fluctuating, degrees of power and influence.

Also, with the unified efforts of World War II the professional military were drawn out of their state of social and political isolation and they accepted many more liberal national values. They maintained complete dominance over the strategy and military conduct of the war as most civilian officials were content to let the professionals direct the conflict. At the same time, the military learned to work with and to influence the civilians who ran the domestic war economy—*not,* however, without some conflicts and struggles for power.

The power center of wartime military leadership was the corporate organization of the military chiefs. Prior to February, 1942, this was the Joint Board, composed of four high-ranking Army and Navy officers. Subsequently, the Joint Chiefs of Staff came into existence as the military leadership of the United States, and they with their United Kingdom counterparts formed the combined Chiefs of Staff early in World War II to provide a supreme Anglo-American military group for the direction of the war. The United States Joint Chiefs of Staff came from the Army, Navy and Army Air Force, and included the President's Chief of Staff, Admiral William D. Leahy. From their creation in 1942 until enactment of the National Security Act, the Joint Chiefs of Staff had no legal status in the statutory organizations for national security. During this time, the Joint Chiefs of Staff as a functioning body was what the President chose to make it. It existed entirely apart from the War and Navy Departments.

During World War II, the fighting forces of the United States were organized into the Department of the Army and the Department of the Navy. The chiefs of these separate departments reported directly to the President in his role of Commander in Chief, and they cooperated with each other on joint missions. The civilian secretaries of the military departments were also members of the President's Cabinet. It became obvious, however, during World War II that this organization should be studied to determine if a more unified and effective arrangement could be devised.

On September 17, 1947, the National Security Act "unified" the armed forces and formally established the Joint Chiefs of Staff as a permanent agency within the national military establishment which became the Department of Defense in 1949 and designated them the principal military advisers to the President and the Secretary of Defense. The Act further provided for a Joint Staff of not more than a hundred officers, operating under a director appointed by and responsible to the JCS. This Act also set up a Department of the Air Force as a separate service, co-equal with the Departments of the Army and the Navy—all under the management and direction of the Department of Defense.

Since 1947, the JCS organization has undergone seven major changes, starting with the Key West agreement of 1948 and extending to the Defense Reorganization Act of 1958. A 1949 amendment created the office of Chairman of the Joint Chiefs of Staff, and General of the Army Omar N. Bradley was sworn in as the first JCS Chairman on August 16, 1949. The size of the Joint Staff was also increased from 100 to 210 officers by the 1949 amendment. Legislation which became effective in June, 1952, placed the Commandant of the U.S. Marine Corps in co-equal status with members of the JCS when considering matters that directly concerned the Marine Corps. Then, in June, 1953, President Eisenhower declared that the JCS was "not a command body" but an advisory group, responsible for formulating strategic plans but not for directing the operations to carry them out.

The seventh JCS change came as a result of the Defense Reorganization Act of 1958. This Act incorporated six major points:

 (1) Operational forces organized into unified and specified commands were separated from the military departments, which had previously been executive agents, and were made directly responsible to the Secretary of Defense through the JCS.

 (2) Operational command of all combat-ready forces was given to the unified and specified commanders. The line of authority extended from the President as Commander in Chief, to the Secretary of Defense, whose orders would be issued to the unified and specified commanders through the JCS.

 (3) The size of the Joint Staff was again increased, this time from 210 to 400 officers, since the operational direction of the unified commands had been added to the other responsibilities of the JCS.

(4) Each Service chief was authorized to delegate major portions of his authority and duties to his vice chief, so that the chief might devote his primary attention to his JCS duties. The duties of the chiefs of the military Services as members of the JCS now take precedence over all of their other duties.

(5) The stipulation that the Chairman should have no vote in the decisions of the JCS was deleted. The Chairman was also authorized to assign duties to the Joint Staff and to appoint its director in consultation with the JCS and with the approval of the Secretary of Defense.

(6) The 1958 Reorganization Act specified that "the Joint Staff shall not operate or be organized as an overall armed forces general staff and shall have no executive authority, but may operate along conventional staff lines" to support the JCS.

The major functions of the Joint Chiefs of Staff are to:

(1) serve as the principal military advisers to the President, the National Security Council, and the Secretary of Defense;

(2) prepare strategic plans;

(3) provide for the strategic and operational direction of the armed forces;

(4) review plans, programs, and requirements;

(5) and provide U.S. military representation to international security organizations, mutual defense boards, and commissions.

The entire JCS organization includes approximately 1,500 personnel—about 700 officers, 400 enlisted personnel, and 400 civilians. Officer positions are divided equally among the three military departments: Army, Navy (20 percent are Marines), and Air Force.

The organizational structure has three groupings:

(1) Joint Chiefs of Staff as a corporate body.
(2) Joint Staff.
(3) Other agencies which assist the JCS, but which are not a part of the Joint Staff. (Since the number of officers authorized for the Joint Staff is limited by law to 400, certain functions must be performed outside of the staff organization.

Wartime Powers

During the war years under Franklin D. Roosevelt the Joint Chiefs of Staff's position of power was reinforced by their relationships with the President. Roosevelt, like his colleague Winston Churchill, considered himself a master strategist. He enjoyed the title Commander in Chief. He experienced great pleasure in planning and charting grand operations with his military leaders. Like many senior civilian officials, he found deep satisfaction in working with the generals and admirals on equal terms. President Roosevelt and his military leaders ran the war without benefit of advice from Cabinet-level officials or any top-level policy or coordinating agency, such as a National Security Council, to help formulate broad national war objectives that went beyond military victory. As a result, the military milled about without a clear notion of the overall war aims of the government.[1]

With an agreed policy of unlimited war, Congress was also satisfied to abdicate its responsibilities of controlling the military establishment. They felt patriotically obliged to provide whatever money and resources the military leaders and the President said they needed. Under the policy of wartime secrecy, it was deemed imprudent for Congress to inquire specifically into military estimates or plans. They trusted in God—and General Marshall—to achieve victory, and so finished the war with some $50 billion in unused appropriations and no post-victory national policy for demobilization, occupation plans, or roles for American power in the postwar world.

During the war years the professional military attitude toward civilian control changed completely. The armed forces reorganization plans which followed the war reflected their new self-conception of the military's role in government. Some military leaders believed civilian control of the military was a relic of the past, with no place in the future. "The Joint Chiefs of Staff at the present time," Admiral Leahy said frankly and truthfully in 1945, "are under no civilian control whatever." He also made clear that "we felt the Joint Chiefs of Staff should be a permanent body responsible only to the President and that the JCS should advise the President on the national defense budget." [2]

Postwar Changes

Although the influence of military professionals upon American society tended to decline during the immediate postwar years, it still remained at unprecedented levels for a "peacetime" period. As we have seen, prominent military individuals moved into many nonmilitary and influential positions throughout government and industry. Military officers and military methods became omnipresent during this period, more so than in any other country.

During the Truman years the administration used many of the distinguished former military leaders for important positions that could benefit politically from their prestige. The professional military did not withdraw from political activity in the tradition of its prewar professional ethic of noninvolvement in other than purely military matters because hard-line foreign policies based upon military power—evolved by civilian leaders—forced the military professionals to accept increased responsibility for the formulation of national policy. The Cold War policies for the containment of communism created by Secretaries of State Marshall and Acheson were usually more power-oriented and belligerent than those offered by the military. The influential State Department anti-communism planner, George Kennan, also laid much stress on the importance of military power.

The military found themselves "experts" defending the administration's hard-line foreign policies to the politicians. They testified in Congress on behalf of foreign aid appropriations, urged the ratification of treaties involving the United States overseas, defended the assignment of American troops to Europe and the "limited" conduct of the Korean War. The JCS explained to Congress the administration's decisions on force levels and budgets and were the advocates of politically biased defense policies. Because of their political involvement, the military became vulnerable to partisan criticism, and the frequent unpopularity of the policies they were advocating resulted in a lowering of their prestige and that of their institutions.[3]

The separate services willingly accepted their postwar responsibilities imposed by world wide defense commitments. Individual officers and top-level military schools worked to broaden their basis of geo-political information, but the separate services also fell back into their old habits of rivalry and parochial dissension over roles, missions, weapons, and budget allocations. They could agree upon no programs or objectives which represented any unified concept of what part they should play in the world of their new responsibilities. Partly as a result of this civilian leadership of the Defense Department gained authority. It was evident that the Joint Chiefs of Staff and their service planners could not agree on the military requirements of national security.

The Korean War brought additional changes to the pattern of civil-military relations at the national level. It created widespread public interest and discord over foreign policy, it fostered opposition in Congress, and further drained the political influence of the Joint Chiefs of Staff. The limited war in Korea was the first in American history which did not enjoy united popular support and the sentiments of a crusade. Public resentment over the conduct of the war eventually contributed to the defeat of the political party in power. (The failure of the Johnson administration to remember the lessons of Korea fifteen years later in their conduct of the Vietnam war again resulted in the ousting of the party in power.) The Joint Chiefs in Washington supported the Truman administration's limited war objectives, the troops fought as trained professionals with no goal other than rotation home. But the field commanders and career officers suffered frustration because they were not permitted to "win." The military professionals were for the most part convinced that a military victory was denied

them in Korea because they were overruled by political considerations.

The Eisenhower administration which came into power in 1953
with the mission of ending the frustrating war in Korea again
changed the role and philosophy of the Joint Chiefs. Eisenhower,
himself a military man of senior stature, did not require the political
support of leading military figures. He desired only their agreement
as members of a team. A subsequent series of defense reorganization plans which were undertaken during the Eisenhower years
were designed to provide for a larger degree of unified civilian-
military thinking. The JCS were directed in 1953 to formulate a
"new look" military strategy that would consider not only military
factors but the administration's fiscal policy of a reduced defense
budget. Army Chief General Ridgeway complained that he was
under pressure to "conform to a preconceived politico-military
'party line.' " [4] The single strategy of massive retaliation by Air
Force bombers was also forced upon all the services.

Also, it was during this period that the military leaders embraced
a detailed anti-communist doctrine based upon the assumptions of
Secretary Dulles. The armed forces began to preach what became
the phobia of anti-communism which was then added to the historic duet of "patriotism" and "national defense" as the basis for
militaristic policies.

Defense and the New Frontier

In his instructions to the Joint Chiefs of Staff in April, 1961,
President Kennedy advised, "while I look to the Chiefs to present
the military factor without reserve or hesitation, I regard them to
be more than military men and expect their help in fitting military
requirements into the overall context of any situation, recognizing
that the most difficult problem in government is to combine all
assets in a unified effective pattern." These instructions have guided
the military into its present position in the current formation of
national security. The prospects of atomic war, the tensions of the
Cold War, the obsession with Communist aggression, the contingencies of national defense have strained the decision-making
processes. The traditional concepts of civil-military relationships

have been transformed while military policy has been welded to national policy and the military has been required to participate in formulating policy in most aspects of national security.

When Robert S. McNamara became Kennedy's Secretary of Defense in 1961, much of the wartime glory and stature of the military had diminished. The great captains of the war years had largely left the scene. Whatever prestige the Joint Chiefs had was dealt a devastating blow in the Bay of Pigs fiasco in 1961. An immediate result was the disassociation of most of the top Kennedy civilian advisers from the military. Henceforth, the professional military were generally ignored by the dashing people of the Kennedy regime. Even the Secretary of Defense studiously avoided any social contact with his "troops." Secretary McNamara rarely participated in any military social events, public ceremonies, nor even visited or spoke to a professional military school. For the next seven years a group of civilian analysts and "whiz kids" in the offices of the Secretary of Defense, under Robert McNamara, ran the defense establishment with a new set of cost-effectiveness criteria; a new planning, programming, and budgeting system; and with a revised national defense policy based upon recognition of limited war and theories of flexible response.

The logistic management of the defense establishment became highly centralized under the control of the Secretary. The strategic concepts evolved largely from the basic views on limited war as an alternative to massive retaliation—which were codified by retired Army General Maxwell Taylor—plus the theories of McNamara, and the civilian strategists and planners gathered by President Kennedy. The civilians usurped much of the professional military's responsibility for strategy formulation because, despite unification, the armed services were bogged down with interservice frictions, disagreements over roles and missions and parochial battles within the Pentagon, creating vacuums in decision-making which the civilians were ready to fill.

The Joint Chiefs at the beginning of 1961 were: Chairman, General Lyman L. Lemnitzer, U.S.A.; General George H. Decker of the Army; General Thomas D. White of the Air Force; Admiral Arleigh A. Burke, Chief of Naval Operations; and General David

M. Shoup, Commandant of the Marine Corps. Within a year, all but Shoup were gone. General Maxwell D. Taylor was brought out of retirement initially to advise the White House on intelligence, paramilitary and counterinsurgency matters. He was eventually named Chairman of the Joint Chiefs of Staff. In the following years General Taylor was one of the most influential architects of the U.S. military and strategic policies. Unlike most of the top military figures of the period, General Taylor enjoyed not only the prestige of a brilliant military record but also the credentials of a coolly debonair intellectual. He was always effective in Congressional testimony and widely respected by the legislators. His reputation also gained him acceptance by the intimates of both Presidents Kennedy and Johnson. General Taylor's substantial balance of influence did not begin to dissipate until 1968, when his theories and predictions about the Vietnam war were caught up in the general bankruptcy of the Johnson war policies.

General Maxwell D. Taylor

General Taylor has been an unusual figure in American military history, a soldier-statesman free of the usual military mythologies and unlike the popular image of the professional soldier. General Taylor had a distinguished academic record, graduating fourth in his class at West Point in 1922, an accomplished linguist, and recipient of eight honorary law and engineering degrees from leading universities. He first directed the creation of the Army's doctrine for limited war during his term as Army Chief of Staff (1955–1959) under President Eisenhower. When he finally spoke out against the strategies of atomic war, his retirement followed quickly. His subsequent book, *The Uncertain Trumpet,* rejected the Eisenhower-Dulles strategy and became the nucleus of the Kennedy-McNamara doctrines of flexible response, functional forces and, forgotten by many, planted the seeds for the ABM concept. During the ensuing years up until 1968, General Taylor was at the center of much U.S. decision-making on Vietnam, serving as a respected senior soldier, Ambassador to South Vietnam, and as a special consultant to President Johnson.

Prior to July, 1964, when he retired from chairmanship of the

Joint Chiefs of Staff, General Taylor shared the views of the other chiefs that a land war in Southeast Asia involving American troops was both unwise and unnecessary. He stated in a 1966 magazine interview that he had "been among the officers who have said that a large land war in Asia is the last thing that we should undertake." He qualified this view to mean a land war against Red China, because that was considered to be the only power in Asia which would require us to use forces in very large numbers.

(In 1969, in light of the over 500,000 American troops deployed and the costs of the Vietnam venture, it became a question of what is considered "large" forces in relation to Asia warfare.—Author.)

The general went on to say that he was slow in joining those who recommended the introduction of U.S. ground forces in South Vietnam but felt something must be done to slow the rate of infiltration from North Vietnam into South Vietnam.[5] (Nothing has indicated that U.S. ground forces have ever substantially affected the rate of infiltration.—Author.)

In the same 1966 interview, General Taylor commented on civilian-military relations in the conduct of the war: "In my period as Ambassador for some thirteen months, I never saw any form of civilian intervention in military matters that I did not think was entirely justified. . . . The kinds of things which were controlled out of Washington should have been controlled out of Washington, whereas the actual day-to-day operations against the Viet Cong were never interfered with." [6]

The miscalculations and decisions to enter the Vietnam war in the spring of 1965 were made by the leaders in Washington, supposedly the brightest men of the generation; the Johnsons, Rusks, Bundys, Taylors, McNamaras—and others, backed by the confidence of the Joint Chiefs and their military planners. The top-level militarists led the country into the quagmire.

Dean Rusk

Secretary of State Dean Rusk was, if not the most "brilliant" of the new Kennedy foreign affairs team, probably the most consistent and steady. He patiently repeated his positions and justifications for the Vietnam involvement like an endless recording. He also remained in office the longest, departing at the end of Johnson's term. He left with dignity if not with great appreciation from his countrymen—but then, President Kennedy had really intended to be his own Secretary of State and Rusk was chosen because he was respectable, older, and had good ties to the establishment.

It is doubtful that Kennedy, had he lived, would have permitted Secretary Rusk to follow the path of militarism in Southeast Asia. As it turned out, however, Dean Rusk by earlier experience was essentially Asia-oriented; he had deep convictions about the honor of U.S. commitments in the area, and was confident that the military would prevail, along with all the virtues of America's missions and powers.[7] He was a leading contributor to the miscalculations, the escalations, and the national discord over Vietnam.

McGeorge Bundy

During the crucial months of 1964 and 1965 as President Johnson moved step by step toward the growing commitment of combat troops in Vietnam, no one supported his decisions more persuasively than his key staff adviser on foreign affairs, McGeorge Bundy. In fact, Bundy was widely recognized as one of the principal designers of Johnson's Vietnam war policies. He was typical of the "brain trusters" who have frequently moved in and out of the seat of government where they enjoy positions of great power and influence and very little responsibility for the execution of the ideas and decisions they so cleverly influence.

Bundy was one of the leading militarists of the period, an advocate of aggressive military action whenever it suited the grand strategy of his foreign policy design. He favored the overuse of military force in the Dominican crisis and he was a strong believer in the military concept of "surgical" air strikes against missile sites during the Cuban crisis. Like many of the young military planners in the Pentagon, Bundy was apparently fascinated by operational problems—organizing, setting up tasks, and planning the scheme of operations—instead of reflecting on the purpose and implications of an operation.[8] His "brother-in-arms," William Bundy, Assistant Secretary of State, initiated the State Department paperwork which

became the Tonkin Gulf Resolution in August, 1964. McGeorge
was visiting Vietnam in February, 1965, at the time of Pleiku, and
recommended to the President the retaliation by air attack which
followed. During the subsequent months McGeorge Bundy continued to be a most influential adviser in the reckless escalation
of the U.S. venture in Vietnam. Then in early 1966, as did other
leading civilian militarists and advisers who had succeeded in mir-
ing America in the fruitless Vietnam venture, he retreated back
into private life and became head of the Ford Foundation, leaving
the military to finish the war which he and his colleagues had so
confidently joined. In October, 1968, Bundy candidly announced
his changed views on Vietnam. "This war," he said, "cannot continue at its present level—not only because of what it means in
Southeast Asia, but still more because of what it means in the
United States. . . . It is now plainly unacceptable that we should
continue with annual costs of $30 billion and an annual rate of
sacrifice of more than 10,000 American lives. It is equally wrong
to accept the increasing bitterness and polarization of our people."
He argued, "There is no prospect of military victory against North
Vietnam by any level of U.S. military force which is acceptable or
desirable." [9]

The education of the aggressive Bundy proved to be very costly
for the nation. Unlike the career militarists in the armed services
who also advocated the strategies of escalation for Vietnam, Bundy
could walk away from his failures and even enjoy the luxury of
publicly changing his views. The professional military must live
with the tragic war to the bitter end—and they don't dare express
any but confident and loyal platitudes.

Walter W. Rostow

Another aggressive militarist who had considerable influence
upon President Johnson was the faceless Walter W. Rostow, who
replaced Bundy as special White House adviser on national security
affairs. Rostow exerted a heavy hand in the administration decisions
and the policies and plans which served to escalate the war effort,
and to get the nation ever more deeply mired in Vietnam. He was
even more dangerous than Bundy. In the words of David Halber-

stam he was "a total ideologue with a captive President, a Rasputin with a Czar coming under siege." [10] Townsend Hoopes, Air Force Undersecretary (1967–1969) dubbed Rostow "a fanatic in sheep's clothing" unwilling to listen to others' ideas.[11] His position permitted him to interpret the combat reports and to brief the President on the war's progress. For years Johnson saw the war through Rostow's militaristic eyes.

With the departure of President Johnson, Professor Rostow, who had been disenfranchised by Eastern academic circles because of his militarism, crept back into the anonymity of a teaching position in Texas, where history will probably neglect his part in the sanguinary episode of Vietnam.

Robert S. McNamara

Militarism attained a pinnacle of power in the United States during the heyday of Defense Secretary McNamara. In many ways he exerted more influence on foreign policy than did Secretary Rusk, as much ability to affect fiscal policy as the Secretary of the Treasury, more direct impact on wages, prices, and consumer goods than the Secretaries of Labor and Commerce—and, perhaps more than any other official of the government excepting only the President, a direct and actual responsibility for the life of the nation.[12]

In the view of Presidents, White House aides, Congressmen, and even many military officers, Robert S. McNamara was the best Secretary of Defense the Pentagon had experienced. President Johnson, it is reported, believed during the 1964–1966 period that Bob McNamara was "the greatest invention since the telephone" and stated that he was the "best Secretary of Defense the nation ever had." But McNamara was a manager, not a leader. Unfortunately, as head of the largest establishment in America, where the professional career officers considered leadership a pre-eminent qualification for high responsibility, the Secretary lacked the touch with his people which could create loyalty, enthusiasm, and high morale.

McNamara and his civilian teammates strived to bring some sort of order out of the chaos they found in the Pentagon. They demolished time-honored military purchasing customs with cost-effectiveness criteria. They eliminated some sacred old branches like the Quartermaster Corps, and they combined others. They established overall procurement policies, unified common logistic services, stepped up quality control, and made efforts to control interservice battles and press leaks by consolidating public information functions. In the name of better management and efficiency, the command and operations of the armed services were unified, techniques of computer analysis and control were introduced, and the "military-industry team" coordinated and strengthened. As a result many of the service administrative inefficiences once caused by overlapping, duplication, and rivalry have been replaced by a powerful organized war machinery which defies effective democratic and Congressional controls.

During the years that Secretary McNamara and his civilian strategists ran the Defense establishment they were no less guilty of stimulating the growing militarism than were the combat-ready careerists. Although the civilians were largely concerned with efficiency in the organization and management of the Defense establishment, they eagerly seized upon the concepts of a new national military program of flexible response expressed by General Taylor. They modernized and expanded the General Purpose Forces, substantially increased the national airlift capabilities, and closed the strategic missile gap. Most of these programs satisfied one or more of the armed services. What irritated the military, however, was the authoritarian approach of the Pentagon's pseudo-intellectual civilian managers. Independent service views and opinions were continuously pressured into line by department policy and security classification procedures which suppressed disagreements with the Secretary and his assistants "for security reasons."

Congressional hearings became a procedural formality, and instructions on how to testify were promulgated by the Secretary of Defense to the services in 1965. The memorandum stated that even "if pressed for his personal opinion" a witness is required to defend the Pentagon's position and make clear "the considerations or factors which support the decision." [13]

Accused of downgrading military influence on purely military matters McNamara denied any intention to usurp the decision-making prerogatives of the military leaders. He said: "To the contrary, I have encouraged the Joint Chiefs to express themselves openly and free of the restraints of their service connections in the interest of the soundest possible defense program for the country."

Also, McNamara, speaking to the American Society of Newspaper Editors in April, 1963, stated that in his view "There is nothing innately desirable about centralization. But the fact remains that when national security decisions affect broad interests they must be made from a central point, not from subordinate points each specially concerned with one part of the forest—and not even by a committee made up of representatives of the forest. For the nature of committees is to compromise their special interests, which is not the same as making the decision from the point of view of the national interest.[14]

Typical of the irritations suffered by the military at the Pentagon under Secretary McNamara was the implication that computer calculations, operational analysis, and abstract theories obtained from books somehow had greater weight in the military decision-making process than the lessons of experience and history. Retired General Thomas D. White, USAF, described the young "whiz kid" types who invaded the Pentagon and the precincts of military responsibility. He stated, "In common with other military men I am profoundly apprehensive of the pipe-smoking, trees-full-of-owls type of so-called defense intellectuals who have been brought into this nation's capital." Other military men were ready to point out that these brash civilians were arrogantly propounding various theories of strategy without having any responsibility of command.[15]

The civilian amateur strategists in the Pentagon even usurped such specialized military functions as target selection in North Vietnam. One anonymous general officer was prompted to compose a ditty about his status:

> I am not allowed to run the train;·
> The whistle I can't blow.
>
> I am not allowed to say how fast
> The railroad trains can go.

I am not allowed to shoot off steam
Nor even clang the bell.

But let it jump the goddam tracks
And see who catches hell! [16]

McNamara's relationship with his generals and admirals was typified by a studied reserve and detachment. While he managed the armed services he never permitted himself to become personally involved with them. He avoided the normal social contacts with the top military figures in Washington where the cocktail party and reception is regarded, next to the official briefing, as the most effective process of establishing communication and short-cutting bureaucracy. The military was never able to approach McNamara on the informal "Old Boy" basis that so many civilian officials find especially flattering. Nor did McNamara succumb to the practice of becoming emotionally involved with the men of the fighting forces by participating in their sentimental rituals and ceremonies. As an ex-reserve officer and a veteran he may have had some of the normal civilians' trepidations when in the presence of senior ranking military figures, but it was rarely evident. He compensated for his non-warrior credentials with a cool detachment from his uniformed subordinates which many found offensive. Secretary McNamara's impersonal attitude toward the military was also reflected in the studiously casual manners many of his young civilian assistants affected toward the proud and senior officers in the Pentagon. For many military professionals their tours in the Pentagon during the McNamara regime was an ego-shattering experience.

The heavy hand of civilian authority in the Pentagon has been resisted in many ways by the military. Every high-ranking civilian official in the Department of Defense has from four to a dozen clever colonels and Navy captains sitting in his outer office. They act as aides and military secretaries to the public official, answering mail, screening phone calls, and determining who shall get in to see the boss. They also act as agents and informers for their own service headquarters. They keep in constant liaison with their parent service to report on whom the civilian Secretaries have been seeing and what they have been saying.[17] They continued to work for their own service as elements of the constant and relentless but submerged resistance of the uniformed planners against their presumptuous young "civilian masters."

During the McNamara years the Pentagon was dominated by the civilian team of militarists whose game was analysis and efficiency and whose only credentials for leading the armed forces was academic accomplishment. They were young men in their thirties and early forties. Many came from Eastern schools and had impressive records of advance degrees and intellectual performance. They were eager to exercise power, and in contrast to most older civilians and civil servants who work in the Department of Defense they were not overawed by the military rank. With Secretary McNamara the "whiz kids" dominated the military establishment for eight years, revamped the armed forces, increased the annual defense budget costs from $44 to over $80 billion, and led the nation into the most unpopular and devisive war of its history. By 1969 they had mostly left the scene—a scene dominated by the Vietnam war, a huge 3.4-million-man establishment, entangled in expensive and dubious weapons programs, and a rising tide of public criticism of the whole defense complex.

McNamara has been accused by former colleagues in the Kennedy administration, such as Richard Goodwin, Marcus Raskin, and John Kenneth Galbraith, of being instrumental in creating a military machine of such enormity and power that it is no longer responsive to political control. The critics maintain that the Kennedy administration had the avowed aim of establishing greater civilian control over the military, but by 1969 the military establishment was in fact playing a greater role in determining American policy than at any time since World War II. McNamara became an advocate of the defense establishment and in a large degree a captive of military programs. He didn't represent political control so much as he and his team exercised civilian management that created an immense and powerful bureaucy which dominates much of the government.

Flexible Response in Vietnam

McNamara has also been accused of being dominant among those who during 1964–1965 led a misinformed President Johnson down the tragic road of expanded war in Vietnam—a battlefield already notorious as the cemetery for the careers of generals and diplomats. One Johnson associate declared that "It was Robert McNamara who persuaded the President that we should go in there and that the war could be won. Of course Bundy and Rusk were saying the same things days after day." At the time there was an apparent belief at the top levels of the Office of the Secretary of Defense that superior administrative efficiency and good management of armed forces power could win the war.

It was largely the decisions and recommendations of Secretary McNamara, not those of the professional military men of the Joint Chiefs of Staff, that guided the early years of the war in Vietnam and shaped the American military-industry war machine. There is little doubt that McNamara was in charge of the intervention in Vietnam—but no responsible or high-ranking active military or naval officer has seen fit to publicly oppose any of the plans, policies, or predictions emanating from the Department of Defense since February, 1965. In the words of Admiral John T. Hayward, USN Retired, "where, for instance, are the [military] people who disagree with Westmoreland or McNamara?" [18] Obviously, as Professor Hans Morgenthau puts it: "No general was going to admit that the U.S. couldn't win this lousy little war against a couple of hundred thousand peasants in pajamas."

With the approval of the President, Secretary McNamara exercised a degree of personal control and supervision of the Vietnam war operations and build-up typical of the way he managed the Pentagon. He used the Joint Staff Operations and Plans staff to attain a high degree of centralized control and rapid decision-making capability. He exercised around-the-clock control of armed forces through the National Military Command Center and its world-wide communications. "Once a decision is made," reported a Pentagon staffer, "we are ready to start moving troops in less than four hours. This compares to a reaction time of eighteen to twenty hours several years ago." The availability of troops, airlift and sealift, and supply status data were recorded in memory banks and computers figured out the problem in the fastest possible time.

During his years of guiding the Vietnam operations, McNamara maintained his own staff of statisticians and analysts who called on the Operations people of the Joint Staff for reports and data from the combat zone. Aircraft sorties, loss rates, bomb tonnages dropped, ammunition expended, killed-by-air claims, weapons losses, prisoners captured, kill ratios and body counts were compiled, analyzed, charted, and graphed to support conclusions that the war was progressing or to be the basis of new plans and decisions.[19] Unfortunately for McNamara, much of the data was at best conjecture—or at worst, fabrication.

Although some insiders have defended McNamara as being privately unhappy about our military venture in Vietnam and supporting it mainly out of loyalty to the President, his public statements did not reveal any such reservations. He said, "I don't object to its being called 'McNamara's War.' I think it is a very important war and I am pleased to be identified with it and do whatever I can to win it." He repeatedly fell into his own traps of miscalculations and public predictions about the course of the war. Until his resignation in 1968, McNamara persisted in his efforts to analyze facts and figures and to relate manpower, firepower, morale, and leadership into a quantifiable matrix that would prove the war was being won. Like so many of his civilian colleagues in the Pentagon, he had no conception of the realities of the battlefield. His chief concern was with the collection of facts and data rather than with an understanding of their significance.

At the same time he could perceive the evident failure of the bombing attacks upon North Vietnam. The effort could be measured in tons of bombs and the results seen in aerial photos. He made his candid opinions known throughout the government and received the antagonism of the military and the irritation of the President. His 1967 disenchantment with the bombing was probably the beginning of McNamara's disillusionment with the war, the erosion of his loyalty to the Commander in Chief, and the festering doubts about the war's purpose. It began to dawn on him, as so many of his fellow intellectuals had already seen, that the U.S.

techniques of fire and military power were immoral and were in fact destroying the peoples we were striving to assist. There was really never any clear objective in the war, there has been no sense of direction. As Dr. Kissinger has stated, direction is the purpose of policy-making.

In fairness to Secretary McNamara and his military advisers, none of them wanted or intended in 1965 to put more than limited combat forces into Vietnam. Their calculations, confidence, and misunderstanding of the nature of the revolutionary war led them to grossly underestimate the resources of the enemy. The subsequent increases in U.S. involvement resulted from the stamina, determination and tactics of the other side.

McNamara, of all the bright young men who influenced the defense policies of President Kennedy and Johnson, was actually probably the least militaristic. His great objective was to get the establishment under control, to have the armed forces make sense, and to preserve the peace at the least possible cost. He didn't really desire to employ armed power. During the Cuban crisis he violated all the principles of military leadership by interfering with subordinate commanders in the details of their jobs. Up until his resignation he tried to evaluate a victory in Vietnam by a variety of statistics and reports to prove that American firepower and equipment was winning the hearts and minds of the South Vietnamese and defeating the Viet Cong.

Each year in office the Secretary announced the substantial economies he claimed to have effected by improved defense management and organization. Yet when he took over the defense establishment in 1961 military spending was running at $44.7 billion a year. He reduced some waste, overlapping and duplication of functions, but he also initiated such billion-dollar boggles as the F-111 and C-5A. When he left office in 1968, defense costs had reached $80 billion and were going up. McNamara's war machine was hardly a bargain-basement model. But even more disturbing was the realization that a small underequipped army of irregulars was fighting to a bloody standstill the finest and best-equipped expeditionary force America had ever fielded. In March of 1968, Secretary McNamara folded his charts and departed the

Pentagon, a puzzled and sad man who had shaken the defense forces from top to bottom in search of efficiency but hadn't learned that successful wars must be fought, not managed.

Eclipse of the Military

Although not always agreeing with them, McNamara reiterated on occasion that his civilian officers were listening to the military advisers more than had any previous administrations. It was, he maintained, the responsibility of the civilian leaders to accept or reject the proposals of the Joint Chiefs. Usually the recommendations were accepted—as they were following the Tonkin Gulf incident. McNamara reportedly called the Chiefs into his office and asked them how the United States should reply. The opinion was unanimous: air attacks should be launched against North Vietnam bases. McNamara passed the advice on to the President, who summoned the Chiefs to a White House conference and subsequently followed their advice in detail. (Twenty-one months earlier, during the Cuban missile crisis of 1962, the Joint Chiefs had similarly advised immediate bombing of Cuban missile sights. President Kennedy rejected the wisdom of his military advisers on that occasion.)

One of the main causes for the relative decrease in the military's policy-making role following Korea and during the McNamara years has been the failure of the services to develop joint and integrated doctrines based upon the capabilities of the defense establishment as a whole rather than upon the special functions and interests of the separate services. Without such doctrines to guide the planners, the decision-making processes of the joint staffs have been based upon compromise and mutual aggrandizement. Positions and proposals are diluted by consensus agreements which satisfied each individual service. The Chiefs perform best on large and broad issues and key decisions, particularly those involving military contingency plans, interventions, and operations. They usually agree on a hard power line based upon readiness. As would be supposed, they find more difficulty on questions related to programs, priorities, and resources which touch the service budget, long-range plans and the details of national security policy.[20] As a result many of the difficult planning, programming, and budgeting decisions fell to the civilians.

The military backwardness and traditionalism in the Pentagon also gave the New Frontiersman sufficient reasons to seize power from the professionals. The "LeMays" persisted in piloting their SAC bombers and neglected the establishment of an effective limited and conventional warfare force. The Joint Chiefs and their planners clung to their old rituals of decision-making which further decreased military effectiveness and prestige. The JCS problem-solving routine involves four stages: A draft or "flimsy" (white paper) is the first effort (by the planners—or "joint action" officers) that requires the formal views of Army, Navy, Air Force, and Marine Corps. In a typical minor JCS paper it is not unusual to devote as many as 1,600 man-hours drafting the first-stage paper. Next, the study or report is typed on "buff" paper by the Joint Staff and is the subject of more coordinating conferences chaired by representatives from the Joint Staff and attended by action officers from each service. Upon attainment of fullest possible agreement at this level, the paper turns "green" and the problem goes on the Joint Chiefs' agenda. Prior to their consideration of the paper, each member of the JCS receives a detailed oral and written briefing by the action officers at his own service headquarters on the content of the paper and the recommended positions of his staff. After approval of the paper by the Joint Staff it is "red striped" and becomes an official policy, directive, or plan.[21] If the Chiefs can't agree, the problem goes to the Secretary of Defense along with the varied opinions, and the Secretary makes a decision. Most of the hundreds of JCS papers considered by the Chiefs each year are agreed upon at the working levels. The big and important problems, however, are frequently the cause of dissension among the Chiefs.

The handicaps of these procedures which hamper the Joint Chiefs stem from their dual roles as members of the corporate JCS and their loyalties to their respective services. Each Chief is expected to consider the problems from the national point of view; yet when he returns to his own staff and debriefs them on the outcome of the JCS deliberations, he is prompted by the desire to report a victory for the positions recommended by his loyal and hard-working staff "Indians." The "Whiz Kids," operating more informally, directly—and objectively, were able to reach decisions rapidly and evidenced scorn for the indirect rituals of the military.[22] The military should blame none but themselves for their declining influence during the McNamara years.

Robert McNamara fully realized the complexity of defense decision-making, and long before he became entrapped by the pressures of militarism and the distractions of the Vietnam war, he stated: "But at heart the problem comes down always to the same questions: What is really in our national interest? What will help this country to play the role we want it to play in this terribly critical period of the world's history? We are interested in saving money—in sound military-civilian relations, in the whole range of issues which tend to dominate the headlines. But the national interest towers above them all; and it is the national interest, above all, that we seek to serve." [23]

Department of Defense energies since 1961 have been largely devoted to creating smooth-functioning administrative apparatus rather than clarifying the criteria on which decisions should be based. Major issues have been reduced to their simplest terms. Decision-making is a group effort by planners and corporate Chiefs. The key executives choose from options and proposals based upon details which are unfamiliar. The defense officials, admirals, and generals dependent more and more on their subordinates' conception of the essential elements of a problem and their skill of oral briefing. In such an environment there is minimum opportunity for creativity.[24] Those responsible for leadership become the captives of their staff planning specialists and briefing officers.

The "oral briefing" is an element of military decision-making and staff ritual which evolved initially during World War II in the Army and Air forces. It came of age in the Korean War and now is an important part of command and staff procedure at every military and naval headquarters. In most major headquarters it often attains spectacular proportions. In these institutionalized, informal, oral-visual briefings, communications are passed upward from staff to responsible decision-makers and commanders. The briefing is both a formal, stylized presentation and an informal meeting where decisions are arrived at by elaborate compromise. Crucial decisions frequently hinge upon the techniques and skill of the briefing officer and staff planner. The oral briefing is a staff procedure which responds to the speed of events and makes use of the latest techniques in data transmissions, communications, and electronics. The briefing is necessary because the flow of paperwork is less effectual in the military than in other bureaucracies. The audience at a normal briefing, in addition to the Chiefs or commanders, consists of the chiefs of staff sections and the young working staff planners. All are expected to speak up and help inform and convince the commander.

The briefing helps coordinate staff action, as it avoids otherwise normal blocks to information flow. Briefings are daily affairs in the Pentagon, in the command control centers in each service, the unified commands, and in every headquarters with a staff in Vietnam. In fact, the briefing productions put on by the military has no counterpart in civilian operations, and the "dog and pony show" spectaculars have contributed no small part to the military's ability to "snow" the civilians in the Department of Defense and Congress during the recent years of waxing militarism. This military style of communications has become a ritualistic recitation of memorized details and a reduction of information to a format of quantifiable data.

The Vietnam war has exposed the dangers of the briefing routine. Frequently the staff briefings in Vietnam have "proved" that the war was being won by the quantity of ammunition expended on suspicious areas and "body counts" of enemy dead that were impossible to verify as enemy, much less as dead. Officials at the highest decision-making levels have often been misled by "canned briefings" which have converted conjecture and assumption into hard facts of figures, charts, and map symbols remote from human efforts or reality.[25] Only lately has Congress awakened enough to look behind the scenery of the briefing shows for the shenanigans going on backstage.

Renaissance of the JCS

Despite the recent criticism of the military establishment and its leaders, prompted largely by the national frustrations over the war in Vietnam, the influence of the Joint Chiefs of Staff paradoxically has been rising within the Nixon administration. In contrast to the practices of the McNamara regime in the Pentagon, Secretary Laird is reportedly giving considerably more weight to the advice and judgment of the Chiefs of Staff. The civilian defense analysts and "whiz kids" have either been downgraded or replaced. The National Security Council machinery, revitalized and managed by Dr. Henry A. Kissinger, now provides a formal channel for the Joint Chiefs to express their own views to the White House. Under McNamara, military advice that reached the White House was usually an "agreed" Pentagon position reflecting the views of the Secretary and his civilian analysts. A number of the miscalculations and mistakes of the Vietnam war and the costly military procurement programs were the fruits of McNamara's procedures. At the same time, the review of the military plans, programs, and budgets fostered by McNamara was sound procedure. The military was forced to justify their proposals to civilian defense systems and operations analysts. Because of the size and complexity of these matters they had not heretofore been carefully examined by the Budget Review, Congressional hearings, nor in National Security Council and White House studies.

The danger of the re-emergent influence of the Joint Chiefs of Staff is the possible reduction of checks and balances at the Pentagon level. The military services represent a most powerful coalition of vested interest with inherent biases, expansionist tendencies, and doctrinal objectives typical of large bureaucracies. Interservice rivalries, prior to McNamara, served to balance the services off against each other as they made the annual drive for their share of the defense budget. Now, as a result of the functional forces approach to budget determination, the services conceal their differences from public view outside the Pentagon and cooperate for their mutual benefit. The Chief of Naval Operations publicly expresses support of the C-5A air transport program when actually the C-5A concept is in direct competition to traditional Navy strategic sealift concepts. It was some years after the Joint Chiefs of Staff "unanimously" recommended deployment of the antiballistic missile system (ABM) before a Congressional committee learned that the Air Chief of Staff was actually opposed to it.[26] The new, expensive, and controversial weapons programs being proposed are originated in the services and are espoused by the Joint Chiefs of Staff. The civilians in the Defense Department, the Secretary of Defense, and the President don't dream up the ABM's, the MIRV's, the new bombers, and the other increasingly costly contributions to the arms race. They are the products of military advice.

So the serious responsibility of controlling the military now appears to fall upon Congress, which hardly has time to comprehend all of the weapons gobbledegook, and upon Dr. Kissinger in the White House who may well become swamped by the details of military paperwork and the determined, ambitious Pentagon planning. The combined efforts of the military careerists and their Chiefs of Staff eventually wore Mr. McNamara down—and he was the sturdiest Secretary to ever attempt control of the Pentagon.

In June of 1969, when Senator Stennis, Chairman of the Senate Armed Services Committee, opened the debate on the Defense Procurement Bill with his support of the ABM Safeguard system, he stated that it should be approved mainly because the President wanted it and whatever the President felt necessary for national defense should not be denied him. This was the old canard which supports the myth that the civilian heads of the defense establishment determine all requirements and set policy, and that the military merely carry out orders. Actually the ABM concept has been promoted off and on by the U.S. Army for over ten years. It was to be a new mission and role for the increasingly vestigial anti-aircraft artillery (missile) command whose job had pretty well disappeared as the possibility of attack by enemy manned bombers became less likely. The ABM promised to open up whole new careers and vast new commands. Neither President Johnson nor President Nixon nor Secretary Laird conceived the requirement for the ABM, and it is even doubtful that its detailed functioning was clear to these busy men. The ABM was sold to the civilian heads of the defense establishment by the convincing Army missile technicians and other vested interests who built a case for the enemy threats and the need for an ABM system. At one time even the Air Force opposed the Army's ABM program, but they eventually closed ranks and went on to suggest that perhaps there should also be an airborne ABM system and the Navy added thoughts on the merits of a shipborne ABM. Merely because the President or the Secretary of Defense is sold on certain programs by defense interests, if history is to teach anything, should no longer be reason enough for Congress to approve the request until after careful analysis.

Once the military and its planning officers are called into administration policy councils, their political power increases enormously. The military has strategic and operational expertise because it is "experienced" and knows the language of the trade. Military vernacular and technical gobbledegook quickly put the civilian official at a disadvantage because in high circles he is reluctant to reveal his ignorance, so he accepts the military rationale and advice. If he has doubts, he hesitates to question the distinguished and bemedaled "experts."

The military controls much of the intelligence coming from the critical problem area and has the photo interpreters, chart designers, and skilled briefing officers who graphically explain the situation. The military planners are usually prepared for crises and contingencies. Or they have preliminary studies, estimates, and photos available which enable military advisers to present their views supported by facts and firm recommendations of what must be done.

The military influence increases with the Congress, the press, and its industrial allies when contingencies arise. The services declare with confidence what they can do if permitted, that is, the proper employment of air power will quickly turn the tide, etc. The military inevitably pushes for more escalation, larger task forces, weapons for every possibility—and overkill firepower. The civilians find it difficult to deny "the troops" whatever they deem necessary to insure success. To do so adds to the civilian mythology that without such escalation they would be holding the commanders back and giving them less than they wanted. In turn, the military feels entitled to demand more and more, and so dominates the planning.

Each service strives to play its role and to be given a mission in the plan. To be left out or to play a minor role means a loss of status. Within the military hierarchy, careerism is at work among the planners, who do not dare to risk a charge of being soft on Communist aggression or of having doubts about the wisdom and prospects of the military venture. The military becomes enthralled with the details of force requirements, task forces, and operational planning—quickly relegating any concern over the purposes or propriety of the venture to the civilian leaders, who are prone to defer to the fighting men. Only a very courageous civilian can resist the tough militaristic solutions of the generals and admirals in an emergency. For most men in high position, being tough and exerting ready power is more attractive than acting sensibly or practicing patience. But it is easy to be tough when toughness means coercing the weak and rewarding the strong, and when men of power and influence stand ready to applaud. It is far harder to hold to principle, standing for firm ideals even when they bring danger. But it is the true path of courage. It is the only path of wisdom—the sure path of service to the United States.

Footnotes

[1] Samuel P. Huntington. *The Soldiers and the State.* Harvard University Press, Cambridge, Mass., 1964, pp. 319–323.
[2] *Ibid.,* p. 336.
[3] *Ibid.,* p. 386.
[4] *Ibid.,* p. 395.
[5] "Top Authority Looks at Vietnam War and Its Future," *U.S. News & World Report,* February 21, 1966.
[6] *Ibid.*
[7] David Halberstam, "The Very Expensive Education of McGeorge Bundy," *Harper's Magazine,* July, 1969.
[8] *Ibid.*

[9] "Bundy's Second Thoughts," *Newsweek,* October 21, 1968.

[10] Halberstam, op. cit.

[11] Townsend W. Hoopes, *The Limits of Intervention.* David McKay Co., New York, New York, 1969.

[12] "The Power in the Pentagon," *Newsweek,* December 6, 1965.

[13] Sec Def Memo, January 11, 1965, signed by Deputy Secretary of Defense, Cyrus Vance.

[14] "McNamara Speaks on Defense Decision-Making; Cites 'Chaos' of Past," *Army Navy Air Force Journal and Register,* May 4, 1963.

[15] Jack Raymond, *Power at the Pentagon,* Harper & Row, New York, 1964.

[16] Richard J. Stillman, "The Pentagon Whiz Kids," *U.S. Naval Institute Proceedings,* April, 1966.

[17] Tristram Coffin, *The Passion of the Hawks,* The Macmillan Co., New York, 1964.

[18] John T. Hayward, "The Second-Class Military Advisor: His Cause and Cure," *Armed Forces Management,* November, 1968.

[19] "The Power in the Pentagon," *Newsweek,* December 6, 1965.

[20] Craig Powell, "Civilian/Military Rapport Reaches a New Maturity in the Defense Arena," *Armed Forces Management,* December, 1967.

[21] Richard Stillman, "The Pentagon Whiz Kids," *U.S. Naval Institute Proceedings,* April, 1966.

[22] *Ibid.*

[23] "Secretary McNamara Speaks on Defense Decision-Making; Cites 'Chaos' of Past," *Army Navy Air Force Journal and Register,* May 4, 1963.

[24] Henry A. Kissinger, *The Necessity for Choice,* Harper & Row, New York, 1960.

[25] Time Essay, *TIME* magazine, October 10, 1969.

[26] "The Military Influence," *New York Times* editorial, July 6, 1969.

Chapter VII

MILITARY GAMESMANSHIP

"One of the tragedies of unification is that there are not, at the top, men who really know enough about each of the services to evaluate all of those services."
Hanson W. Baldwin in The New York Times, *1949*.

The Services' Roles and Missions

At the end of World War II, steps were taken by the Truman administration and a few Army and Navy leaders to design a postwar organization of the defense establishment that would resolve some of the problems of rivalry and command relations. The Army War Department, with the concurrence of the administration, favored merging the services under a single Department of War. The proposed concepts for the unification of the armed forces under a single general staff involved, among other changes, a considerably reduced and restricted role for the Marine Corps and transfer of naval aviation to the new Air Force. The general idea was to transform the Corps back to its 1939 size and posture —minus its aviation, which would also go to the new Air Force. In addition, a proposed Senate bill included authority for the Secretary of Defense to prescribe service "roles and missions" without need of Congressional sanction.* The National Security

* There has been no official definition of *roles* and *missions* as they pertain to the separate services. Existing laws and directives have also used *duty* and *function* to describe what each service shall do and its relationship to the other services. "Function" is now probably a more appropriate term than roles and missions.

Act of 1947, as passed, reflected the wisdom of Congress and their sympathy and concern for the traditions, pride, and morale of the naval services. The bill included substantial roles for the Marine Corps as well as retention of the Navy's air arm.

Despite the 1947 Defense Act, however, controversy over service roles and missions continued to boil behind the façade of the newly "unified" Armed Forces. So a harassed Secretary of Defense, James Forrestal, gathered the Joint Chiefs of Staff at Key West, Florida, in March, 1948, to discuss the interservice problems. Functions of the armed services and the Joint Chiefs of Staff were agreed upon and spelled out. Elaborating on the basic National Security Act of 1947, the Department of Defense then published a directive known as the "Functions Paper," or the "Key West Agreement." Subsequent revisions in the National Security Act of 1947 and the Functions Paper were eventually codified and published as doctrine in *Joint Action Armed Forces*. Its successor, *Unified Action Armed Forces,* which followed the Defense Reorganization Act of 1958 is the current guiding doctrinal source of service roles and missions and defines *how* the services are to operate in joint operations. It emphasizes the principle of "Unity of Effort."

Defense Reorganization Act of 1958

The practice, which began in 1947, of specifying roles and missions in legislation was seriously challenged again in 1958. President Eisenhower, seeking to streamline the Department of Defense machinery for the rapid response required in the atomic weapons age, presented a number of reorganization proposals to Congress.

Included in these proposals was one giving the Secretary of Defense the power to transfer, reassign, abolish, or consolidate functions authorized by law. Speaking for the administration, Secretary of Defense Neil McElroy explained the purpose of the proposal as follows:

> There is no desire for authority to emasculate any of the four services. The desire is simply for the Presi-

dent and the Secretary of Defense to have authority to
eliminate overlap and duplication in the application of
the statutory language to specific instances or situations
so that two services will not be claiming that each is
entitled to do the same thing.[1]

The law, as enacted by Congress, granted, in part, the powers
requested by the President for the Secretary of Defense. The
language of the Defense Reorganization Act, however, did provide
for the organizational integrity of the departments and services.
Congress described the basic policy embodied in the Defense
Reorganization Act of 1958, in part as follows:

> In enacting this legislation, it is the intent of Congress
> to . . . provide a Department of Defense including the
> three military departments of the Army, the Navy (in-
> cluding naval aviation and the United States Marine
> Corps), and the Air Force under the direction, author-
> ity, and control of the Secretary of Defense; to provide
> that each military department shall be separately or-
> ganized under its own Secretary . . . ; to provide for
> their unified direction under civilian control of the Sec-
> retary of Defense but not to merge these departments
> or services. . . .

Despite these prolonged and repeated efforts to curtail rivalry
between the armed services and to achieve agreement as to who
does what and where, the problems of roles and missions or functions and command relations have remained very much alive.

Command Relations

Because of routine security classification, much that goes on
within and between the services is rarely made public. "Command
relations" is a continuous, even traditional, and longstanding area
of interservice rivalry. It is a subject for intrigue and behind-the-
scenes maneuvering in Washington, among the unified commands,
and in joint contingency planning which is usually kept secret and

within the sanctums of the high commands and their staffs. It revolves essentially around the questions: Who will provide the commanding officer for a joint task force or joint command? Which service will provide officers for the key joint staff billets, such as Chief of Staff and operations officer, and what will be the chain of command to the several service components making up the joint command? What forces will make up a joint command? In other words, Who will be in charge? Command relations have a direct bearing upon service status, pride, functions, publicity, and the doctrines governing the conduct of the operation.

Prior to Pearl Harbor and the subsequent large combined operations with allies and the joint Army-Navy World War II landing operations, command relations between the Army and Navy and the Marines were largely academic matters. For years the Army and Navy each generally went its own way with little concern about what the other did except at the annual confrontation before Congress, where each presented its case for a fair share of the defense budget pie. Army and Navy officers met at their clubs in Washington, faced each other at the football game, but otherwise were usually remote in life, habits, training, and strategic concepts. A small number of service planners had been meeting since the early 1920's at the Washington level on the old Joint Army-Navy Board to define general missions of the two services. In 1927 the Board had produced "Joint Action, Army and Navy," a significant doctrinal guide for joint operations and eventually, early in World War II, the Joint Army-Navy Board evolved into what is now the Joint Chiefs of Staff. But joint training exercises, joint task forces, and joint contingency planning—even direct and close liaison—were mostly lacking between the services and their operating forces prior to December 7, 1941.

During the years before World War II the Marines alone were concerned with the refinements of command relations in joint operations because the Corps, while an element of the Navy, had occasionally served for prolonged periods under the Army in land campaigns. World War I had not clarified or enhanced the Marines' function within the Navy, and during the postwar years the Marines were desperately seeking a mission and reason for existence. They found in Gallipoli, the amphibious fiasco conducted by the British forces at the Dardenelles in 1915, an operation which, instead of demonstrating the futility of modern landing operations, could be used to prove the need for specially trained amphibious forces. The Marine students of Gallipoli concluded that the British had failed to take the Dardenelles because of faulty doctrine, poor techniques, ineffective leadership, and lack of coordination between the services. The Marine Corps concentrated on command relations with the Navy in amphibious operations and developed a tentative doctrine for joint landing operations which served as the basis of all subsequent World War II amphibious invasions.

In theory, the Fleet Marine Force was only under the administrative command of the Navy and many operational command difficulties were supposedly avoided by the existing doctrine for landing operations. In the beginning, however, at Guadalcanal in 1942, and frequently thereafter in the Pacific War, the Marines suffered the efforts of admirals who also wanted to be generals. The Marines had problems with the Army too. During that war the Marines deeply resented the loss of the 4th Marine Regiment on Corregidor while serving under the Army and General MacArthur and so bent every effort to get the 1st Marine Division out from under MacArthur's Sixth Army command after the battle for Cape Gloucester in 1944.

In turn, the Army high command in the Pacific often criticized the Marines' fitness to command large-scale operations and never forgave nor forgot the summary relief by Marine Lt. General "Howlin' Mad" Smith of Major General Ralph Smith, Commander of the Army 27th Infantry Division. This episode occurred during the battle for Saipan in the summer of 1944 when the Army division was serving under the Marines' amphibious command.

At the same time, the Navy was never happy about its Seventh Fleet being assigned to MacArthur's Southwest Pacific forces and chose to concentrate its main efforts in a primarily all-Navy and Marine Corps Central Pacific campaign.

In the European theater, command relations problems were mostly between the allies rather than between the U.S. Services. The Army was making the major U.S. contribution, so General

Eisenhower and his Army generals dominated the joint American commands. There were some problems with the Navy during the planning and execution of major amphibious landings which preceded each land campaign, but for the most part the Army ran the show and the Navy had its second team assigned to the European war. The Navy's main efforts were concentrated upon the naval campaigns against the Japanese in the Pacific where the admirals were in command. The basic issue in the Pacific theater was whether the Navy or the Army forces would spearhead the attack against Japan. Suspicions arose that each service, Army and Navy, was trying to dominate the other in the Pacific.[2]

Command relations between the Army, Marines, and the Navy in the field were never entirely resolved during World War II, nor have they been since, in spite of postwar doctrine for unified action and joint commands.

Unity of Effort

The guiding doctrinal concept of our military establishment as an effiicent team of land, naval, and air forces is based on the principle that effective utilization of the nation's military power requires the efforts of the separate military services to be closely integrated. Unity of effort among the services at the national level is obtained by the authority of the President and the Secretary of Defense, exercised through the military departments and the Joint Chiefs of Staff. It is also attained by the strategic planning and direction of the Joint Chiefs of Staff. Unity of effort and close cooperation among service forces assigned to unified or specified commands is achieved by exercise of operational command, by adherence to common strategic plans, and by sound operational and administrative command relations and organization.[3]

Lack of unity and joint doctrine as well as operational rivalry is, nevertheless, evident in the conduct of joint planning, joint exercises, and in joint combat operations such as Vietnam. Doctrinal differences consist of the varying concepts of the four services on the tactics, techniques and organization for combat. Each service has a different view of its own importance and role in war and in relation to the other services. The individual members of the services also have opinions about how well the sister services are performing. Such opinions are usually critical.

Some of the major and long-standing areas of doctrinal differences and interservice rivalry have been:

1. The relative effectiveness and cost of land-based air power versus carrier-based air power (Air Force vs. Navy).
2. The policies governing command and control of all air power in the combat zone (Air Force vs. Navy and Marines).
3. The organization, control and techniques of close air support (Air Force vs. Army vs. Marines).
4. The relative values of strategic mobility by airlift or sealift (Army-Air Force vs. Navy-Marines).
5. Airborne assault operations versus amphibious assault operations (Army-Air Force vs. Navy-Marines).
6. Command of Marine ground forces in land combat under a Field Army (Army vs. Marines).
7. Command of SAC bombers performing tactical-type missions in support Army forces (Army vs. Air Force).
8. Unified and special logistic support of Marine and Army forces in joint operations (Marines vs. Army).
9. Land-based, sea-based and airborne ICBM's and ABM's (Army vs. Air Force vs. Navy).
10. The nature and size of Army aviation (Army vs. Air Force).
11. The need and value of manned bombers and air defense interceptors (Air Force vs. Army).
12. The short atomic war concept (Army vs. Air Force).
13. The Navy-Marine team as the answer to limited war (Navy-Marines vs. Army-Air Force).
14. Forward deployment of ground forces versus U.S.-based mobile strategic reserve forces (Air Force vs. Army and Marines).[4]

Many of these doctrinal differences stem from the varied methods and traditions of the services, and they are further bolstered by service pride, a lack of understanding of the other services, and a natural desire on the part of each of the armed forces to fight a war in its own manner, under its own commanders, thereby insure its share of success and glory. In Vietnam Generals Westmoreland and Abrams, commanders of Military Assistance Command Vietnam (MACV), have not only had to unify the efforts of their U.S. air, ground, and sea components despite these longstanding differences, but have also been handicapped by a command relations structure imposed upon them by the politicians in Washington and the admirals at Pearl Harbor.

Actually, the top level civilians around President Johnson in Washington controlled the basic decision-making and strategy formulation during the winter of 1964–1965, as the nation moved doggedly into the Vietnam war. In this respect Vietnam was a civilian-run war. At the same time in Saigon the United States military completely dominated the civilian side of the country team. But in MACV the concerns were mainly operations, tactics, bombing targets in the South, pacification, and data gathering for reports to Pearl Harbor and Washington.

The headquarters of the Commander-in-Chief Pacific (CINCPAC) overlooking Pearl Harbor at Oahu, Hawaii, has also been influential in the command and conduct of the Vietnam war but has been generally neglected by news media and analysts looking for either paragons or culprits. The Pacific Command is one of the United States' major area unified commands which control the planning and operations of all the four service components assigned to the strategic area.*

Commander-in-Chief Pacific has always been a naval officer. Under his command are U.S. Army Forces, Pacific; U.S. Air Force Pacific; the Pacific Fleet; and Fleet Marine Forces, Pacific. All have their headquarters on Oahu.

Military Assistance Command Vietnam (MACV) in Saigon is also a unified type of command in that all services were repre-

---

* Other area unified commands are the European Command, Atlantic Command, and the Alaskan Command.

sented, but Commanding General MACV has been under the direct chain of command from CINCPAC. MACV also frequently dealt directly with the JCS and even the White House on some matters during the war, but, in the winter of 1964–1965, as the nation moved toward large-scale entry into the Vietnam war, the role of CINCPAC was a dominant one, as evidenced by its role in the Gulf of Tonkin events.

The U.S. command structure in Vietnam has been one of the most confusing of all wars: General William C. Westmoreland (and his successor, General Creighton H. Abrams) has had operational control of all U.S. forces in the country and as Commander of MACV has also been Commander U.S. Army Republic of Vietnam (COMUSARV). Under COMUSMACV the day-to-day U.S. Army operations are run by the Deputy Commander for USARV. Operational control of all Army ground units in the II, III, and IV Corps areas is assigned to First and Second Field Forces under U.S. Army generals.

The Air Force component of USMACV is headed by an Air Force lieutenant general who is COMUSMACV's deputy for air operations and is also commander of the 2nd Air Division at Tan Son Nhut air base in Saigon.

The III Marine Amphibious Force (III MAF), under a Marine lieutenant general, has had command of operations in the northern I Corps and this general was also the Navy component commander under COMUSMACV. The Marine commander has also been senior adviser to the Army of the Republic of Vietnam (ARVN) in I Corps. In each of the other corps areas the advisory group (with the ARVN) is headed by a U.S. Army officer.

The commanding general MACV commands all U.S. Army troops and Marine divisions in South Vietnam as well as soldiers sent there from South Korea, the Philippines, Australia, and New Zealand. He has control of the tactical air forces based in South Vietnam supporting these ground troops, but he has not been in command of the U.S. naval forces in the South China Sea. Nor has he commanded the B-52 bombers of SAC based on Guam, Okinawa, and Thailand. They remained under the United States-based Strategic Air Command. Also, all of the fighter bombers of the Air Force based in Thailand, which conducted the bombing of North Vietnam, have been under the control of CINCPAC. The fleet carriers and their bombers which conducted strikes against North Vietnam were also directed by the Navy and CINCPAC. In fact, the commander of MACV had no responsibility for the air war against North Vietnam. It was all he could do to get limited authority to make counterattacks against targets across the DMZ with his aircraft based in South Vietnam.

Except for specific missions American commanders have not commanded large Vietnamese military forces. There has been no unified or combined command of ARVN and U.S. forces. In the words of Secretary McNamara, the battlefield has been "split into segments," with the ARVN operating under their own commander in one segment and U.S. troops "supporting" the ARVN in another segment. While the U.S. military commitment has been to *assist* the government of South Vietnam in the conduct of its counter-insurgency and defense efforts, in fact, between 1965 and the proposed de-Americanization of the war in mid-1969, U.S. forces increasingly fought the war *for* South Vietnam.

In addition to the complexities of organization which have typified the military effort in Vietnam, there has never been an American war with a higher ratio of generals, colonels, and rear-area support types of troops. According to reports, eighty generals have found jobs in and around Saigon; colonels are sufficient to command a few hundred regiments, and throughout the American forces about 75 percent of the troop strength has consisted of logistic support men and clerks in service organizations.

"Pentagon East," the sprawling headquarters of MACV, and its satellite Army Air Force, and ARVN headquarters located at Tan Son Nhut air base, is replete with hordes of staff officers and special sections such as MACSOG and MACMAP (Military Assistance Command Studies and Observation Group and Military Assistance Command Military Assistance Program directorate). The vast and baffling organization created by the military to manage the Vietnam venture would be a joy to Professor G. Northcote Parkinson.

Top-ranking military analysts have maintained that the war,

third largest in American history, should have had a single commander for all forces. Military critics have further maintained that the unified commander of all forces, including allies, should have been the Commanding General of the Military Assistance Command, Vietnam, instead of the existing arrangement under which the MACV command's immediate superior is an admiral commanding the Pacific area with his headquarters thousands of miles away in Honolulu.

The Army and the Air Force officers in Vietnam supported a unified command concept for Vietnam, a command which would consist simply of an Army component, a Navy component, and an Air Force component, all with headquarters in Saigon at the Headquarters of a "Commander in Chief Southeast Asia" (CINCSEA). It would have been an area unified command directly under the JCS in Washington. Such a concept has been opposed by—among others—top Marine and Navy people who desired to maintain the historic sanctity of the U.S. Navy's command dominance of the entire Pacific area.[5]

Lt. Gen. Ira C. Eaker, USAF (Ret.), a close student of the war in Southeast Asia, stated that "all the wars we and our allies have won in this century clearly support the need for unified command and demonstrate that war is not a venture that will ever be a successful, cooperative enterprise managed by committees with divided responsibility in the battle area." Many service professionals recognize this truth but in practice they are frequently their own worst enemies.

Even though major strategy decisions at the White House level were "civilian" and "unified," their details were often left for implementation to the divergent interests of the four services. The most frequent disagreements have, however, been between the Washington-level civilian-military planners who consider both national and interservice political factors, and the MACV command which has to contend with the enemy, the GRVN, and the four U.S. services, each of whom is fighting a different type of war.

Comments by fighting men returned from Vietnam and outspoken and frustrated retiring officers reiterate the recurrent problems of command relations and interservice rivalry in the tragic war. Despite the efforts of public affairs officials in the Pentagon to control criticism and to direct the nature of statements by military men, a mass of evidence dramatically portrays the continuing problems of command in Vietnam. Administration defenders counter by accusing the dissidents of not understanding that Vietnam has not been a military war, but rather a war run by civilians to achieve civilian objectives. Considering the cost in blood and money and the failure to achieve most objectives, such a civilian-run war has not demonstrated convincing success. The command relations and the organization of U.S. forces, as well as the relations with the forces of South Vietnam, have violated the basic American doctrine of unity of command. Despite the lessons of history, civilian leaders have tolerated, for political reasons, a command relations policy which fosters inter-service differences, hampers combined operations with allies, and thus undoubtedly has contributed to the difficulties of the war.

The one area where unity of effort seemed to make the most progress and achieved the greatest impact has been the reporting on the daily, weekly, and periodic accomplishments of each major command. The propaganda designed to shape public opinion and attitudes, about the progress of the war put out by the Department of Defense was created by the four services. Each has its own point of view and its own purposes, but the total result is a united effort to sell the war to the nation.

Footnotes

[1] Hearings, House Armed Services Committee, 85th Congress, Second Session, on H.R. 12541, 1958, p. 11.

[2] Iseley and Crowl, *The U.S. Marines and Amphibious War,* Princeton University Press, 1951.

[3] Joint Chiefs of Staff, *Unified Action Armed Forces, JCS Pub. 2,* Washington, D.C., 1959.

[4] Maxwell D. Taylor, *The Uncertain Trumpet,* Harper & Brothers, New York, 1959, Chapter VI.

[5] Claude Witz, "The Case for a Unified Command: CINCSEA," *Air Force Magazine,* January 1967.

Chapter VIII

A WAR FOR EVERYBODY

"News flowing from actions taken by the Government is part of the weaponry."
> Attributed to Arthur Sylvester,
> Assistant Secretary of Defense,
> 1962.

The months between Tonkin Gulf (August, 1964) and Pleiku (February, 1965), when the President decided to employ combat troops in South Vietnam, was an intriguing period for the student of militarism's influences on national opinions and policy. The late Robert F. Kennedy is reported to have stated that it was his understanding that the Joint Chiefs of Staff sold the White House on the commitment by indicating that it would be temporary. The Chiefs had judged that the small initial force of Marines and Army from Okinawa would be enough to contain the insurgency and then could be withdrawn before the end of 1965. But by the end of that year 200,000 American troops had been committed and more were on the way.[1] Whether the report is correct or not, the military led by their civilian Secretary of Defense, Robert S. McNamara, were consistently optimistic in their war reports and estimates and they were repeatedly proved wrong by events. The subsequent years of faulty reports, incorrect predictions, and miscalculations did more to damage the prestige and credibility of American military and defense leadership than any previous period in our history.

The Army's War

The U.S. Army has determined the operations, tactics, and much of the strategy in the Vietnam war. It has been essentially a land war, which is the Army's functional responsibility. The Army Military Advisory and Assistance people had been in South Vietnam in growing numbers since 1954, and the Army led the way in developing counterinsurgency doctrines to contend with Communist-inspired "wars of national liberation." The Army Special Action units, including the "green beret" Special Forces, were actively involved in counterinsurgency efforts in South Vietnam between 1961 and 1964. In December, 1964, there were almost 23,000 American Army men on duty in South Vietnam, and by their very presence it was rapidly becoming a U.S. war theater, dominated by the U.S. Army. The aggressive conduct of the Vietnam war has been according to Army doctrines and principles of long standing: find the enemy, fix him in position, fight him—and finish him off.

At the beginning of the American combat involvement in Vietnam in 1965, General William C. Westmoreland, U.S. Commander in Vietnam (MACV), planned to employ ground combat troops to hold key bases and to back up the South Vietnamese Army in the field where necessary. The Pentagon-Westmoreland plan was to build coastal bastions of U.S. troops at the Da Nang, Hue-Phu Bai, Chu Lai areas; at Bien Hoa and Vung Tau and Camranh Bay; at Pleiku-Qui Nhon, and other combat bases later. From these bases superior air and sea power would be applied and U.S. combat power could be projected for offensive operations inland as needed. This was similar to the coastal strategy, based upon the flexibility of sea power as viewed by the Navy and Marines. It was estimated at first to require only 130,000 U.S. troops including 27,000 Marines. But by late 1965 the frustrated military high command began to propose larger and more extensive offensive operations. These courses the President rejected; the bombing of Hanoi, a naval blockade of Haiphong and the northern ports, and an all-out offensive including invasion of North Vietnam. Such options remained uppermost in the military's minds for the duration but were never seriously considered by either President Johnson or President Nixon.[2] But the Johnson administration approved a steady buildup of U.S. forces to conduct large offensive operations in South Vietnam.

Lieutenant General James M. Gavin, who retired in 1958, was Chief of Army Plans and Operations in 1954 and had then advised against any U.S. ground operations in Vietnam. He has been a consistent and outspoken critic of American policies and strategies in Vietnam since the decision to intervene in 1965. In 1966, General Gavin advocated the "enclave" strategy in Vietnam. He maintained that the United States had sufficient forces there to hold several base enclaves on the coast, where sea and air power could be made fully effective. He suggested that Da Nang, Camranh Bay, and other coastal bases were logical American enclaves. Such a holding strategy would avoid stretching forces beyond reason in an endeavor to secure the entire country of South Vietnam from Viet Cong penetration, he maintained.[3] Gavin also pointed out that bombings would not stop the penetrations of North Vietnamese troops into the South. He subsequently wrote a courageous book, *Crisis Now,* dealing with both Vietnam military and American domestic problems. In his book General Gavin noted that he "was convinced from . . . personal knowledge and expertise that as a military operation Vietnam made no sense." [4] Because, he pointed out, unless the people of the country prefer the government supported by foreign troops to the guerrillas, the mere introduction of large numbers of ground troops with modern equipment would not resolve the military conflict. The wisdom of General Gavin has been repeatedly verified in Vietnam. Unfortunately, he retired from active service years too soon; the Army and the Pentagon needed him.

The strategic concept of holding key coastal enclaves is, as Walter Lippmann has said repeatedly, a strategy "built upon our sea power, which is our strong right arm, not upon the ability of American soldiers fighting 8,000 miles away to make secure 2,500 villages." Lippmann also explained that such a strategy would enable us to eventually disengage our military forces from the

Asian mainland and to retire to the sea and islands where our power is at its maximum. To do so would be to act "honorably, humanely, and wisely." [5]

General Earl G. Wheeler, U.S.A. (Army Chief of Staff, October, 1963–July, 1964, Chairman of Joint Chiefs of Staff since July, 1964) has been the senior proponent of the offensive and aggressive tactics since the beginning of the Vietnam venture. He consistently advocated the strategy of bombing North Vietnam and rejected the concept of containing U.S. forces in coastal enclaves and base areas. Wheeler felt that such tactics would surrender the initiative to the enemy and permit him to concentrate his forces and weapons at any chosen point of attack. The country would in effect be left in the hands of the enemy.[6] So the costly Army policy of "seek and destroy" dominated the offensive operations in Vietnam for over four years and Wheeler remained essentially committed to pursuit of a military solution.

The long-standing Army tactics of keeping the enemy "off balance" by countless patrols and spoiling attacks, large "sweep and clear" offensive operations deep into enemy country—to "maintain maximum pressure"—had for some time been successful in killing large numbers of Vietnamese and had helped protect the lavish American base installations from attack, but they had not accomplished any substantial strategic gains. Even with favorable "kill ratios" the strategy had been expensive in U.S. casualties, resulted in the destruction of much of the social, political, and economic fabric of South Vietnam and has been the cause of most criticism of the war.

For four years (July, 1964–July, 1968), Army Chief of Staff General Harold K. Johnson was a leading spokesman in the explanation and defense of the conduct of the war. Like General Westmoreland, Johnson was constantly "turning the corner" with encouraging appraisals and optimistic predictions on progress in Vietnam, despite reports to the contrary.

In an exclusive interview with *U.S. News & World Report,* September, 1967, some six months before the enemy Tet offensive, General Johnson stated:

We are very definitely winning in Vietnam and I say
that for this reason: There has been a marked turn-
about in most areas of the country in the last year. . . .
If my observations are borne out . . . I recently returned from my eighth visit to Vietnam . . . then I
believe we will see some real evidence of progress in the
next few months.

I estimate that somewhere in the next year to a year
and a half there will be a restoration of Government
control over most of the country—we can expect to see
a gradual reduction of U.S. forces—as the Viet Cong
are reduced to banditry.[7]

In the same interview General Johnson discussed the efforts
being made then to improve the ability of South Vietnamese defense forces to deal with the enemy: The Marine program in
I Corps involved *combined-action* companies where a squad of
Marines worked with a platoon of South Vietnamese Popular
Forces (local home guards). The theory was that after a certain
period of time the Popular Forces would be instilled with sufficient
professional skills to permit the Marines to move on to another
hamlet. The Army 199th Brigade worked with three South Vietnamese Ranger units at battalion, company, and platoon level and
trained side by side. The 1st Infantry Division, U.S.A., ran a
training camp for Regional Forces on basic tactics and weapons
and they conducted unit training for ARVN battalions. But the Tet
offensives of early 1968 set all of these programs back, and by
the summer of 1969 the most optimistic reports on the future
capabilities of South Vietnam's military forces were disheartening.

The general was essentially correct, however, in his estimate of
when withdrawals of American troops would commence, but not
for the same reasons. In the summer of 1969, when token American troop withdrawals began, it was not because the enemy had
been reduced to local area banditry, but rather because America
was sick of the unsuccessful and bloody war—and the Nixon administration wanted to be rid of the burden. The new strategic
plan established by the administration in July–August, 1969, was

to de-Americanize the war; reduce offensive operations, cut costs, cut losses, and turn the problem back to the government of the Republic of Vietnam.

The highly trained career officers of the Army and the other services have found the Vietnam war a frustrating but fascinating professional challenge. The very size and scope of the American military force has also generated unceasing pressures to satisfy such military demands as trying out new weapons and using the war as a military testing ground and laboratory. Helicopter assault theories, air mobile operations concepts, new helicopter types, new weapons and organizations, and counterinsurgency tactics were all ready for trial by the Army in Vietnam. It was not a life-or-death war in defense of the United States, but rather a remote and limited conflict where training and equipment could be tested and combat experience renewed or attained by the professionals. In Vietnam the U.S. Army has been able to create the most professional, best equipped expeditionary force for limited war in our history.

The application of the combat power of this force under President Johnson was, however, hardly flexible or even very limited— it has been massive. It has been the creature of what *Washington Post* editor Philip Geyelin calls the "escalation machine." This machine is the product of the military-civilian-scientific decision-making system which kept enlarging the war "for reasons only marginally related to military need." The overwhelming size of the American Army presence in Vietnam created pressures to view all problems in military terms and to subordinate all else to military demands. Or as Sir Robert Thompson, British guerrilla warfare expert, noted of the American strategy in the war: "There was a constant tendency in Vietnam to mount large-scale operations which had little purpose or prospect of success, merely to indicate that something aggressive was being done."

The Marines' War

The enclave strategy proposed by General Gavin was essentially the concept of operations visualized by the Marines when they first deployed to Vietnam. They planned to apply their amphibious doctrine to the counterinsurgency limited-war problem by first establishing beachhead enclaves with the friendly sea under U.S. Navy control at their backs. Then as they consolidated their beach-head bases they would spread their control along the coast and inland in an "inkblot"-fashion. Their tactical areas of operations would expand by means of their mobile air-ground team operations concurrent with an aggressive civic action program in the villages and hamlets within the security of their areas of operations.

Lieutenant General Leonard F. Chapman, then Marine Corps Chief of Staff, explained the Marines' concept of their operations in Vietnam:

> Thus our Navy-Marine Corps team is making its unique contribution to the over-all effort in Vietnam. Most important, in my mind, is the fact that *we* have chosen the battlefields and intend to fight on *our* terms. The Viet Cong must either fight us where *we* want to fight or quit the field and let us consolidate our perimeters uncontested.
>
> I don't suggest that the total U.S. effort should be made along the coastline or challenge the wisdom of establishing a redoubt in the central highlands of Vietnam. How much of our total U.S. resources should be employed along the coast and how much in the interior is not an appropriate topic for me to express myself on today. My point is that we Marines are making our contribution at the places where our experience, training, equipment and tradition best prepare us. Using our "inkblot" concept, *we* can "call the tune" in our prosecution of the Vietnam campaign.[8]

Such a concept was based on Marine Corps amphibious doctrine which had evolved since the Eisenhower "New Look" period when the services all concentrated upon atomic war tactics and techniques. At that time, the Marines' solution was an all-helicopter concept of dispersed landings by assault helicopters from ships spread out at sea. Operations ashore, supported by tactical nuclear bombs and artillery, were typified by schemes of maneuver using the mobility of helicopters and wide-ranging sorties from secure logistic-air bases. In subsequent years, with the revival of interest in more conventional nonnuclear war, the Marines modified their concepts to include a substantial mix of conventional surface amphibious landing and ground vehicle mobility with their growing helicopter capability. They also renewed training and interest in small wars and counterinsurgency after 1961 when the subject became the new fad in military and official Kennedy circles.

During 1965–1966 and again in 1967, the Marines included frequent amphibious "assault" landings and shore-to-shore operations along the coasts of I Corps as part of their mobility concept and to find and destroy the enemy. Some of these operations such as Operation Starlite, August, 1965, were notably successful; others were mainly landing operations to exercise naval amphibious forces and to keep the amphibious function prominent in the scheme of events. After Tet in 1968 there were few amphibious operations of any importance attempted by Marines. The III Marine Amphibious Force (III MAF) was too busy holding its many base installations throughout I Corps and fighting the land battle. Operations in 1968 were dubbed "inland beachheads" and "inland amphibious operations," but they were actually conventional land-combat operations using helicopters and Army-style airmobile tactics and techniques.

The mission assigned to the Marines in the I Corps area has been fourfold: to "search and destroy" enemy forces; to "clear and hold" selected tactical and key areas; to conduct "revolutionary development" of the civilian social, political, and economic fabric; and to "defend bases" in the beachhead enclaves and at inland localities.

When the Marines moved into Vietnam and the I Corps area in 1965, they were quick to stake out a claim to the entire Corps zone which soon became known as "Marine country." They also hastily expanded their initial brigade and division-wing-size task forces into the III Marine Amphibious Force and promoted the senior Marine to Lieutenant General so that he could cope with the generals of both the ARVN and U.S. Army in the area. The

scheme was for the III MAF command to run its own war in
I Corps to include its own Marine air force, its own supporting
naval amphibious and gunfire forces, its own logistic command,
and a minimum of operational or logistic interference from U.S.
Army generals. The Marines hoped to avoid the pattern of Korea
where the Marine division and air wing became standard elements
of Eighth Army and Fifth Air Force. The Marines cooperated
with and coordinated their efforts with the ARVN units in I
Corps and tolerated U.S. Army units in the area as long as they
were under Marine command. III MAF was under direct command
of General Westmoreland's MACV headquarters, and the general
made every effort to support his Marines and keep them happy.
He approved of the Marines' aggressiveness, admired Marine Lieutenant General Lewis Walt, and had sufficient problems in his
other Corps areas without bothering the Marines 400 miles north
of Saigon, so he let them fight their own war. Nevertheless, there
were other Army and Air Force generals who had designs on the
Marines from the start. They wanted to get the Marines' air-ground
team under the operational control of the Army Field Force and
the Joint Air Operations Center where they believed they belonged.

The Marines were so determined, however, to keep the Marine
air-ground team together under one Marine commander in III
MAF, that they forsook the opportunty to develop a new functional mission and related doctrine for riverine warfare in the
Mekong delta. As a result, the Navy teamed up with the Army's
9th Infantry Division and a new body of tactics, techniques and
equipment for amphibious operations in river and delta areas was
developed. Any Marine units detached from III MAF for duty in
the Mekong delta would have fallen under the operational command of the U.S. Army in the IV Corps area. In avoiding such an
arrangement, the Marines have missed a unique chance to work
with their Navy teammates in the new river warfare—a logical and
challenging habitat for Marines.

As always happens when Marine ground and air units are
involved in prolonged combat operations under a joint command,
the problems of command relations with the Army and Air Force
developed soon after the Marines began to perform in their areas

of operations in the northern I Corps and along the Demilitarized Zone (DMZ). The Marines found they had to fight the war U.S. Army style, and by 1967 they had abandoned the enclave-base defense and "inkblot" concept in order to fight the Army "search and destroy" type of war. They began to roam the entire I Corps area, to establish fire bases and combat bases many miles from their beachheads, and to man the DMZ border on the 17th parallel as far as Khe Sanh near the Laotian border. By 1967, most of the available Marines in Fleet Marine Forces Pacific had been committed, including the 1st Marine Division which had joined the 3rd Division and 1st Marine Air Wing in Vietnam.

As a result of the enemy's Tet offensive early in 1968, the increase in enemy strength along the DMZ on the northern "front" of I Corps, and the siege of Khe Sanh, the Army-Marine command relations began to show strain. General Westmoreland had successfully protected his Marine friends from the designs of his Army generals, but the setbacks of early 1968 throughout Vietnam rekindled the fires of interservice criticism which had been kept submerged in the secrecy of staff planning councils. It had finally become an open secret in Vietnam that many top staffers in General Westmoreland's Saigon high command were dissatisfied with the Marines' conduct of the war in the critical I Corps battle zone.

So at the end of February, General Westmoreland was prompted to assign Army Lieutenant General William B. Rossen permanently to I Corps as Commander of "MACV-Forward," an Army headquarters which a few weeks earlier had been established by Westmoreland's deputy, General Creighton Abrams to coordinate the defense of the DMZ in case of a major attack.

During the three preceding years, a U.S. Marine three-star general had maintained full operational control of all U.S. troops in the I Corps area and technically the responsibility was continued. But in fact, the battles at Hue and Khe Sanh, as well as the increases in enemy strength in and around I Corps, caused much concern to the MACV command, so the Army provisional headquarters and some 30,000 Army troops, the bulk of three divisions, were moved north into what had previously been known as a U.S. Marine preserve.

Historically the Army had reservations about the command of large Army forces by Marines, and there was a long-standing doubt about Marine officers' qualifications to command and support corps-size operations as part of a field Army. By 1969 enemy pressure slacked off in the I Corps area, MACV-Forward became a Provisional Corps headquarters (eventually XXIV Corps) with a direct line to the Army high command in Saigon, and Commanding General of III Marine Amphibious Force continued to run the war in I Corps, but he had a permanent Army headquarters looking over his shoulder as continued evidence of the same old problems of command relations and interservice gamesmanship.[9]

At about the same time that the U.S. Army moved in strength into the Marines' I Corps area, the U.S. Air Force announced that it had taken from the Leathernecks their operational control of Marine air support in the beleaguered northern corps zone. The move angered most Marines from generals to privates because it repeated the historic pattern of separating the Marine air-ground team when participating in prolonged joint operations with the U.S. Air Force. The precedent had been set in the Air Force command of all air operations in Korea and was basic to Air Force doctrine. Centralized control of air operations is also indicated in "Unified Action Armed Forces," the doctrinal guidance established by the JCS for joint operations. Nevertheless, the Marines had maintained the operational control of their own air wing between 1965 and 1968 and in effect had been able to command their own air support and air war in I Corps according to their doctrine for amphibious operations. Under the pressures of Tet, the Air Force was successful in taking over operational control of Marine tactical aircraft for "closer coordination and more effective use of resources." Air Force officers welcomed the change as a step toward increased efficiency and effectiveness. A typical Marine retort was, "Now we are faced with the tragic aspect of having this Marine air-ground team broken asunder simply because of the ambitions of the Air Force brass." In fact, the result of this modified air-control system has not been very damaging to the effectiveness of Marine close-air support.

The issue of control of Marine tactical air operations in South

Vietnam had arisen early in 1968 and divided the Joint Chiefs of Staff in Washington. Air Force General William Momyer, Commander of the Seventh Air Force in Southeast Asia, had urged that the Air Force should coordinate all tactical air missions in the I Corps area just as it did elsewhere in South Vietnam. The Marines would be permitted some limited control over their own air operations, but not to the degree established by Marine air-ground team doctrine. Momyer received the backing of Westmoreland in this matter as well as the concurrence of Admiral U. S. Grant Sharp, Commander in Chief, Pacific; General Earle G. Wheeler, chairman of the Joint Chiefs; and General John P. McConnell, Chief of the Air Staff. The Marine opposition was backed by General Leonard F. Chapman, Marine Commandant; Admiral Thomas H. Moorer, Chief of Naval Operations; and General Harold K. Johnson, Army Chief of Staff. Eventually, the controversy reached Deputy Secretary of Defense Paul H. Nitze, who decided in favor of the Air Force.

These depredations upon Marine organizational integrity and operational capabilities eventually, in May of 1968, prompted retiring Marine Lieutenant General Victor H. Krulak to speak out strongly both in public and in private in defense of his Marines. Krulak had been the top-ranking Marine general in the Pacific since before the Marine deployment to South Vietnam. As Commanding General Fleet Marine Forces Pacific, he commanded all Marines under the Pacific Fleet and had been an influential voice in the Pacific command at Hawaii. Krulak also had a well-established reputation as a determined and effective interservice "Indian fighter." His ambitions for Marine participation in Vietnam were well known, and although the essentially counterinsurgency-military assistance type of war had little relation to the Marines' primary function of amphibious assault and the seizure and defense of advance naval bases, the Marine commander was determined to establish a substantial claim to the battlefield.

With the Army-Air Force incursions into the affairs of III MAF in 1968, General Krulak felt obliged to warn his Leatherneck comrades of the implications and new threats to the Marine Corps. He called upon his Marine colleagues to stand up to their Army critics and to extol the "proud" record of the Marine Corps in the Vietnam war. He indicated that even before the war ended, Marine officers should commence to prepare to defend the Marines' existence against Army efforts to dismember the Corps. Marine officers, he said, "are going to have to defend the Corps' right to fight by reciting its record of achievement" in Vietnam and "our postwar survival may well turn upon our ability to articulate our contribution."

Krulak's secret talks to senior Marines prior to his retirement attempted to refute criticism, reportedly spread by some Army officers in Saigon, asserting that the Corps was basically an amphibious force, poorly equipped for the kind of fighting encountered in Vietnam and had become bogged down in position warfare such as at Khe Sanh. He reiterated old claims about Marine readiness to deploy and be the "first to fight," their success with civic action programs, and defended their frequently questioned logistic capabilities for wide-ranging land warfare.

By 1969 most such concerns by Marines had simmered down, and some senior Marine officers were even ready to withdraw the Leathernecks from the stalemate of Vietnam, recognizing that there was little about the frustrating expedition in Vietnam resembling the Corps' special functions—except fighting. The "right to fight" had lost some of its appeal after over four years of bloody battles in the same old hills and valleys of I Corps. (Also, most senior officers were facing their second tour in the prolonged war with only dim enthusiasm.)

Talks by assistant Marine Corps Commandant, Lieutenant General Lewis W. Walt, to the effect that "Vietnam is the most misunderstood war in our country's history" and that our involvement is "a great step toward preserving the free world" have not been widely convincing. If, as the General implies, the American people, the Congress, and the press have all failed to comprehend the nature and realities of Vietnam, there is little evidence that the defense establishment has understood it any better. Interservice differences over commands, roles, and operations not only confuse civilians but are evidence that the military itself has been unable to grasp the significant issues at stake in Vietnam.

The Air Force's War

The doctrinaires of U.S. aerospace power have also had their own ideas of the functions and effectiveness of air forces in counterinsurgency and limited war. Air Force public affairs efforts and the aerospace publications have consistently described the unique effectiveness of air power in Vietnam:

> The USAF had written a brilliant chapter in military history long before the first jet took off on a strike mission across North and South Vietnam. . . . It is true that the guerrilla war must be won finally on the ground, among the people and by the people. But it is equally true that this war cannot be won without air power. Air power has kept the government effort alive and prevented defeat; air power will eventually point the way toward victory.[10]

The Department of the Air Force in its speech-making guidance for Air Force officers was even more glowing in its description of the Air Force's war in Vietnam:

> Tactical air attacks—which are aimed primarily at supply routes from the north—and at large concentrations of guerrillas in the south—are having a telling effect. They have helped to slow the flow of supplies—and they are keeping the Viet Cong off-balance.
> Our massive B-52 bombing raids have denied the enemy the sanctuary he once enjoyed in the dense jungle.
> Day and night our airpower—like our groundpower —seeks out the enemy from his swampy strongholds— his jungle hideaways—and his mountain strong points. The hunters have now become the hunted.
> There is no sweeter sound to the ears of our soldiers and marines in South Vietnam than the roar of jet and conventional aircraft. They know they're ours—and

they have come to provide help when and where it is
most needed . . . pilots displayed true professionalism
and delivered their weapons with precision. They—in
fact—turned the tide of battle.[11]

In fact, the "sweet sound" of aircraft in the Vietnam war has
been such a dominant, expensive, and debatable aspect of the
military venture in Southeast Asia that the following chapter is
devoted to the "Great Bombing Hoax."

The Navy's War

The U.S. Navy wasn't above making its claims either. The Navy
has participated in the game of quantifying its contributions to the
joint U.S. war efforts by monthly reports summarizing Seventh
Fleet operations in the waters off Vietnam. Naval operations have
fallen generally into four categories: naval gunfire, naval air strikes,
amphibious operations, and the in-shore counter-infiltration patrols
and riverine-delta warfare of the "brown water navy."

Not much public attention has been given to the scale and scope
of naval gunfire employment and to naval air strikes, largely because they have been daily routine for some four years, but the
magnitude of munitions expenditure and the results reported by
these forces in this type of war bears examination. Take naval gunfire, for example: the typical inland ranges of naval gunfire destroyers and cruisers lying several miles off shore is about ten to
fifteen miles. Because of the flat trajectory and high velocity of the
main and secondary guns on U.S. warships, their most appropriate
targets are well defined and identified "point" targets rather than
"area" targets, like those fired upon by field artillery batteries.

The naval gunfire siege of the city of Wonsan in North Korea
during 1952 and 1953 demonstrated that naval gunfire employed
to harass and interdict general target areas had very limited effectiveness. Naval gunfire on shore targets became effective only when
precisely controlled by ground-based naval gunfire spotter teams.
Such teams, as well as air observers, have been employed in Vietnam along coastal areas within naval gunfire range and have directed much of the fire of supporting warships to augment artillery

and air bombing. During April, May, and June of 1969, the 7th Fleet Operations Summary of naval gunfire reads like the description of fires upon Iwo Jima in 1945 where the three-day preliminary bombardment by six battleships and five cruisers consumed 14,000 shells. The three months in 1969 are typical examples of naval operations for the preceding thirty-six months:

April: Enemy positions throughout South Vietnam took a heavy beating from naval gunfire during April, as 7th Fleet ships fired in support of allied forces ashore. Gunners of 26 ships left 1,104 enemy military structures and 793 bunkers destroyed or damaged.

In addition warships destroyed or damaged 138 weapons positions, 54 sampans (most sampans are native fishing craft), 31 caves and 22 enemy supply routes. A total of 53 were killed in action by 7th Fleet guns which also touched off 112 secondary explosions. (The nature of "secondary explosions" caused by naval gunfire is always questionable)

May: Enemy bunkers and structures throughout the Republic of Vietnam were the primary targets of ships in their gunfire support missions. Air and ground spotters reported a total of 757 military structures and 702 enemy bunkers destroyed by shells and rockets. A total of 25 warships fired from the gunline on targets in all tactical zones of the Republic.

Other damage included 131 secondary fires and 124 secondary explosions ignited, 2,435 meters of trenchline, 875 meters of supply routes, 117 weapons positions, 50 water supply craft (sampans) and 40 caves destroyed or damaged. A total of 44 enemy were also reported killed as a result of Navy missions.

June: The guns of 24 warships pounded enemy targets throughout the Republic of Vietnam during the month. Navy gunners left 690 bunkers and 986 military structures damaged or destroyed.

Shells from the warships also were responsible for 148

secondary fires and 26 secondary explosions, cuts across
23 enemy supply routes and 64 enemy killed according
to air and ground spotters. Additional damage reported
included 45 sampans, 33 caves, two weapons positions
and 63 meters of trenchline damaged or destroyed.[12]

During this typical three-month period U.S. naval gunfire reportedly destroyed or damaged 2,185 bunkers, 2,847 military structures, and 257 weapons positions—all located in coastal areas
within range of naval gunfire. The difference between these three
target categories is not clear, but inasmuch as the enemy have
not normally built many "military structures" other than underground storage and base complexes in their jungle assembly areas,
the idea of over 5,000 such targets along the coastal zones is difficult to accept. These targets were more likely "suspicious" native
huts and village bomb shelters.

Naval fires claimed 104 caves, all of which were deemed to be
in enemy hands, were facing the sea, observable and large enough
to hit with guns firing up to ten miles away. Very unusual gunnery!

More than fifty supply routes were damaged. How a supply
route is differentiated from a native path or local road is not clear.
At best, naval shelling on primitive roads can do little permanent
damage, and even shell holes are easily by-passed by foot and
bicycle traffic characteristic of enemy supply operations in South
Vietnam.

All of this gunfire, involving the efforts of two dozen warships
and thousands and thousands of expensive shells, for the three-
month period could finally claim only 161 enemy killed—and
these by the estimate of distant observers and air spotters. Obviously most of the enemy structures, caves, and supply routes
were uninhabited or not being used. But such tabulations have been
typical of the data the Pentagon and its analysts require of the
combat forces. The Navy has played the game and kept its charts
up.

In addition to the two dozen destroyers and cruisers firing on
shore targets during the winter of 1968–69, the battleship *U.S.S.*

New Jersey had also pounded the countryside with some 5,500 16-inch shells at a cost of $1,681 each and 13,000 five-inch shells at $111.52 apiece. Proponents of naval gunfire sponsored the revival of the great battleship as a long-range, all-weather gunfire support ship appropriate for destroying enemy dirt and wood structures. It was taken out of mothballs and reconditioned at a cost of over $21.5 million and then operated at a cost of over $1 million per month. It remained in Vietnam waters for about six months providing mainly moral support to Marines in I Corps. In the spring of 1969 it quietly returned home to the mothball fleet. There have been no reports that its effectiveness in such a war justified its cost. The *U.S.S. New Jersey*'s war effort will probably be recorded as another miscalculation in the long list of expensive gimmicks—such as defoliation, the electronic DMZ barrier, and others —that have typified the war.

During the same period, 300 to 400 naval aircraft from three to five aircraft carriers off the coast flew sorties, mostly in I Corps, to supplement the bombing efforts of over 150 Marine Corps tactical jets. The Fleet summaries reported the naval aircraft destroyed 314 supply routes, 720 military structures, 440 enemy bunkers plus additional caves, weapons positions, and trenchlines during the period April–June, 1969. After some thirty-six months of intensive air strikes throughout the length and breadth of I Corps, it is difficult to understand how so many identifiable "enemy structures," "bunkers," and the other military targets could remain to justify such a scale of air operations. It is apparent, however, that the naval air effort was keeping up its periodic total of sorties, bomb expenditures, and targets destroyed in order to fulfill data requirements—as well as to help win a war.

It is also noteworthy that such firepower expenditure has not been confined to air and naval gunfire. The harassing and interdiction fires, as well as the concentrations of fire on observed targets, practiced by American and ARVN field artillery is probably the most lavish, indiscriminate, wasteful, and technically proficient in the history of warfare. The Israeli General Moshe Dayan described a small action he observed where, "along the 200-yard-wide strip between jungle and fence the American support units laid down no less than 21,000 shells—more than the total volume of artillery fire expended by the Israeli Army during the Suez Campaign and the War of Independence together." In reply, Army Chief of Staff General Johnson lamely explained, "We have not enough information. We act with ruthlessness, like a steamroller bombing extensive areas and not selected targets based on detailed intelligence." [13]

The Propaganda War

Throughout the Vietnam war various high-ranking military and civilian officials of the Defense Department have made optimistic statements about the success and progress attained by the allies of South Vietnam. Yet the Viet Cong insurgents and their North Vietnamese supporters have become stronger, better armed, and have continued to control most of the South Vietnam countryside. As the United States escalated the war, the enemy forces received better equipment from China and the USSR. As the American units won more battles, they also found their base areas under increasing attacks. Body counts of enemy killed increased and so did the size of enemy units. More young men in North Vietnam came of military age each year than the exaggerated totals of estimated enemy killed by allied operations in the South—yet every responsible U.S. military and naval headquarters persisted in the myths and self-deceptions of "considerable progress."

The war gamesmanship practiced by the separate services in Vietnam is understandable in light of their natural tendency to visualize the war through the framework of their own particular doctrinal interests and functional specialties. What has been far less palatable for the outside observer is the numbers game of misleading, confusing, and phony reports on the war's operations. Both the civilian and the military leaders have played this game, and much of the action has originated in the Pentagon offices of the Assistant Secretary of Defense for Public Affairs, where control of military public information has been practiced in the "interests of national security."

The President and the Pentagon have from the beginning desired facts and figures to show progress in the war. Early in 1965, the Pentagon chart and graph experts began to quantify the war in order to establish measures of progress upon which plans and decisions could be based. Secretary McNamara created his policies from such grist. So with even slight pressure from the top to gather operational data it becomes heavy pressure at the bottom as each link in the chain of command adds its weight. Reputations, promotions, and service prestige are at stake.

Such pressures worked in many wondrous ways. At one stage General Westmoreland instructed subordinate commanders to make reports emphasizing "the positive combat accomplishments of the South Vietnamese Army." The pacification effort was "reported" in the same way. Wishful thinking and optimism improved at each higher level of command, despite evidence of contrary facts.

The escalation of the Vietnam war effort fed upon the data and information transmitted to Washington by the war machine. Never has the country's civilian and military leadership been more deceptive and misleading in its reports to the American people than it has been with the flim-flam about the conduct and progress of the Vietnam war. The figures on enemy strength have been consistently confusing to the ordinary citizen, as well as to the defense official. President Johnson on April 4, 1966, said that 50,000 of the enemy had been killed since the beginning of the year. Four months later, the *New York Times*, on August 10, noted that "according to official figures," the enemy had suffered 31,571 killed in action since January 1—a notable decline of 20,000 in enemy killed during the period. The *Times* also noted that "the latest intelligence reports" from Saigon revealed an increase in enemy strength in South Vietnam of 52,000 since January 1, 1966, to a total of 282,000—and this despite our heavy air attacks! The infiltration estimates ranged from 35,000 as "definite" to 54,000 as probable. The growing Viet Cong strength hardly supported the concurrent reports about the decline in Viet Cong morale.[14] Sweep-and-clear operations designed to cut the Viet Cong out of the friendly population produced impressive "body counts" of enemy dead and resulted in favorable "kill ratios" between enemy and friendly casualties, but at the end of the first year of war there were more enemy in control of larger areas in South Vietnam than in 1964.

Also, the number of North Vietnamese troops in South Vietnam has remained a mystery, and reports from MACV in Saigon have done little to resolve it. Despite the reports of bomb tonnages dropped, targets destroyed, and enemy killed in North Vietnam and on the Ho Chi Minh trail, supplies and reinforcements continued to move into South Vietnam in growing quantities right up to the 1968 bombing halt. From the beginning Air Force and naval aviation reports of "killed by air" claims have totaled year after year more than even the most liberal estimates of Viet Cong and North Vietnamese strength.

The *New York Times* reported on August 7, 1966: "About 40,000 North Vietnamese troops are believed by allied intelligence to be in the South." But a week later the Associated Press reported from Saigon:

> The South Vietnamese Government says 102,500 North Vietnamese combat troops and support battalions have infiltrated into South Vietnam.
>
> These figures are far in excess of United States intelligence estimates which put the maximum number of North Vietnamese in the South at 54,000.

In the same week, August 14, General Westmoreland told his Texas press conference that the enemy force included "about 110,000 main-force North Vietnamese regular army troops. Three months later, in a magazine interview the General stated that he believed "approximately 50,000" North Vietnamese regulars were in the South.

In 1967 General Westmoreland and Ambassador Bunker reported that two-thirds of the villages in South Vietnam were under friendly RVN control. This sounded like extraordinary progress, but more detailed reports by the supervisor of the pacification program in Vietnam, Robert W. Komer, revealed the mistaken and distorted nature of those claims. Komer confirmed that of the 14,660,000 persons in South Vietnamese hamlets in 1967 only

659,000 were considered under complete government control and 3,462,000 were in hamlets "almost secure." So actually, only about one fourth of the villagers were in friendly hands. Further analysis revealed that actually about 30 percent of the peasants were under Viet Cong control and only about 5 percent were under total government control. This situation deteriorated further after Tet in 1968 and then improved somewhat—but a candid and complete assessment of the pacification program is yet to be reported by official sources.

Even recognizing the needs for security of information possibly of value to the enemy, the military's treatment of information to the news media has usually been lacking in candor. In official reports American casualties have been described as "light," "moderate," or "heavy." "Light" losses typified most after-action reports, yet weekly casualty figures released by the Department of Defense frequently revealed relatively heavy U.S. losses.

American offensive operations employing massed firepower were designed to "keep the enemy off balance" and all Vietnamese killed in the actions were counted as enemy. In contrast, the enemy's offensive operations have been reported as "terror tactics" which resulted mainly in the killing of "children, women and old men."

Estimated enemy killed in ground actions also tend to be blown up by reporting troops. In spite of the Viet Cong practice of removing their casualties from the battlefield, our after-action reports have been typified by liberal estimates of enemy killed, to make it seem that we won the battle. "Body counts" in many actions can only be hasty at best, and at worst are simply conjecture. Busy troops in battle don't take time from their primary duties to go around counting enemy bodies. The body count of enemy and suspected enemy includes countless numbers of innocent bystanders—but there has never been a category for reporting "noncombatants killed by mistake."

There has been a natural reluctance by American authorities to admit that U.S. aircraft have mistakenly bombed areas causing casualties to noncombatant South Vietnamese, but such incidents have been far more frequent than reported. Some 150,000 civilians are estimated to have been killed annually by combat operations between both sides.[15] The lavish firepower used by U.S. forces suggests that a large share of the casualties are caused by "friendly" fire and bombings.

The nature of the statistics on enemy strength and casualties reported by the military establishment during the Vietnam war are summed up by Richard Goodwin: "If we take the number of enemy we are supposed to be killing, add to that the defectors, along with a number of wounded, much less than our own ratio of wounded to killed, we find we are wiping out the entire North Vietnamese force every year. This truly makes their continued resistance one of the marvels of the world."

The headquarters of each service participates in the contest of charting the war's progress on graphs and tables which reveal how the war is being won. The accumulation of body counts, enemy structures destroyed, defectors received, hamlets under control—all add up to the components of an impressive victory—but in some other war and in some other place. Yet with all the accumulated evidence it is understandable why the high ranking military are prone to blame the political leadership for the military's frustrations. The war was always about to turn the corner they believed and could be won; if only the American people and their politicians had tried a little longer, a victory was possible. American militarists will probably never forgive nor forget that in the Vietnam war it was the civilians at home that *wouldn't let the military professionals win and who failed the fighting men in the field*. But the deceptions, the fabrications, the deliberate distortions have revealed to the perceptive that during much of the Vietnam war the decision-makers didn't know what they were talking about. Or to be more kind, in the words of General Walt, it has been a "most misunderstood war." Though much of the distortion has been meant in the "interests of national defense," it has, as Arthur Schlesinger noted, "cost both domestic and foreign: the ebbing away of belief in the American government."

Each of the competing services, as well as the Office of the Secretary of Defense, has contributed to the propaganda and flow of misleading and contrived information about ground and sea operations, their purposes, progress, and costs—but the most extensive and extravagant delusion has been the defense establishment's explanation of the air war in both North and South Vietnam.

Footnotes

[1] Ward S. Just, "Notes on Losing a War," *Atlantic Monthly,* January, 1969.

[2] Lloyd Norman, "Anatomy of a Decision," *Army,* September, 1965.

[3] General James M. Gavin, "Hold Enclaves, Stop Bombing," *U.S. News & World Report,* February 7, 1966.

[4] James M. Gavin, *Crisis Now,* Random House, New York, 1968, p. 56.

[5] Walter Lippmann, "The Holding Strategy," *Newsweek,* January 31, 1966.

[6] General Earl G. Wheeler, "Gavin Plan Will Not Work," *U.S. News & World Report,* February 7, 1966.

[7] Harold K. Johnson, General, USA, "End of the Vietnam War in Sight?" *U.S. News & World Report,* September 11, 1967.

[8] Remarks by General L. F. Chapman, Jr., Chief of Staff, Headquarters U.S. Marine Corps to the Capital Hill Lions Club, Washington, D.C., October 19, 1965.

[9] William Tuohy, "Marines May Be Downgraded in Viet Command Structure, *Los Angeles Times News Service,* March 1968. In March, 1970 the Army XIV Corps replaced the III Marine Amphibious Force in command of U.S. forces in the I Corps zone.

[10] Jerry Greene, "Airpower's Buildup in Vietnam," *Airforce/Space Digest,* June, 1965.

[11] "The U.S. Air Force in Southeast Asia," U.S. Air Force Aerospace Speech Series. Secretary of the Air Force Office of Information, Washington, D.C., February, 1966.

[12] Source: Seventh Fleet Public Affairs Office, and as reported in *Navy Times,* Washington, D.C., 1969.

[13] Arthur M. Schlesinger, Jr., *The Bitter Heritage,* Fawcett Publications, Greenwich, Conn., 1968, p. 60.

[14] *Ibid.*

[15] *Vietnam 1969,* an American Friends Service Committee White Paper on Ending the War, Philadelphia, May 5, 1969.

Chapter IX

THE GREAT BOMBING HOAX

"Strafe the town and kill the people,
Drop napalm on the square,
Get out early every Sunday
And catch them at their morning prayer."
                              Pilots' ditty, Vietnam

On February 7, 1965, while inhabitants of the central highlands of South Vietnam stirred restlessly in the predawn darkness, Viet Cong guerrillas initiated a surprise mortar and machine-gun attack on a U.S. military advisers' barracks at Pleiku, killing eight American soldiers and wounding 126. It was the worst attack yet suffered by an American unit in Vietnam. The U.S. retaliation came with swift and violent force. Within thirteen hours after the attack on Pleiku, forty-nine U.S. Navy jets launched from carrier decks in the South China Sea sped through tropical rain squall clouds, streaked across the 17th parallel into North Vietnam to the Communist training camp at Dong Hoi which they proceeded to attack with rockets and bombs. The U.S. bombing of North Vietnam had begun. It was the opening act of the employment of massive U.S. air power in both North and South Vietnam and what was to become the most expensive and wasteful hoax ever put over on the American people by its defense forces and their civilian leaders.

"We seek no wider war," President Lyndon Johnson had told the nation after Dong Hoi. But in fact it appeared that Johnson had just about decided late in 1964 to employ his bombers in the

North. The counter-guerrilla war in South Vietnam was not going at all well. It seemed clear that unless the U.S. made a strong military move, the Viet Cong would overwhelm the Saigon forces within weeks or, at most, a few months. The most effective action the President's top military and close civilian advisers could think of—something that would both hinder enemy infiltration into the South and strengthen Saigon's deteriorating morale—was to bomb North Vietnam. It so happened that when the Viet Cong attacked Pleiku, presidential adviser McGeorge Bundy was in South Vietnam consulting with MACV on the advisability of bombing the North. After receiving the routine wining, dining, briefing, and protocol treatment reserved for VIPs to all military headquarters in Vietnam, Bundy was taken to visit the wounded at Pleiku. He was duly impressed and can hardly be blamed for agreeing with his hosts' wishes. He cabled a recommendation to the President to go ahead with the bombing, and Mr. Johnson acted upon that advice with the full support of Secretary McNamara and the Joint Chiefs of Staff.

The first air attacks in 1965 were largely restricted to North Vietnam's southern panhandle. But phase by phase, targets were selected further North until, by June of 1965, U.S. fighters had shot down their first MIGs of the Vietnam war during a raid near Hanoi. By the end of 1966, Air Force and Navy aircraft were permitted to hit rail and military targets on the outskirts of the capital itself.

The Administration announced that there were three basic objectives of the bombing of North Vietnam: (1) To raise the morale of the South Vietnamese (a dubious reason, in that the average Vietnamese citizen probably didn't understand the scope or nature of the bombing). (2) To reduce the flow of the enemy infiltration or to increase its cost. (This was accomplished in some degree no doubt, but has not really hampered enemy operations in South Vietnam. In fact, during 1965 and 1966, the rate of infiltration of supplies and equipment into South Vietnam increased. Since that period the enemy has generally moved his forces about the combat zone as he desired in spite of aerial interdiction.) (3) To push the North Vietnamese to the conference table. (We may never know how successful or important this factor has been. Actually, in the end, the bombing program and its implications forced Washington, not Hanoi, to the conference table.)

As the U.S. bombing intensified, so did the public outcry against it. Partly because of the dissension and partly because of the desire to get Hanoi to the negotiating table, the President ordered ten temporary suspensions in the bombing. Finally, in March, 1968, when he announced his decision not to run for office, he again confined the bombing to an area below the 19th parallel and then in November of 1968 stopped the bombing of the North altogether.

The total Air Force strike aircraft in South Vietnam had reached a peak of about 600 by January, 1967. This was in addition to the two or three naval carrier aircraft groups maintained on station in the South China Sea and Tonkin Gulf, which added another 250 fighter bombers. The latest and most sophisticated attack aircraft in the U.S. inventory were employed, such as the F-4 Phantom II, F-105 Thunderchief, and Navy A-6A all-weather bombers. Numbers of the older Douglas A-1Es and A-4Es also participated in the strikes upon the North.

The typical basic load of the Republic F-105 fighter-bomber is six 750-pound bombs, and the McDonnell F-4 carries eight 750-pound bombs. These aircraft were the mainstays of the Air Force and Navy attack force which had been hitting North Vietnam. In spite of the recurrent restrictions, when the bombing of the North ended in 1968, after forty-five months U.S. planes were flying an average of 300 sorties against North Vietnam each day. More bomb tonnages had been dropped on the North than the total American tonnage dropped on Nazi Germany during World War II. The cost to the United States has been heavy in every respect. The beneficial results of this gigantic effort are still not apparent.

The Bombing Costs

The specific costs of our bombing operations are difficult to determine, as the Department of Defense lumps total figures for our air efforts in both North and South Vietnam. But at the end of October, 1968, when bombing of the North halted, the total bomb tonnage dropped in both North and South Vietnam was given as

2,948,057 tons. (Total tonnages dropped by U.S. aircraft in World War II, in both European and Asiatic theaters, was 2,057,244.) So we dropped almost 50 percent more bombs on Vietnam than in both Europe and the Pacific. The total bomb tonnage dropped in the Korean War was 635,000. We had dropped five times that amount in Vietnam by November, 1968. The Pentagon calculates that bombs cost about fifty cents a pound, so the bombs alone had cost about $3 billion. Only about one fifth of the total bomb tonnages were dropped on North Vietnam, or about $600 million worth of bombs.

As of the end of October, 1968, the United States had lost 915 fixed-wing aircraft and 10 helicopters over the North. (The combat losses in the South during the same period was 315 fixed-wing planes and 906 helicopters.)* An attack or fighter-bomber type aircraft price averages about $2 million, with the popular F-4 costing over $2.5 million. A helicopter costs about $250,000 so another $2 billion can be added for jets and helicopters lost in combat over the North. That amounts to a total of $2.6 billion for the bombing of the North.

There is, however, yet another category of air losses not due to ground-to-air or air-to-air fires. These are the parked aircraft hit by enemy mortar and rocket fire and those damaged by accidents, or lost through other causes. The total of these losses suffered in both North and South Vietnam is 1,198 fixed wing and 1,214 helicopters. These are worth another $2 billion for fixed wing and $300 million for helicopters. If half of this cost is allocated to air operations in the North it would bring the total costs of the attack on the North at the end of 1968 to $3.75 billion.

Then there is the sad cost of pilots lost. The Pentagon has revealed that there were "more than" 450 pilots killed or missing in the air war over the North. The cost of training a combat pilot is at least $450,000. That would add another $202 million to the cost, bringing the total up to almost $4 billion.

Most disturbing of all, the cost of bombing North Vietnam was five times the dollar value of enemy targets destroyed, according

* By June, 1969, 365 fixed-wing and 1,157 rotary-wing aircraft had been lost in South Vietnam.

to a 1967 Congressional Committee investigation and the testimony of Secretary McNamara. The short-term effects of the bombing were emphasized when Congress was told in testimony released in July, 1969, that "practically everything" in North Vietnam has been rebuilt since the U.S. bombing halt went in effect October 31, 1968. General John P. McConnell, who has since retired as Air Force Chief of Staff, told the Senate Armed Services Committee: "Everything is operating up there now very nearly as if it had not even been touched. I would say the repair is 75 percent completed." [1] Never were more money and effort wasted with less results to show for it!

Targeting

In addition to the measurable costs of the bombing in Vietnam, the selection of bombing targets in North Vietnam has also been questionable. The targeting was done by military planners at CINCPAC Headquarters but approved by the Defense Department and White House officials, frequently by the President himself. So, by early 1967, Air Force and Navy pilots were complaining that they were flying politically dictated missions against targets they regarded as militarily useless. The Deputy Commander of the 7th Air Force for sixteen months in Vietnam, Major General G. L. Meyers, testified before the Preparedness Investigating Subcommittee[2] in August, 1967, and detailed the political restrictions which hampered the air war effort. General Meyers described the nature of air operations in Vietnam, indicating the politics—both national and interservice—which affected the conduct of this aspect of the war. The total number of sorties over the North was carefully controlled by allotment to each service for a two-week period, regardless of weather or technical military considerations, he said. This procedure was to insure that the Air Force and the Navy each received its fair share of the action so that their periodic reports would not reveal that one service was more effective or efficient than the other. As a result, sorties were often ordered in bad weather to meet what commanders considered to be a "quota." In good weather, partly damaged targets sometimes had to be ignored because the authorized number of sorties for the period had been flown. Controls and interservice gamesmanship at CINCPAC Head-quarters, Hawaii, at the Pentagon, and at the White House, all contributed to the bombing hoax.

One Air Force officer quoted in *Air Force Magazine*, January, 1967, discussed the command relations and interservice rivalry problems General Westmoreland had to contend with in conducting the air war in South Vietnam: "He [Westmoreland] is really getting the job done despite a hell of a lot of interservice rivalry. He has violated so-called Army doctrine time and time again, to favor the Air Force." [3] This officer made it clear that the interservice rivalry did not originate so much in the armed services as it did in the Defense Department. He confirmed the claim of the USAF and Navy pilots that "there is a numbers game involving sorties flown, bomb loads delivered, targets destroyed and planes lost." The game, he noted, results largely from pressure applied by the Department of Defense which plays one service against the others. Civilian defense officials in Washington demanded to know why the Air Force flew more sorties than the Navy during a period or why the Navy lost more aircraft than the Air Force. They compared bomb tonnages and target destruction reports. Such questions were to develop statistics for operations evaluation purposes and for oversimplified and misleading reports upon which policies and decisions were then based.

The B-52 Charade

In June of 1965 the Strategic Air Command's B-52 bombers made their first appearance over targets in South Vietnam. Their subsequent employment in this type of war has been an interesting example of military "me too-ism," waste, and delusion.

Prior to the Kennedy years, when the armed forces were directed away from their obsession with atomic warfare back to more likely conventional and counterinsurgency warfare, the Strategic Air Command had little interest or capability in the use of "iron bombs" for conventional or limited wars. In fact, SAC actually had very few bomb racks available for converting the atomic bombers to conventional bombers. The LeMay-indoctrinated SAC forces largely considered recognition of limited war, in contrast to the doctrine of massive atomic retaliation, as a form of heresy. However, as "limited war" became the new "thing" in the defense establishment, SAC jumped on the bandwagon and procured iron bomb racks for B-52s. They dug up old 500-, 750- and 1,000-pound bombs left over from World War II and rationalized a "new concept" for B-52s in "guerrilla warfare." The SAC orientation and propaganda briefings employed to sell civilians and government officials on the SAC mission added filmed scenes of B-52s spewing hundreds of "iron" bombs on the test ranges at Eglin Air Force Base. As the countryside disappeared under a storm of high explosives it was vividly explained how this was just the ticket for dealing with "communist aggressors" and guerrillas.

So when the air attacks by Air Force and Navy fighter-bombers in Vietnam began in 1965, SAC desired to join the action. It was expected to be good experience for SAC crews and beneficial for SAC morale to contribute. However, these great bombers, designed for the atomic destruction of Soviet Russia in a massive strategic effort, have been entirely restricted to what amounts to tactical use in South Vietnam. The mere existence of old Russian-made SAMs (surface-to-air missiles) guarding many strategic targets in North Vietnam has served to deter use of the bombers in the North. These obsolescent missiles are the same type that for years ringed key target areas in Russia. One is led to wonder: if the B-52s can't operate over North Vietnam can they be expected to deliver the goods over the USSR? If they can't penetrate modern Russian air defenses, then why do we have them? They are exceedingly expensive conventional bombers for use against "area" targets in the wilderness of South Vietnam.

As Vietnam expert Bernard Fall pointed out in 1965, the use of B-52s involves some special considerations. The population density in the Mekong Delta area and other major population centers is about 250 persons per square mile and in some sectors 1,000 per square mile. With an average bomb load of 500 tons per thirty-plane attack and a known bomb dispersion pattern of about 2,000 yards by 1,000 yards in a routine attack, the devastating effects of such bombardment on heavily populated areas can be readily seen. So the B-52s have been largely used in target areas of known or suspected enemy concentration away from heavily populated areas. Jungle highlands, the wild hills surrounding Khe Sanh and communications defiles in the mountainous border country have been typical target areas. While this use of the B-52s quite properly avoids destruction of the civilian population and innocent hamlets, there is little evidence that the bombers have been of much effect against guerrilla-type targets such as small infantry forces, supply trucks and bicycles, unimproved supply roads, and kilometer-square target areas of suspicious jungle—against all of which targets, saturation bombardment is of dubious value. It has been generally agreed, however, that the psychological effect of the heavy bombs falling from unseen aircraft has probably been tremendous: they have terrorized the enemy, the inhabitants, and even nearby friendly troops.

Air Force Chief of Staff General J. P. McConnell claimed that air power in Vietnam has been used in two new areas of operations which are truly "unique in the annals of aerial warfare." He called them "strategic persuasion" (whatever that may mean), and "the employment of air power in counterguerrilla warfare." He further explained the use of B-52s against Viet Cong targets: "There are several compelling reasons for choosing the B-52 for the job that it is now doing in South Vietnam. For one, this airplane can carry a total of 51 conventional 750-pound bombs which makes it ideally suited to thoroughly cover a large area within a matter of minutes. Equipped with advanced bombing and navigation systems, it can bomb with utmost accuracy from a wide range of altitudes, day and night, and in any kind of weather."

It has yet to be revealed whether this is the appropriate means for destroying small fleeting targets, or for saturating suspicious kilometer-square areas on the target map because no one really knows whether the enemy is there or not. The B-52s have, in fact, turned South Vietnam into a land of round rice paddies! The ultimate effectiveness of the B-52s as counterinsurgency weapons has yet to be demonstrated.

In the spring of 1969 the B-52s were carrying much of the American offensive effort in Vietnam. More than 105 of the big jet bombers stationed in the Pacific area were making as many as

1,800 sorties (one mission flown by one plane) per month from their bases in Guam, Okinawa, and Thailand. This was mass bombing of area targets on a scale difficult to rationalize. Between 1965 and 1968 the bombers dropped 886,000 tons of bombs, or over $880 million worth of explosives during 35,680 sorties. By the middle of 1969 they had probably logged well over 50,000 sorties. Up to 1,800 bomber sorties per month with each bomber dropping as many as 100 bombs meant that 180,000 bombs per month, or 2,160,000 bombs per year could be dropped by these aircraft alone.

Tactical Bombing in the South

Never has a small, underdeveloped nation like South Vietnam been so devastated by "friendly" bombing such as we have imposed upon that hapless country from 1965 to the present time. While the enemy has been conducting an essentially guerrilla type of war throughout South Vietnam, the United States has been conducting a mechanized war. Fantastic as it seems, the U.S. policy of firepower in lieu of skilled counterinsurgency operations is inadvertently destroying the very country we are supposedly protecting.

In the populated coastal provinces of South Vietnam, such as Quang Tin and Quang Ngai, approximately 70 percent of the villages have been destroyed by our bombing, artillery shelling, and fire. In Vietnam we have created desolation and called it pacification.

Most of the aerial bombing in South Vietnam is considered to be tactical or close air support of friendly ground-troop operations. Since the Viet Cong have normally had the tactical advantage of choosing the time and place of battle, close air support by Air Force strike aircraft and the Army's armed helicopters often has provided the saving factor for infantry units ambushed or besieged by the enemy troops.*

* Most close air support of ground operations in the South has been provided by U.S. Air Force, North American, F-100 fighter bomber jets, which can fly at speeds in excess of 900 miles per hour and have a combat ceiling of 47,000 feet. They are armed with bombs, rockets, napalm and 22-mm cannon, and their base price is about $700,000 each.

Close air support bombing is usually conducted at the request of ground units or the Air Force pilots of the small Cessna, 0-1, Forward Air Control (FAC) planes which are assigned to make daily visual reconnaissance over the hundreds of tactical areas of operations of interest to the ground units. The prescribed altitude for these FAC planes has been at least 1,500 feet. (At this distance it becomes difficult to distinguish people, much less to identify them as friendly or enemy.)

The FAC pilots are key performers in the bombing operations, and they have had two main purposes: First, to fly over repeatedly their assigned areas and recommend targets for destruction by air strike. Such targets are not normally examined by troops on the ground for positive identification as to enemy or friendly character. They are bombed unless they are near friendly troops or in "no-strike zones." A second duty is to direct fighter-bomber pilots to the targets. The FAC pilot does not on his own authority, however, call aircraft to bomb a target. The system established by joint Air Force-Army doctrine prescribes that the Army has to give its clearance in every request. This means that when a FAC pilot spots a prospective target he radios its position with a request for a flight of fighter-bombers to the Direct Air Support Center (DASC), which controls close air support at Army corps level. The DASC officers judge the urgency of the request for bomber aircraft in relation to other requests in the area, the nature of the target and the availability of aircraft on strip alert or aloft and nearby. There must also be overall approval by the Tactical Air Control Center (TACC) in Saigon and the area province chief. Such approval is usually attained in advance for entire areas undergoing ground attack or clearing operations.

The Air Force divides air strikes into two categories, termed "pre-planned strikes" and "immediate strikes." A pre-planned strike is one scheduled from twenty-four hours to two weeks in advance, while an immediate strike is carried out within a few hours of its request by ground troops or the FAC. Pre-planned strikes are usually of the interdiction type upon remote areas of known or suspected enemy activity and are not directly related to friendly ground troop operations. In such strikes, targets are considered to be anything that moves. The immediate strike in close support of ground-force operations are considered the most productive in KBA ("Killed By Air") results because enemy locations and bombing effects can be better determined by troops on the ground.

Designation and identification of targets for air attack is normally done by means of the pilot's map. The map's grid squares are one square kilometer and the squares are identified by numbers. The target location on the map can be located within about one tenth of a kilometer, and the fighter-bomber pilot at 15,000 feet or more, moving at jet speeds, must identify and then plan his direction of attack in relation to this imaginary spot on the terrain below. At best he can reduce his target to an identifiable area about 100 meters square. Such typical targets as "suspected enemy troop concentration" in a patch of woods or an "infiltration route" in a wilderness of hills usually requires considerable help from the FAC who, flying lower and slower, can make a better attempt at spotting the area. The procedure is then for the FAC to mark the target with a smoke rocket and talk the fighter-bomber pilots into the target. The usual results are not pin-point bombing.

A close support air strike is not completed by an apparent hit on the target. The typical strike involves eight or nine low-level passes by several fighter-bombers and usually requires ten to fifteen minutes to complete the bombing. If all bombs are not dropped in the target area they have to be dropped on secondary or other targets of opportunity, because it is not desirable for aircraft to return to base loaded with unexpended bombs. Thus thousands of tons of bombs have probably been wasted on targets already hit by initial passes or by previous strikes—or on "suspicious" localities.

Bombs are also wasted, of course, by normal inaccuracies or mistaken identity of targets. The pilots of the Forward Observer Aircraft observe every pass and help the fighter-bomber pilots adjust for inaccuracies in their bomb deliveries, but it is virtually impossible for the full bomb loads to land only within the target area—even when it is as large as a target village.

The "unfriendly" nature of a village is not usually known by the bomber pilot, and is mainly a matter of conjecture on the part of the FAC pilot. A village is frequently considered unfriendly if it has been warned to evacuate by leaflet drop or airborne broadcast. The fact that the people can't read or may not hear the warning—or that they don't know where to go—puts them in the "unfriendly" category. Their main refuges then are the bunkers and shelter trenches in the village areas. Because these protective entrenchments have also been used by the Viet Cong, all such shelters are classified by the air observers as "military structures," the village is an "enemy hamlet," and it becomes a fair target. Judgment as to the nature of the target is left mainly to the FAC pilot. As one Danang-based fighter-bomber pilot reported, "We are going four or five hundred knots and we can't see much ourselves. I've never seen a body or a person yet and I've been on over a hundred missions. It's virtually impossible to see any movement on the ground. The FAC is the expert. We're only experts on delivery." [4]

Typical pilot descriptions of methods employed to distinguish Viet Cong soldiers from the rest of the people while flying hundreds of feet above them in observation aircraft were: "You know that they are V.C.s if they shout at you, or if you see them carrying a weapon, or if they run, or if they look up and appear nervous." And "If they do suspicious things such as stand in tree lines." Any Vietnamese building made of stone and cement is classified as a "permanent military structure," wooden buildings and native houses (called "hooches") are "military structures" in the Bomb Damage Assessment Reports.

It has not been unusual for ground troops to request close air support to suppress enemy sniper fire or to destroy individual riflemen who were interfering with an American advance. For this purpose fighter-bombers heavily laden with 500-pound or 750-pound bombs or napalm plus hundreds of rounds of 22-mm cannon shells would be called to strike and "flatten" all "enemy structures" (houses) and "suspicious activity" (people) in the area of the suspected sniper. A 750-pound bomb will make a crater about twenty-five feet across and six feet deep—quite big enough, no doubt, for the destruction of snipers and any type of native military structure.

After such air strikes the FAC pilot flies over the area again and makes a Bomb Damage Assessment Report to DASC and to the fighter-bomber pilots who, by and large, have no idea where their bombs actually landed. The BDA Report includes the percentage of "Bombs on Target" and the percentage of "Target Destroyed." The pilot also reports any "Military Structures Destroyed." There is no reporting category for "Homes Destroyed" or "Civilians Killed." (Many unofficial reports from Vietnam have indicated that friendly bombing has killed and wounded tens of thousands of noncombatant South Vietnamese and made at least four million of them homeless and displaced.) At best, the BDA Reports are inaccurate; at worst, they are contrived to avoid reporting a doubtful or wasted mission, and the claimed results have been in totals highly misleading.

Phony Reports

The reporting of such results of the air war in Vietnam has been largely distorted to suit the purposes of the air components and their commanders. As the periodic air action reports make their way from MACV in Saigon, through CINCPAC Headquarters, the Joint Chiefs, and to the President, they get condensed for quick comprehension and reduced to catch words or clichés. As noted in Chapter VI, under the McNamara regime the military amplified its proclivity to report combat operations, not in terms of human efforts but in numbers suitable for computers or for display in glib statistics and on charts. No matter how carefully qualified or specifically limited the original report may have been, the end product usually had the appearance of unquestioned fact. For example, the production of "Killed By Air" claims used by the air components in Vietnam. The effects of bombing attacks are estimated by a highly involved computation based on the size of the area hit, the number of people that *must* have been in it, the number of bombs that *should* have landed in it. The reporting headquarters then put these two unknowns together, come up with an apparent "known," and dispatch the figures off to Washington. The figures become part of the weekly totals of "enemy forces killed," and are announced by the Defense Department.

Pilots of high-flying B-52s and fast-flying fighter-bomber jets have rarely been able to even see enemy casualties resulting from their attacks. "Body counts" for "Killed By Air" claims are made by the Forward Air Controllers. All people observed in the target area—enemy, friendly, or unfortunate civilians—are considered to be "enemy" in the body counts.

The hoax of the bombing effort in Vietnam is that it has been conducted and reported as if it was the siege of Leningrad where the measure of success is bomb tonnages dropped, buildings smashed, and fortifications destroyed. In fact, however, the numbers of actual enemy personnel killed by air action has been largely ritualized conjecture. Such claims of damage inflicted upon the enemy by our air attacks in both North and South Vietnam have been exaggerated, have involved many innocent noncombatants, and have misled and confused the nation.

In 1968, U.S. bombers *of all types* were making an average of 300 sorties per day—or 9,000 per month. Following the halt in bombing of North Vienam the effort and cost of bombs was not reduced but was diverted to South Vietnam. U.S. bombers from Thailand, Okinawa, and South Vietnam made 13,000 sorties in November, 1968, over supply routes in Laos and South Vietnam, and 15,000 in December. The bombers concentrated on dropping huge tonnages of explosives on "chokepoints" at mountain passes and constricted road nets. Despite the November, 1968, bombing halt total tonnages of bombs dropped on Vietnam increased, except for a slight decrease in February, 1969. In November, 115,000 tons were dropped; in December, 127,700; in January, 129,700; in February, 115,800. The January figure represents the highest monthly tonnages dropped during the war up to March, 1969.

Eventually, in July, 1969, President Nixon ordered the Pentagon to cut down on B-52 bombing in South Vietnam. What was officially explained as a budget move was in truth much belated recognition of the fact that such bombing does not work. Marine Colonel William R. Corson in his candid dissection of the Vietnam war, *The Betrayal*, stated the simple truth that "the bombing does not promote our objectives in Vietnam." [5]

The bombing of Vietnam has had precisely the effect that the analysis of the United States Strategic Bombing Survey after the Second World War would have forecast—and as General Matthew B. Ridgeway said, "The Korean War taught that it is impossible to interdict the supply route of an Asian army by airpower alone." So the notion that strategic bombing or aerial interdiction can stop guerrillas runs contrary to all experience—yet the great bombing hoax continues.

Before his untimely death in Vietnam, Dr. Bernard Fall said, "What changed the character of the Vietnam War was not the decision to bomb North Vietnam: not the decision to use American ground troops in South Vietnam: but the decision to wage unlimited aerial warfare inside the country at the price of literally pounding the place to bits." The people of South Vietnam are in a worse situation today than they were in 1965. As a result of our "help" an entire nation is being physically, morally, and spiritually destroyed. What kind of people are we to presume that this is the proper way to aid our friends, safeguard the Free World, and to defend our honor?

Footnotes

[1] "Air War in North Vietnam: Adding Up the Score," *U.S. News & World Report,* August 18, 1969.

[2] Senate Armed Services Committee.

[3] Claude Witze, "The Case for a Unified Command: CINCSEA," *Air Force Magazine,* January, 1967.

[4] Jonathan Schell, "A Reporter at Large, Quang Ngai and Quang Tin," *The New Yorker,* March 9–16, 1968.

[5] William R. Corson, *The Betrayal,* W. W. Norton Co., New York, 1968.

Chapter X

CITIZENS AND SOLDIERS

*"Military philosophies, bred and crystallized in the crucible
of war against the elements and other adversaries, may
not convincingly register on mentalities trained and experienced in totally different circumstances."*

Admiral R.B. Carney USN
Address to the Naval War College
May 31, 1963

Selling the Program

Prior to World War II the military establishment lived a life
apart from civilian affairs. Most army posts and naval base societies were separate from commercial, political, and community
interests. Much of this has changed since the war, and the services
now conduct highly sophisticated public relations efforts.

One of the "publics" receiving priority attention from the armed
forces is the Congress. The military maintain over 330 Congressional liaison officers and DoD employees serving Capitol Hill
and do a great deal of lobbying. In addition the services set up
elaborate tours, flights, visits, and demonstrations designed to influence Congressmen and gain their support. "Visiting the troops"
is a favorite Congressional pastime. Although visits of VIP Congressmen are considered a real nuisance by enlisted men and officers, because they always entail extra effort and expenses for the
command, most Congressmen seem to enjoy the experience, especially if they are veterans of relatively low rank. The attention
shown by generals and colonels to legislators who may have once

been enlisted men or reserve lieutenants is usually a pleasant switch.

For the military leaders, the inconvenient visits are looked upon as worthwhile efforts in Congressional relations which they hope will pay off in budget allocations and in good reception for favorite weapons, construction, or personnel programs. So the local commanders turn out the troops for parades, reviews, demonstrations, and weapons displays. Senior officers are assigned to escort the visitors. Staffs put on elaborate command briefings (known in civilian business as "sales presentations"),* and the visits or tours usually end up with a command reception and dinner. Officers and wives are designated to appear; they share the expense of the drinks and food; and the whole show is considered to be a matter of duty and loyalty to the command and its public relations responsibilities. Such affairs go on regularly in all the services. For the military people, the visits are generally an imposition and a bore, leavened only by the ample flow of cocktails which are part of the reception routine.

The Congressmen frequently display ignorance of military matters as well as boredom, but they always hope to make political hay by having their pictures taken with troops from their constituency. Platitudes about the importance of the host service, the sacrifices and courage of the men, and the preservation of peace in the face of Communist threats are offered for the benefit of the local press.

Visits by VIPs and Congressmen to the armed forces in a combat zone, such as Vietnam, are a special inconvenience for the troops, but also usually pay dividends to the defense establishment. It takes a wise and level-headed citizen to maintain the objectivity of his views on warfare and military operations after seeing the fine young American fighting men in the environment of the battlefield. The dirt, the danger, the wounded men, and the spirit displayed add up to a different impression of military service than found in large rear-area bases or U.S. facilities. The normal VIP civilian

* Governor Romney called it "brain-washing" following his 1968 visit to Vietnam.

visitor, Congressman, or Cabinet member who visits the operating forces in a theater of war usually returns home with the opinion that "nothing is too good for the troops." And no wonder. Certainly our forces are made up of the nation's healthiest and finest. Their hair is nicely trimmed, they have military manners, and they are as neat as possible under the circumstances. The average mature adult and civilian official finds contact with America's young military people an inspiring experience. It is also a sentimental happening that tends to gain emotional, if not always rational, support for all sorts of militaristic ideas. No one is immune to the appeal of flags, uniforms, and the impressions made by the armed forces in their rituals and ceremonies. Every good general and admiral makes the most of these assets in selling the program.

Presidents and members of Congress are often invited by the armed services to attend special demonstrations which display the troops, their equipment, and their firepower. Such affairs are planned well in advance, carefully rehearsed, and usually are conducted with precision and showmanship. Firepower demonstrations costing hundreds of thousands of dollars are the military's favorite spectaculars and can be counted on to make a deep impression on the civilian officials from Washington. The aircraft, tanks, ships, gunfire, noise and smoke invariably thrill the visitors. The obvious power displayed gives confidence to the civilian leaders and stirs their pride in America's fighting forces. So while happy admirals and pleased generals beam upon their important guests from Washington, the President or perhaps a Senator says a few words to "the troops." He invariably tells them how proud he is of their skills and dedication, how the American people are all for them as they stand ready to "defend freedom" anywhere, any time, and implies that nothing is too good for the defense forces. The only problem is to make America realize how important all the ships, jets, guns, and tanks are to the welfare and happiness of the Free World. Bands play, officers salute, officials compliment the generals—and then fly home. Everyone has a good feeling of rededication to national defense and a rejuvenating joy and strength through firepower.

Presidents and Their Fighting Men

Shortly after his inauguration in 1969, President Nixon made personal calls and brief talks to the senior executives and staffs of each of the major departments of the Federal government. His opening remarks to the Department of Defense people in the Pentagon tell us something about the relationship between top-level civilians and the military. The new President commented on his slight discomfort, as a former junior naval officer, in the new routine of admirals and generals standing up in his presence, calling him "sir" and showing deference to him, when his normal reaction was to snap to attention in the presence of the high rank. This is the usual tendency in veteran enlisted men or junior officers who find themselves in high civilian positions where they officially outrank the top military leaders. They rarely completely overcome their awe, respect, or fear of high military rank that resulted from their early training and experience.

It takes a confident and courageous civilian official in the DoD, in Congress, or in the White House to face up to a roomful of hard-faced, well-decorated generals and admirals and either to stare them down or talk them down. Robert McNamara and some of his "whiz kids" demonstrated such confidence and courage. But McNamara is gone. The services now are well populated with upcoming, determined, and impressive officers who are aware of every technique of influencing, cajoling, selling, and "psyching" their civilian masters. It is still standard procedure for military officers to wear uniforms and decorations when they testify at Congress. Their impressive appearance puts the drab Congressman at an immediate disadvantage, and the officers know it.

During periods when the nation is at war the President frequently officiates at White House ceremonies where Medals of Honor are awarded to combat heroes or their kin. These are always moving affairs with the numbers of erect young uniformed heroes, sometimes visibly scarred—or even more touching, the very young widows and children, and the parents of those fallen in battle. On such occasions Presidents are inclined to obligate themselves to the fighting men. As the stern-eyed generals and admirals, the serious

Secretary of Defense and other high officials who attend these ceremonies stand by, the President expresses such platitudes as "America goes to war because it is devoted to peace," and the whole gamut of similar clichés.

Civilian officials are bound to feel humble and inadequate in the presence of these exceptionally brave men. Only a combat-experienced man perhaps can maintain a perspective of such heroism, for he knows that gallantry in battle depends on circumstances and that many heroic deeds go unrecognized along with those men who did not live to relate them. Nevertheless, as time passes a President becomes more and more emotionally involved with his military heroes. Each awards ceremony makes him more personally committed to the servicemen and their families, and he makes statements and promises which indicate an increasingly close and sentimental association with the armed forces and their codes of service and sacrifice. It then becomes ever more difficult to deny the recommendations and wishes of the military establishment.

The Culture of War

The American people have become more and more accustomed to militarism, to uniforms, to the cult of the gun and to the violence of combat. Whole generations have been nurtured on war news and wartime propaganda. The relatively few years of peace since 1939 have been filled with a constant diet of novels, movies, comic strips, and television programs, all with war or military settings. For many young Americans the military experience is merely a realistic extension of the entertainment and games of childhood. Even the weapons and equipment they use at war are similar to the highly realistic toys of their youth. Soldiering loses appeal for some who experience the blood, terror, and filth of combat; for others it is an exciting adventure, a competitive game, and an escape from the routines and responsibilities of civilian life. The prospects of military duty and possible combat service in Vietnam have, however, been rejected by many of the nation's youth as "unjust, illegal, and immoral." Many young people are now rebelling from a surfeit of militarism and war.

In addition to the widespread influence of prominent military men and military methods, so evident in American life from World War II to the present, American culture has become infused with other expressions of militarism.

There has been a sustained production of postwar military novels and memoirs of distinguished leaders which contributed to the nation's knowledge and interest in war and military matters. Most of the novels tended to have social implications in their analysis of the military stereotypes and the military system. The first outstanding postwar "war" novel was Norman Mailer's *The Naked and the Dead*, published in 1948. It presented the traditional liberal's stereotype of the regular army officer who is a fascist at heart, in contrast to the liberally educated reserve officer hero. It was solidly in the American tradition of antiwar, antimilitary literature. Then there was James Jones's *From Here to Eternity* with its more sympathetic presentation of Army life and ethics. *The Cain Mutiny*, by Herman Wouk, is the classic naval novel which draws out characterization of a variety of officer types and in the end glorifies the Navy.

Probably of more lasting impression upon the millions of veterans and civilians seriously interested in how the war and the military forces were managed and led were the biographies and memoirs published by many prominent wartime military figures. General Eisenhower's *Crusade in Europe* was a top seller for years and has probably been read by more adult males than any of the war books. General Omar N. Bradley's *A Soldier's Story* was also very popular. *War As I Knew It* by General George S. Patton, *Brave Men* by the correspondent Ernie Pyle, books about General Marshall and General MacArthur—and a whole rash of excellent war histories—all oriented and informed the American people on military matters. Military literature of all types, about wars old and recent, continue to be a popular subject for a nation steeped in militarism.

In contrast to postwar literature and drama, the military comic strips and cartoon books have tended to be more romantic, idealistic, and have less criticism of the ranks and systems of the armed forces. "Sad Sack" and "Beetle Bailey" made gentle fun of life in the service and of military types, in the same manner that the Phil

Silvers Show on TV burlesqued and ridiculed basic aspects of Army life and leaders. But the popular "Terry and the Pirates" and "Steve Canyon" created by Milton Caniff, an Air Force disciple, have over the years maintained a glamorous image of sex, adventure, and patriotism in the U.S. Air Force. "Buz Sawyer," the naval reserve aviator, has been in and out of active duty for years and has probably represented the most normal picture of military life. Then there have been a large ration of war comic books devoured for years by the young and simple-minded. They have been generally violent, bloody, and concerned with the militant destruction of "Commies," "Reds," "Nazis," and all the other "bad guys" who threaten the "good guys" on our side. The images and attitudes created by the steady diet of this form of entertainment and the resulting beliefs formed in the immature minds of young generations are hard to define. The influence has probably been considerable.

For the more mature and educated, television has provided a wide variety of combat and military oriented shows. In the years following World War II, the services each sponsored documentaries of their campaigns which were generally excellent. "Victory at Sea" was probably pre-eminent, with excellent musical score and a fine commentary. Others of historical value and technical merit were "Tarawa," "Crusade in Europe," and the British film "Desert Victory," which has been repeatedly shown in the United States. There have been countless movies produced with war settings and most of them continue to appear as TV re-runs. In fact, a steady dose of TV serials, both comedy and situation drama, with war themes has been offered during the past twenty years.

This abundance of entertainment with military themes and characters has covered the spectrum of quality from good to horrible. Most professional military men and combat-experienced veterans find much of the war fiction and military drama to be exaggerated and misleading. Hollywood's version of military people is usually one of stock characters. If nothing more, such forms of entertainment and literature have made the American people more aware of the military and familiar with their armed forces. At worst, however, they have created some misleading images of military life and people as well as deceptive ideas of the "bad guy" enemy.

By 1968, with the growing public revulsion for the Vietnam war, a reaction to war and militarism began to be felt in many aspects of American life. One of the most evident expressions of rejection was seen in the decline of the military toy market. For years there had been a multimillion-dollar business in military models, realistic toy weapons, G.I. dolls, and children's uniforms. Suddenly parents turned away from such items and by 1969 they no longer dominated the toy counters. But for some fifteen years American children had access to a complete arsenal of weapons and equipment which stimulated their imagination and helped indoctrinate them in the nomenclature, characteristics and purposes of the real thing.

The prolonged and unhappy preoccupation with the fruitless war in Vietnam resulted in a general disillusionment and disenchantment with the culture products of militarism. A letter to the editors of *Life* magazine, in 1969, spelled it out:

> I grew up on a diet of Hollywood war films. The heroism, the romance, the adventure and even the death excited my interest. For these were men. When I entered the service I was astonished that no Fredric Marches, Clark Gables, Humphrey Bogarts were to be found in my barracks. Only young kids like myself (17), half frightened, confused, immature kids stumbling through the senselessness of combat.

Youths: Duties and Attitudes

The recent resurgence of antimilitarism expressed by the students and young people should be of considerable concern to the administration and the defense leaders. It is a different reaction from the waves of antimilitarism and pacifism typical of the interwar years of the 1920's and 1930's. After World War I, antimilitarism was only one aspect of the reaction to the war and evidence of the emergent social liberalism of the times. According to Dr. Huntington, the pacifism of the period also reflected the rejection of militarism by business and the conviction that the military were a holdover from a barbarous past. Business and industry had not yet teamed up with the defense establishment.[1]

The current attitudes of youth were brought to focus by the spreading reaction among the students and intellectuals against the "immoral and unjust" war venture in Vietnam. Despite administration and military efforts to explain and justify this "most misunderstood war in our history," the young people have become well aware of the miscalculations, the cruelties, the misinformation, and the vested interests so typical of this war. The war has been described from every angle, and the discerning observer can't help but be cognizant of the distorted official reports. Of even deeper significance perhaps than the revolt against the war and the draft, which are matters of direct personal concern to most young people, are the attitudes of youths and students toward the defense establishment, national military policies, and ideologies of patriotism. These changes would seem to reflect a growing awareness of the country's militaristic character and a feeling that it is not what they want or believe it should be.

In October, 1968, *Fortune* magazine made a survey of young people aged eighteen to twenty-four to determine their attitudes toward major current social and political issues. The findings appeared in *Fortune* in January, 1969, and are of interest because they (1) reflect the opinions of the young people who provide the future officers and men of the armed forces, (2) reveal the degree by which the defense establishment and the government have failed to sell their ideals and military programs to young people, and (3) provide identification of the problem areas and unfavorable attitudes which the defense leaders should attempt to overcome in the future.

Of special interest are the attitudes of the college students as compared to non-college youth. College-educated people are considerably more critical of war, the defense establishment, and military values. Yet this is the group that will have to provide the future officers and leaders of the armed services. The less critical and more conservative opinions of people who haven't attended college favor military values—a dubious endorsement. Some of the significant attitudes related to military matters expressed by the young people are revealed by the *Fortune* survey:

Fifty-nine percent of the college students think the United States made a mistake sending troops to Vietnam and 47 percent of the non-college youths believe it was a mistake.

Patriotism affects the attitudes toward the war of only 28 percent of the college students versus 46 percent of the non-college group.

Disgust with the government's war policies is felt by 47 percent of the college students and 30 percent of the non-college.

The values believed to be worth fighting for are especially significant. *Protecting the national interest* has the support of 73 percent of the non-college group—and only 52 percent of the college students.

Other relative values considered to be worth fighting for:[2]

		PERCENT		PERCENT
Containing Communists:	No college	68	College	43
Counteracting aggression:	No college	65	College	62
Fighting for our honor:	No college	64	College	31
Protecting allies:	No college	53	College	44
Keeping a commitment:	No college	30	College	19

A subsequent special report on youth which appeared in the June, 1969, issue of *Fortune* made some additional observations on the attitudes of youth:

> Resistance to the draft is growing among all groups of young Americans. Among both moderate and conservative college students, the belief in war as an acceptable strategy is declining. A majority of college students no longer hold patriotism to be very important. Non-college youth are not, however, ready to throw off their beliefs in patriotism to the same degree.

Inasmuch as the attitudes reflected in these survey reports are generally contrary to all the basic values and creeds of the military establishment, the only conclusion is that the Vietnam war has tended to bankrupt the moral and spiritual credit and credibility of the armed forces and their leaders insofar as their influence on the opinions of young people is concerned. From the peak of prestige and respect attained by military leaders following World War II, the profession with its civilian leaders has fallen to a new low point of esteem. The military establishment can blame no one but itself and the forces of militarism which led it into the Vietnam morass—long known as the "graveyard of diplomats and generals" and now, apparently, the quagmire of American militarism.

Whereas today's veterans and fathers went to war for their country, their sons are increasingly ready to go to jail for their country. Although the young dissenters and nonconformists have been sadly unable to articulate their objectives or to make clear to the rest of society what it is they want, an observer can see in their music, dress, manner, and language what they are rejecting.

The whole subculture of the youthful dissidents is the antithesis of the values and attitudes taught and upheld by the military profession. Appearance, form, and manner are important to the military way of life. There is probably nothing so irritating to a professional soldier as the sight and sound of an "odd ball" hippie type —unless it is a dirty rifle or a sloppy salute. The young people apparently sense this irritation, and so their revolt contains many antimilitary expressions: the long hair and beards, the unkempt, dirty, and feminine dress, the burlesque items of old uniform, the weird music, the cultivated slouch, and the disrespectful language. Yet it has been little more than a protest by a minority trying to express itself. Thousands of this same type of young men have been trained and indoctrinated to become contributing members of the most professional expeditionary forces the country has ever fielded. Despite the relative harmlessness of the youth revolt, insofar as its outward expressions of dress and taste are concerned, the adults and the military should realize that it is also evidence of a larger rejection of old values and beliefs which the military establishment must face up to.

So it behooves the leaders of the military-industry power establishments, which are now the objectives of the young people's attacks, to carefully examine their own ethics, values, and purposes. The gaps between succeeding generations can only be closed by agreeing upon the basic values which motivate our lives, and the strength of the nation requires unified and continuous direction of all of our citizens. De Tocqueville observed: "Each generation in a democratic society is a new people." Leadership in the right direction is the obligation of the adults. Purposeful and constructive effort should be the desire of the new generations. If defense of the nation is to be a part of this teamwork, all concerned must come to a better understanding of the problem.

(For what ever comfort it may afford, the Soviet military establishment is also concerned about the young people of the USSR. The Communist Party journal *Kommunist Vooruzhennikh Sil* complained that some Russian youth were pacifists and lacked the hatred the older generations held for the Soviet Union's enemies. The publication, mouthpiece for the Soviet's militarists and lobbiest for heavy spending on defense, deplored the lack of understanding by Russian youth who failed to see that the United States imperialists were preparing for a new war against the Soviet Union and other socialist countries. The journal said, "We must not for a minute forget that in case of war we will be fighting an enemy who has been nourished on a fierce hatred against us, an enemy who is morally depraved by unbridled anti-Soviet propaganda and who is prepared to carry out the work of the most ferocious beasts.")[3]

How simple life would be for the world's militarists if all young people would just hate the "other side" without question or reservation!

The war in Vietnam and its meaning to the young people of America is a basic cause of their revolt. It is the most doubted war in our history. It pollutes their plans and purposes. They are forced to interrupt careers, forego prospects of marriage and family, lose limbs, and sacrifice lives—all for a highly dubious purpose. In the eyes of many students, the war is evil; the employment of massed American firepower on a small and remote nation in the throes of a civil war is both unjust and wicked. Washington has failed to make a case for the nation's military actions in Vietnam; as a consequence, the military establishment has become the objective of a new wave of antimilitarism led by the young people—the military's most important public.

The class of 1969 at Yale dedicated its commencement to opposition to the war. Some of the graduating seniors pledged to refuse induction if drafted. The vast majority of Yale seniors indicated that they wanted to serve and protect their country and their commencement spokesman stated, "Patriotism is not dead on the college campus today." But, he added, patriotism is not "blind obedience," it is the "constant search for good and better policies. When old policies are shown to be wrong, patriotism generates efforts to implement new ones."

Concerned observers maintain that it is a mistake to assume that only a handful of radical and revolutionary students are dissatisfied with their society, with the way colleges are operated, and with the defense establishment. Actually, large numbers of bright, normal, and serious young people are as deeply disturbed as the more active dissenters. Their revolt against militarism also stems from their widespread repudiation of the Vietnam war venture. They have concentrated their dissent and their attacks upon the draft and the ROTC system mainly because they are the first points of contact between the society of youths and the military establishment. The need and validity of the draft and ROTC are really not the central issue—they merely are the most convenient symbols and representatives of the military system within target range of America's youth.

The Draft and ROTC

The draft has been present for many years, but between the Korean War and the Vietnam conflict it touched the lives of only a small percentage of those eligible to serve. An average of hardly more than 100,000 men were called each year. Deferments were easy to come by, and those selected for duty accepted the draft as a tolerable opportunity for travel, adventure and perhaps some technical training. The escalation of the Vietnam war changed the draft picture. Draft calls rose to 30,000 men or more per month. During the war build-up years of 1966, 1967, and 1968, a total of 882,390 men were drafted into the Army and Marine Corps (23,380). And many draftees went into the combat units where the casualties and the killings were.

As of December 31, 1968, there were 37.4 million men registered with Selective Service. Of this number, 20.8 million were between the ages of eighteen and twenty-six, and of these, 1.5 million were considered to be immediately available for military service. The rest had completed their military service (three million), were not qualified (5.2 million), were deferred (6.8 million), were exempt (126,000), or were already in the active or reserve forces (3.9 million).[4]

The recent reaction to forced military service has been different because of the nature of the Vietnam war; it has not been officially sanctioned by Congress as a "war," there is no visible or feared enemy threatening the United States, there has been little national martial spirit—nor even widely popular support of what the military has been called upon to do. As a result, the draftee feels not only a normal dismay at going into the service but resentment at being made to serve as a conscript in a mercenary venture.

How to make a draft system both just and palatable will always be difficult as long as some men are called and others are not. The draft reforms proposed by President Nixon on May 13, 1969, which are keyed to a lottery, may be considered a more acceptable system. Beyond its efforts to improve the draft, the administration is also fostering the concept of an all-volunteer armed forces subsequent to a withdrawal from Vietnam and a planned reduction in armed forces. Army men, however, almost unanimously oppose the concept of the all-volunteer armed forces. Many career soldiers argue that this would cut the military off from civilian society and it could foster a withdrawal of the armed forces into a social isolation such as experienced in the latter half of the nineteenth century. The Army professionals also know from experience that a 1.5-million-man peacetime Army—or even a one-million-man Army—is an almost impossible prospect without the pressures and provisions of the draft. The draft has historically also driven volunteers into the Air Force, Navy, and Marine Corps—and although those services have traditionally promoted their volunteer image it is highly doubtful that they would benefit from a termination of the draft. If the defense forces are to remain at a strength of over two million men in the foreseeable future, it would appear to be in the national interest to continue the draft with the fairest possible system.

The students' attack upon the college ROTC system is unfortunately a concern with symptoms rather than causes. Like the draft, the ROTC is not a cause of the national militarism nor is it to blame for the miscalculations and tragedies of the Vietnam war. In fact, the sound future direction and leadership of the military establishment may well depend, in large part, upon the influence of the men trained in liberal civilian educational institutions and upon reserve officers with college educations.

A young Dartmouth College alumnus expressed his concern over student attacks upon the ROTC at his school:

> One of the best methods of insuring a growing and increasingly powerful military machine is to provide a more and more tightly knit officer caste system. The best possible method of insuring this is to centralize the development of more and more military academies under the direct and exclusive control of the Military. In order to preserve the purity of the military bloodline one must make certain to block the infusion into the military caste of men (and women) educated in the traditions of the liberal arts, sciences, and humanities. By far the best method of preventing this infusion from diluting the military is to destroy the source of the infusion. Only by diligently destroying the ROTC and all other groups that foment and encourage the assimilation of civilians into the military can we ever hope to, someday, have complete military control over all facets of American life. And tomorrow the World! [5]

Total ROTC enrollment dropped in 1968 by about 35,000 to some 213,000 students, owing to the abandonment of compulsory training at some schools; in 1969 the downward trend continued, reflecting student anti-war attitudes. The number of ROTC units, however, has been increasing: the Navy has a list of 130 schools requesting units, the Air Force has had four student applicants for every opening in the program. Over 353 schools offer ROTC programs, and in 1968 nearly 23,000 ROTC graduates were commissioned, an increase of 1,700 over 1967. They provided about 50 percent of the Army's new officers, 35 percent of the Air Force's, and 20 percent of the Navy's. All three services maintain that no other program could provide as well qualified young leaders.[6] Although many students are motivated to take ROTC training and attain reserve officer status in order to avoid a draft into the Army, most young men are sincerely interested in the opportunities and satisfactions of leadership and responsibility offered by service as a commissioned officer, as well as a desire to fulfill their obligation to their country.

The ROTC is considered vital to the nation's security. The officer corps should be structured so that it represents a broad blend from various sources including the service academies, ROTC programs, officer candidate schools, and men and women commissioned from the ranks. Such programs provide leadership opportunities to a significant percentage of American youth and provide added assurance for sound, responsible and representative military leadership in the future.

The Military's Think Tanks

Perhaps one of the most startling bits of evidence of thriving militarism in the defense establishment was the rapid increase of civilians employed by the Defense Department. In 1960 there were 169,000 employees in DoD; this number grew to 1,300,000 by 1969. Other defense-related agencies increased by some 500,000 people during the period.[7]

In addition to civilian government employees there has also been a steady rise in Defense Department-sponsored research and analysis carried on by civilian colleges, universities, and other institutions. Between 1958 and 1968 Federal research and development expenditures increased about $1.7 billions.

By June, 1969, a total of $2.2 billion in Federal research contracts were held by colleges and universities and by institutions they manage. About half of this money goes to military, space, and atomic energy projects. Among the institutions being funded are sixteen Federal Contract Research Centers (FCRC) or "Think Tanks." These serve as specialized consulting firms to the Department of Defense. They are nonprofit (but extremely well paid) research and analysis organizations of a type first created during World War II to evaluate air operations. The FCRC's are relatively independent, being aligned neither with government nor industry. Although heavily staffed with retired officers and some 7,000 talented professionals of other disciplines, they claim to strive for objectivity. Many of their projects, however, are ones conceived by the military and DoD civilian specialists. The FCRC staffs have many capabilities not usually found among the more transient planning officers on the military service staffs. It is these research and analysis institutions and organizations working within the university systems which have drawn the ire and the criticism of the student dissenters. Although the Federal dollars have become very important to colleges and universities, some schools and independent research organizations, such as Stanford Research, have recently commenced to draw away from defense-oriented projects. The present trend is to let the defense establishment do a good deal more of its own thinking.

Regardless of the nationwide criticism by students, however, many schools and universities persist in feeding at the public trough of Pentagon-sponsored research. In October, 1969, the Department of Defense signed a $600,000 contract with the University of Mississippi to determine if crows, ravens, jays, hawks, and vultures could replace humans in such "dangerous, difficult, expensive, or boring facets of war as aerial photography, gunnery, steering of missiles, detection of mines, and search-and-destroy missions." The three-year contract was disclosed in a Pentagon circular seeking ornithologists to work on the project.

The Domestic Front

Despite these trends which show dissatisfaction with the military's conduct of the Vietnam war, renunciation of militarism, and reduced confidence in the defense establishment, the leaders of the Department of Defense have tried to further extend military influence into the lives of the American people. Without having yet resolved the problems of its own values and its role in the nation's affairs, the defense establishment is seeking new roles and missions in the social sector.

On September 26, 1968, in a speech made to the National Security Industrial Association, Secretary of Defense Clarke Clifford boasted that the United States has a military-industrial team with unique resources of experience, engineering talent, management, and problem-solving capacities which could be used to find the answers to complex domestic problems in education and social welfare.

The Chief of Staff of the Army, General William C. Westmoreland, found the prospects of new battles on the domestic front also appropriate for the Army. In a speech at Kansas State University in April, 1969, he visualized today's Army blending its military capabilities into an integrated whole, involving all of the instruments of national policy—political, economic, diplomatic—all a part of a well-orchestrated national effort. The general declared, "The Army must not only be prepared and flexible to meet new and unforeseen requirements to support national programs, it must also be prepared to do so effectively within the bounds of our national style."

The new "zone of action" has also received the strong personal endorsement of Secretary of Defense Melvin R. Laird. The Defense Department's new Domestic Action Program will be established to help resolve domestic problems. The program is designed through the use of the Defense Department's extensive resources and human skills to join other government agencies and private institutions in trying to overcome some of the serious domestic problems which face the nation today. By meeting this challenge, the Department believes it will enhance its ability to provide total national security. (In other words, the defense establishment is becoming concerned about the security of its rear, the Zone of the Interior.) Secretary Laird has pointed out, "This call to social consciousness will be accomplished without impairing our primary mission of military readiness." [8]

The Secretary believes the Department of Defense can contribute toward resolving domestic problems in certain areas of the country: some of the $40 billion in procurement funds can be diverted to purchases which will benefit areas with social and economic problems. In many cases, areas with concentrated unemployment have already been the objects of beneficial defense contracts. Thus, *Project Transition* will provide civilian skills to over 60,000 men about to leave the services, and *Project Value* is aimed at providing employment for 5,600 disadvantaged youths.

In another program the Department intends to see that its vast resources in plants and facilities when inactivated are converted to the economic advantage and benefit of local areas.

The armed services will continue to lead the nation's institutions in fostering and exemplifying racial integration and equality of opportunity (although racial bigotry and related problems are by no means absent in the military establishment).

A most striking example of the militarism of our society is that we have sought to meet the local crises of race and poverty by training more than 400,000 regular soldiers, National Guardsmen, and police in riot control. The pervasive use of military means to solve our social and political problems is a most disturbing indication of the failure of other conflict-resolving institutions.

There is no doubt about the need for a growing awareness of domestic and social problems on the part of the powerful defense-industry team but the extent of their participation in the national efforts on the domestic front bears close watching. Considering the history of military misjudgments such as evidenced by the Vietnam and Dominican Republic interventions and the stupendous and costly miscalculations for programs such as F-111, C-5A, the Lockheed Cheyenne armed helicopter, the M70 tank, the Skybolt and Bomarc, and others made by the defense-industry team, such proposals are alarming. The defense establishment, operating behind the screens of technical gobbledygook and secrecy, is capable of gigantic mistakes which are motivated by careerism, profits, and military empire-building—as well as the national interests. There is no reason yet to expect that defense planners, analysts, and computer programmers offer any new magic for solving the nation's social problems.

Unwittingly, perhaps, Secretary Clifford recognized the limitations of the Department when he made the understatement of the year: "I do not regard the Department of Defense primarily as an instrument of social welfare."

Footnotes

[1] Samuel P. Huntington, *The Soldier and the State,* Harvard University Press, Cambridge, Mass., 1964, p. 290.

[2] Daniel Seligman, "A Special Kind of Rebellion," *Fortune,* January 1969.

[3] Bernard G. Wertzman, "Youths' Pacifism Scored in Soviet," *The New York Times,* July 6, 1969.

[4] Robert S. Horowitz, "The Week in Congress," *Navy Times,* August 13, 1969.

[5] Jay Stuart Haft, *Dartmouth Alumni Magazine,* June, 1969.

[6] Robert Keatley, "Student Soldiers," *Wall Street Journal,* July 2, 1969.

[7] *Statistical Abstract of the United States,* Department of Commerce, Washington, D.C., 1968.

[8] *Commanders Digest,* Department of Defense, Washington, D.C., July 12, 1969.

Chapter XI

ATTACK IN A
DIFFERENT DIRECTION

*"Overgrown military establishments are under any form
of government inauspicious to liberty, and are to be regarded as particularly hostile to republican liberty."*
George Washington

During a ten-day period in December of 1950, 105,000 allied
troops were withdrawn from the port of Hungnam in Communist
North Korea following the entry of massive Chinese Communist
forces into that war. The U.S. X Corps, consisting of the veteran
1st Marine Division, the 3rd and 7th U.S. infantry divisions, plus
Republic of Korea forces, had been stopped cold in their drive
from Hungnam to Chosin, deep into northeast Korea. The subsequent retreat and evacuation by sea was an unprecedented and
unhappy experience for the American people and their armed
forces.

At the time Major General O. P. Smith, commanding the Marine
Division, made one of those typical Leatherneck remarks; he
announced that the Marines weren't retreating, but were "attacking
in a different direction." The press and public found this a palatable
explanation. The allied troops were redeployed into South Korea,
refitted, and went on to fight many battles in the counteroffensives
of 1951. However, the Korean War has yet to be won.

Now, eighteen years later, in Vietnam, we have a larger U.S.
field army with a force of almost a million allies—all of whom
are bogged down in the bottomless morass of another Asiatic land
war. The United States has suffered more than 40,000 killed in

action, more than 260,000 maimed and wounded, and has very little real progress or profit to show for the efforts made since our intervention in March, 1965. Furthermore, Defense Secretary Laird and General Wheeler both reported in the summer of 1969 on the grim prospects for any immediate success in "Vietnamizing" the war.

The Army of the Republic of Vietnam, they stated, will require years before it can stand on its own against even the Viet Cong irregulars, to say nothing of being able to contain the supporting allies from North Vietnam. This in spite of the fact that we have already provided the South Vietnamese with $1.5 billion worth of armored vehicles, trucks, field artillery, light aircraft, radios, and other aid and equipment not generally available to the Communist forces. The South Vietnamese armed forces of over 800,000 men are about four times larger than the forces of the National Liberation Front rebels and their North Vietnam allies in the country. Yet it is highly doubtful that extravagant dollar aid or the planned additional $1.25 billion worth of more modern and expensive equipment will ever provide the Army of the Republic of Vietnam with the spirit, skills, and inspiring leadership it needs to dominate its dedicated opponents. The U.S. military commanders in Vietnam have often said that it will be several years before the Republic of Vietnam can fend for itself.

In fact, the whole concept of Vietnamization of the war is questionable. The militarists who desire to prolong the American withdrawal and who talk about the massacre of South Vietnamese that may happen at some future date if our troops leave the battlefield are apparently oblivious to the fact that a massacre of the Vietnamese people has been going on for five years and much of the bloodshed has resulted from U.S. firepower. What has to be done is to stop the fighting.

The planned continued presence of hundreds of thousands of American military advisers, pilots, technicians, and special support personnel will present the same risks of casualties and losses from guerrilla attacks as were experienced in 1964 and 1965. Historically, America has been inclined to retaliate and intervene in situations where U.S. military personnel are exposed to attack and suffer casualties. As long as Americans remain in the war zone, there will be reasons to defend both their safety and their honor.

The price Americans will have to pay for their dubious and ill-calculated investment is continued loss of 100 to 250 young American fighting men per week, or over 10,000 killed each year; a cost of $28 billions a year; widespread domestic dissension and criticism of our government's war policies; and continued lack of support by the rest of the world's nations who deplore our strategy and intervention in the affairs of Vietnam.

Patience has run out, the cost has already been too great, the military establishment has revealed no acceptable plans or ability to find any new solutions—and the Paris meetings show no sign of progress or hope of a cease fire. Peace and negotiations are bogged down as the United States seeks an "honorable" settlement when actually there has been very little that is honorable or even very honest about the U.S. participation in the war. The Nixon administration is not *yet* to blame for the frustrations of the Vietnam war, but it is now time to make some sincere and forthright moves away from the hazards to which three decades of militarism have brought the nation. It is time to swallow our pride and begin to "attack in a different direction."

The present program of gradual U.S. withdrawal from Vietnam should be accelerated; first by an American cease fire and a phased redeployment of U.S. forces to major coastal enclave bases behind a screen of security provided by the South Vietnam army. This maneuver should be followed soon by substantial and rapid reductions of U.S. forces in-country to include brigade, division, and air-wing-size units with their logistic support forces.

By withdrawal of these forces back to their home bases we can rapidly reconstitute the depleted strategic reserve forces, reduce combat losses, and cut war costs. The American people are not so arrogant and proud that they won't quickly be able to stomach a new strategy disengagement from Vietnam. The first order of national business, then, should be to get *all* American forces out of Vietnam—and *to stop the killing of Americans*.

As the national defense effort is redirected away from the quagmire of Vietnam, it should also be steered clear of the forces of militarism which have so powerfully influenced the nation's course in recent years. Our ideologies, our motives, and the enemy must be re-evaluated in terms of today's realities and in relation to other national issues and problems. The result should be a new national security policy which is feasible, acceptable, and provides clear direction upon which the defense establishment can determine its functions and its needs.

The new basic national security policy should recognize two fundamental facts:

1. There are limits to the power of the United States.
2. The United States is strategically essentially an air/ sea power—not a land power.

The influence of the career military professionals upon the nation's defence and martial spirit should not be hampered by any reactionary effort to change the long-standing codes of duty, honor, and loyalty to country—or the creeds of discipline, *esprit,* and courage. The nation will always have need of its soldiers, sailors, airmen, and Marines. These fighting men require the unique spiritual and ethical values upon which to base their beliefs in service and sacrifice. We cannot expect generals and admirals to stop thinking like generals and admirals. If they did they wouldn't be very useful.

Nor is it reasonable to expect the professional military leaders to be anything less than vigorous, ambitious, and competitive in the pursuit of their careers and enhancement of their profession. It will be the duty of the Congress, the media, and the people, however, to recognize that the disciples of national defense are not completely selfless and altruistic when they foster national defense programs—they too have vested interests. Their ideas must be judged—not sanctified.

The entire vast and powerful defense establishment, the uniformed members and their civilian leaders, in the words of John Kenneth Galbraith, simply have to be kept "under firm political control."

The Sacred Trinity

The connotations of "national defense," "patriotism" and "anti-communism" must be continually evaluated in terms of the real world. They cannot be merely sacred shibboleths used by doctrinaires and demagogues to support special interests. The basic values of militarism should be examined with enlightened perspective and an objective understanding of their significance and purposes.

Patriotism in its essence is simply devotion to one's country. It is not limited to ceremonies, flags, and bands—or to uniforms and warfare. It is also a concern for the peace, prosperity, and progress of the nation. It is service and sacrifice for country in combat *and* in peaceful duties. It includes service for the poor, the ill, and underprivileged at home as well as fighting for allies in foreign lands. Creative productivity that will benefit the nation and bring it honor and respect is just as patriotic as sitting at the trigger of an atomic missile capable of destroying distant cities. Patriotism in its martial form, however, has been extolled by the disciples of the new militarism.

The dangerous patriot is the one who drifts into chauvinism and exhibits blind enthusiasm for military actions. He is a defender of militarism and its ideals of war and glory. Chauvinism is a proud and bellicose form of patriotism that includes a zealous devotion to military policies and programs. It is an extreme militarist point of view which identifies numerous enemies who can only be dealt with through military power and which equates the national honor with military victory.

National defense in its literal sense means defense of the United States and the republic's sovereign islands and bases against foreign attack or seizure. The Constitution assigns Congress the responsibility to provide for the common defense under the principle that national defense is a national responsibility.

Containment of communism, military aid and alliances, forward deployment of land, air, and sea forces, doctrines of rapid reaction, and large powerful in-being forces inculcated with the spirit of the offensive must all be weighed in terms of the real needs of national defense. We should determine whether a nation with 3.4 million men under arms and with powerful forces numbering over 1.2 million people overseas, far from American shores, is maintaining a defensive or actually an aggressive posture. Who are we defending against? For the past twenty-two years, the nation's and the militarists' enemy has been "aggressive communism," the product of the world-wide Communist conspiracy.

So the third basic creed of American militarism is *anti-communism*. The patriots who man the national defense establishment are prepared to defend the country, its friends, and its allies against *Communist aggression* wherever and whenever it is judged to be at work against the interests of the United States and the countries we find it desirable and feasible to support and defend. Many of our political, military, and editorial opinion-makers have acquired an anti-communism syndrome. They either think they see threats of Communist aggression on all sides or they dub any social or political dissent that they don't understand or they oppose as evidence of a Communist conspiracy. The military, for its part, always has to focus upon a potential enemy. Communist aggressors are the most convenient, current, and identifiable enemy. If there were no Communist bloc and no such enemy threat, the defense establishment would have to invent one. If Soviet Russia and its satellites were all constitutional monarchies with large and powerful armed forces, they would be the enemy. If Great Britain were still a major sea power, it would be considered a potential enemy by U.S. naval war planners—as was believed in 1914. So Marxist communism in itself is not the real threat to the United States: it is the *military power* evident in much of the Communist-dominated world which constitutes the presumed danger to the United States.

Who Is the Enemy?

World War II and the subsequent Cold War have moved the professional military leaders along the conservative path and away from popular liberalism in a trend which was begun toward the end of the nineteenth century. The military has long realized that its existence depends upon the probability or possibility of war and so are rarely optimistic about the intentions or good nature of any potential enemy. The military emphasizes the evil in man and seeks out threats of aggression and danger wherever they may be found. To most military officers human nature is unchanging and no institutions or wishful thinking can result in peaceful civilization. Wars can be perhaps prevented or delayed by military power, they can be won only by armed strength, and by and large, wars are considered inevitable. The standards and needs by which American military strength should be measured, they believe, have been "the estimated force which the strongest probable enemy could bring against us." [1]

Some sociologists insist that everyone in the modern world is either a conscious or unconscious nationalist. Any appeal to international peace or brotherhood is likely to be a form of nationalism in disguise. The conscious nationalist fights for his country in concrete terms and with full awareness. The unconscious nationalist, if he fights, fights always in the abstract for "humanity," or "freedom," or "peace" or "anti-communism," and remains completely blind to the fact that the way he defines these ideas and ideals is most often determined by a nationalistic frame of reference, or of which he is unaware.

It is true that most people, the world over, want peace. But whether they are conscious or unconscious nationalists, they will define peace in such a way that it is synonymous with the power interests of their own nation and, therefore, detrimental to the power interests of some other nations. Most men desire peace, but they are unprepared to appease or to accept the power aspirations of another nation when they do not coincide with those of their own.

One of the more common human failings is the tendency to react to new phenomena with old reflexes. Generals are often the slaves of strategies designed for other wars, and diplomats are prone to retain postures and policies based on conditions of a world that no longer exists. In today's rapidly changing world, this kind of perceptual lag can be dangerous and costly. Testifying before the Senate Foreign Relations Committee in February, 1966, General Maxwell Taylor stated that "it would be disastrous" for the security of the United States to pull out of South Vietnam. He said, "I think it would start our troubles on a world-wide basis. The repercussions would not be limited to Southeast Asia but would affect every country with whom we have relations, particularly in all our alliances which would be adversely affected." [2]

Despite such fearful warnings, the world of 1970 is not the world of 1950 or even 1960. Today the situation has improved. The virulent hostility that marked the Stalin era has diminished, and the United States and the Soviet Union are seeking accommodations in areas of mutual interest. Power alignments are more confused, and the world is generally less polarized.

Most military people know very little about communism, either as a doctrine or as a form of government. But they have been provided with reasons enough to presume that it is bad and represents the forces of evil. For example, naval personnel indoctrination stresses the moral obligation to fight Communist aggression—and emphasizes the merits of naval forces as the instruments of anti-communism:

> The record of communism is a record of deceit, dishonesty, and tyranny. The evil of communism is not static, it is a cancer that grows ruthlessly. Unless it is checked it expands and chokes off all other forms of government and all freedom of belief, thought and speech. Our moral obligation to fight communism includes the necessity to maintain a strong Navy.
>
> Our institutions and our citizens are *free* to the extent that they fear no interference. If our shores and borders were ringed with powerful, watchful enemies, many of our citizens, our institutions, and in particular, our government would have to be careful what they said and did. Always we would be afraid that the enemy might come in and threaten us for saying or doing things he disfavored.
>
> Similarly the citizens and institutions of other free nations must know that they are protected—and protected in their home waters—by our forces. Otherwise, they will be pressured to become timid and subservient to a powerful and ambitious neighbor.

The nations of the free world look to the United States for leadership and inspiration as well as for protection and support. For them to read about our land forces and our air forces is not the same as for them to see our ships and carrier-based aircraft in and over their harbors.

The Communists—and for that matter any enemy—bow only to force—to force they see and fear. Therefore our naval forces, even as they strengthen the moral courage of the free world dishearten by their presence the bravado of the totalitarian nations, and chill their schemes of war and conquest.[3]

The Naval Officers Guide provides the young naval officer with additional anti-communist ideologies:

The Communist strategy encompasses a program of infiltration, economic penetration, subversion and occasional armed aggression. The United States is their principal opponent and the eventual target of all Communist efforts. . . . This country's ultimate goal is the elimination of every type of servitude in the world.

We must recognize Russian and International Communism for what it is—an international conspiracy for power and conquest. It is powerful, militarily and economically, but it is weak morally, for there is no basis in ethics for the Communist philosophy of moral good. The motivating force of Communism is lust for personal power and position and their perquisites.[4]

These and other oversimplified concepts of anti-communism stem from the basic national policy (developed following World War II) of "preventing the expansion and extension of Communist domination by the use of force against the weaker nations on the perimeter of Communist power." [5]

By "Communist power," this policy implies the USSR and Red China. To the Department of State, it has meant a combined centralized Communist conspiracy aimed at the monolithic world revolution. The military threat is in the form of the tired cliché of "Communist aggression" which supports insurgency or rebellion against "our side" by what the Communists on the "other side" call "wars of national liberation." Regardless of where we identify Communist aggression, in a small Caribbean nation or in remote Southeast Asia, the real enemy is "Communist power," or specifically, the USSR and/or Red China. The power of American militarism and the defense bureaucracy has been born of the fear created by these Communist hobgoblins. If "anti-Communism," then, is all we can agree on as a national credo, we will never be able to cure the psychosis of force and destruction which has become the American tragedy.

"Who is the enemy, anyway?" *Time* recently asked. "The Russians, with whom Washington has been signing treaties, and exchanging musicians? The Chinese, who have been shooting Russians lately? Those scrawny North Vietnamese, visited often by American journalists? Assorted revolutionaries in distant and backward countries, who might be influenced by Communists?" [6]

The doctrinaires of the military establishment, the Department of State careerists, and administration leaders have attempted to define the Communist enemy in simple and generalized terms. There has been a determined effort to perceive communism with the same view as of ten or twenty years ago. East Asian communism has been regarded as a homogeneous and disciplined movement of international aggression which poses a threat to the United States comparable to that of Hitler and the Japanese in the thirties or Stalin in the forties. "The contest in Vietnam," President Johnson explained, "is part of a wider pattern of aggressive purposes."

Defense and administration leaders have been obsessed with the idea that the United States is being challenged not by lightly armed bands of young guerrillas and North Vietnamese infantry formations—without heavy supporting arms, no air power and no naval forces—but by a heavily armed, dangerously strong military power which is committed to world expansion and which is a threat to the United States.

There has actually been no evidence to sustain the thesis that the war in Vietnam is the spearhead of Chinese Communist aggression. Indeed, most evidence indicates that Asian communism is as fragmented as is European communism. The idea that we are fighting in Asia to stop Chinese Communist aggression today so that we will not have to fight it in Hawaii tomorrow is the product of an anti-communist mythology. It is a stereotyped concept of the militarists in constant search for an enemy and for reasons to justify the establishment. In fact, the evidence in Vietnam strongly indicates that the opponent is not aggressive Chinese communism but a local insurgent party led by Communists who desire to take over the government of South Vietnam, not for Peking but for themselves. The Vietnamese people have historically fought any Chinese domination.

The conspiracy myth has been perpetuated in spite of the very evident fragmentation of the Communist bloc. We are fighting the native Viet Cong rebels in Vietnam, not because they pose any threat to the United States or its interests, but because they desire to overthrow a corrupt government which we have chosen to support. We support it, not because we admire it, but because it is "anti-Communist." The real enemy, then, is not the Viet Cong whom we are killing but Red China and the USSR who are providing arms aid to North Vietnam and the National Liberation Front. So we have justified the scale and cost of the war in which our main military objective has been to kill large numbers of Vietnamese in their own country by believing we are frustrating Chinese Communist aggression and thereby containing Communism in Southeast Asia. The proof of this basis for war rests on ideology and analogy, not on rational argument or concrete illustration. The Viet Cong, North Vietnamese and Chinese as Communists have strong bonds of common interest and certain ideological affinities —but they also have greatly divergent interests and purposes.

There is also a belief by many that the conflict with communism is man's ultimate battle and some extreme military doctrinaires apparently would not hesitate to destroy all mankind if Communist aggression seemed a serious threat. This belief fosters acceptance of the atomic arms race regardless of the dangers.

Typical of the military point of view on the threats to national security is the statement of policy made by the Air Force Association in 1969:

> *We view the threat to our nation's security as greater than ever.* Now it is three-pronged. The Soviet Union has tightened its grip on its satellites by naked force while continuing its buildup of both sophisticated advanced weaponry and conventional forces. Red China continues its domination of the landmass of Asia by sheer weight of numbers while at the same time thrusting toward full-fledged status as a nuclear superpower in its own right. Both Communist powers urge, aid, and abet so-called "wars of national liberation" in the less-developed areas of the world. Any one of these developments poses grave risks for the United States in its position as leader of the Free World. Taken together they represent a threat of greater magnitude than any this nation has faced to date.

But Harvard's George Wald says that "the thought that we are in competition with Russians or with Chinese is all a mistake, and trivial," and Under Secretary of State Elliot L. Richardson has stated, "National interests, not political ideologies such as world Communism, are the primary influence determining international behavior. The unity of Communist discipline and dogma is a thing of the past." The term "Communist" now covers such a multiplicity of states, parties and tendencies as to have little meaning or usefulness. "With the decline in the unity of world Communism there has come a decline in the appeal of Communism to the underdeveloped countries," the Secretary added. The resurgence of nationalism has been accompanied by a decline in the ability of the great powers to impose their will and enforce their authority on their allies.[7]

And finally, from the enemy point of view it is not surprising that a band of bellicose and dogmatic Marxist-Leninists in Peking should interpret the deployment of U.S. Army, Navy, and Air Forces totaling over 600,000 combat men in Southeast Asia and the western Pacific—almost ten thousand miles from the American mainland—as an aggressive strategy designed to encircle, contain, and threaten China. If an Oriental power were to deploy such an expeditionary force in Mexico, Americans would be justly outraged. So the guilt of aggression in Vietnam hinges a good deal upon the point of view from which the map is oriented.

"It would be a gross oversimplification," Secretary McNamara once said, "to regard Communism as the central factor in every conflict throughout the underdeveloped world."

Policies and Guidance

It is generally agreed among students of national policy that the United States should have a national strategy. During the Eisenhower years U.S. policy was under the influence of a policy paper known as "NSC-1" (National Security Council Paper No. 1) which was at best an ambiguous document. Then during the "agonizing reappraisal" of strategy in 1961, an effort was made to write a truly meaningful "Basic National Security Policy," known as BNSP. This proposed national policy guidance underwent five major attempts at agreement by top military and civilian leaders. But it was never approved and remains merely as a guideline for U.S. policy abroad.

Since the Kennedy years there has been no formal statement of Basic National Security Policy on which force levels and military structure could be based. There were annual and detailed defense posture statements by Secretary McNamara which spelled out the force levels and requirements for the forthcoming year—but not an agreed national policy. Without an agreed national strategy, there is no clear concept of American objectives or priorities for foreign and domestic goals, and the military services are left to visualize missions for every possible product of their imaginations and doctrinal interests.

The National Security Policy guidance coming from National Security Council decisions should be the basis upon which the defense establishment formulates its missions, its concepts and its requirements. The military must have a clear idea of the capabilities it is expected to create and what tasks it is expected to perform.

The premises upon which past strategic policies were determined must be periodically reviewed in light of current realities.

The present system of defense budget formulation for defense structure funding is a businesslike, although piecemeal, approach. It, too, must be more clearly related to changing national commitments and BNSP requirements. The defense programs and budget stem from the Joint Strategic Objectives Plan (JSOP) which is formulated each year by the Joint Chiefs of Staff and their Joint Staff in the Pentagon. This planning effort involves the digestion of masses of intelligence data to arrive at an estimate of the capabilities and proclivities of all potential enemies. Then there is an assessment of the present capabilities of U.S. forces and weapons, (these are rarely deemed adequate), and consideration of the technological advances expected in the near future from the large defense research establishment. The annual JSOP ("Jaysop") is a military judgment as to the forces and programs which the defense establishment believes should be supported in the ensuing five to eight years.

Presidential guidance is incorporated in the system by means of Draft Presidential Memoranda which inform the President about major issues and studies. He can accept or reject their advice and conclusions. In general, however, the planning and budgeting for defense has become a complex and ritualistic procedure for determining, propagating, and financing the services' programs, rather than a means of providing military capabilities consonant with grand national strategy. Concepts of new systems must be analyzed as well as their costs and effectiveness. Forward deployment, military aid, rapid reaction, atomic deterrence, and even civil defense should be analyzed in light of feasibility and acceptability—as well as estimates of enemy capabilities.

Defense spending has continually increased because requirements are based on strategic assumptions that have remained generally unchallenged and unchanged since the early Cold War days when the enemy and the threats were quite different. The force structures and force levels are now composed by military chiefs without any clearly stated national security policy guidance from the White House.[8] This is partly because the civilian leaders depend upon military intelligence estimates of enemy capabilities which are never anything but grim and the civilians rarely question them. Then during war periods the civilian control of the military tends to diminish because only the military "experts" understand the details of requirements, and the civilian officials do not want to be guilty of withholding from the troops what the military claim is needed.

For purposes of budget planning and programming, the active armed forces are considered in terms of four main functional categories: Strategic retaliatory forces; Continental air and missile defense forces; General purpose forces; and Airlift and sealift forces. (For a detailed composition of functional forces, see Appendix 4.)

The U.S. strategic retaliatory and air and missile defense forces which require 40 percent of defense expenditures have been built since 1961 on the assumptions of a credible minimum deterrence. A credible minimum deterrence is based on a second-strike capability with power enough to destroy two fifths of an enemy's population and three quarters of its industry, thereby effectively eliminating it as a twentieth-century power.

The general purpose, airlift and sealift forces which account for 60 percent of the defense budget, are designed to allow the United States to control a land or sea area or deny it to the enemy in a limited war or counterinsurgency situation. It is not designed for general war against a nation's armed power, population, and industry. The general purpose forces have not been related to the defense of U.S. territories as much as they have to the defense of other allied countries on the rim of the Communist world and in the execution of the doctrines of containment and forward deployment.[9]

The strategy of forward deployment is evidenced by the location of sixteen of the nation's twenty-three active divisions in Europe, Korea and Vietnam; and by the overseas basing of nearly half of the 5,000 tactical and attack aircraft along with about one third of the Navy's general-purpose ships.

These commitments have continued more because they are routine, almost traditional missions on which the services have based their planning than because they have strategic justification.

The validity of the threats which led to these deployments in the 1940's and 1950's is long overdue for review and analysis.

The main faulty planning assumption of the recent past is that American ground forces and their supporting arms have proved unable to deal with events on the Asian mainland or any similar underdeveloped land being torn by local civil war and insurgency. The pertinent question now is not only the feasibility of our commitments, but whether a particular commitment is truly in the best interests of the United States.

Defenders of the strategy of large general purpose forces deployed to forward areas in support of military alliances say that any large defense cuts would undermine the policies of collective defense which have guided defense planning since World War II. In fact, however, the policy of collective defense is also overdue for reappraisal and revision. Not only have possible enemy threats changed in recent years, but American military presence on foreign soil is not as urgently needed. West Germany and the other NATO allies are quite capable of assuming a larger share of the provision and costs of the European defense forces. Economically, militarily, and politically Japan is now capable of once again becoming a Pacific power and assuming a large share of responsibility in the Western Pacific. For a quarter century American military and economic aid has nurtured these and other nations where now a renaissance of nationalism is making the presence of American armed forces not only undesirable but irritating. Historically, no sovereign people have relished the presence of foreign troops stationed on their soil for prolonged periods, even as allies, but the American military continues to garrison the outposts of the Free World on others' lands, in the manner of the Roman legions. It is now time to bring the legions home and to divert their costs to the repair of the decaying cities and the nation's social fabric.

A policy of withdrawal from our deep involvement in the affairs of Asia should be designed to avoid future military entanglements on the mainland of Asia. Our past strategy in the Pacific has been a peripheral one which extends our influence and military presence throughout the Pacific Ocean areas and to the littoral of Asia.

It has not normally included plans or policies involving invasion or occupation, or large-scale ground combat.

Essentially it is a maritime and an airpower strategy, based upon our dominant strength, mobility, and advantages in those elements. It permits the presence of our air-sea forces up to the coastal perimeters of hostile Asiatic countries but does not commit us. It permits amphibious incursion and even limited intervention, but also allows us to avoid large-scale participation in land operations. A peripheral strategy is made possible by the freedom of the seas and the mobility of sea-air power.[10]

At the same time that we avoid involvement on the mainland, we should strengthen our alliances with the more dependable and promising island nations which have common interests with us in the Pacific areas: Japan, Australia, New Zealand, and the Philippines. These nations have the industry, stability, strategic location or resources to be reliable allies. They should be allies who have a direct concern about any dangerous threats or aggression in that part of the world. They are economically developed nations with considerable reason to defend their interests. Also, by concentrating our efforts and investments on a more selective, logical, and promising alliance for our collective security, we should then expect more substantial contributions from each of them when needed.

If we learn anything from our sanguinary experience in Vietnam we will return to this maritime strategy in the western Pacific that will avoid commitments, and our own national interest and welfare will determine the extent of future ventures to aid troubled nations in that part of the world. The paranoid concern about Communist aggression, which has typified our contingency planning in recent years, will not be the primary factor. Such a defense strategy will utilize modern and powerful combinations of mobile sea-air-ground forces. These general-purpose, conventional war forces, in combination with modern nuclear deterrent weapons, will guard our areas of interest, using the vast reaches of the oceans and the skies above as their battle grounds. At present we have few challengers in these realms—and we can keep those few under close surveillance. Nor should strategic policy of military withdrawal to key island bases in the Pacific area define any defense perimeter or sphere of interest in the manner of Secretary of State Dean Acheson's list which omitted Korea in 1950. The U.S. can reduce the provocation and expense of its presence on foreign soil in the western Pacific, but its interests in the affairs of the area will be decided by specific events and their bearing upon the national welfare, not by outworn policies and meddlesome contingency plans. Our intentions need not be broadcast in detail, but there should be no doubt about our capabilities.

The withdrawal of American military forces and the reduction of U.S. military facilities on the soil of other sovereign nations is not a prelude to isolationism. The fact is that the United States is now bound to the rest of the world by so many ties, by such a variety of institutional and private forces, and by transportation and communications systems which have shrunk the globe that there can be no isolation. Actually, the reduction of the American military presence world-wide should enhance communication between peoples because it reduces the evidence and connotations of imperialism and removes the irritants caused by the arrogance of armed power. In the modern world arena, power depends on social, political, and economic strength as well as military capability. The inflated notions of U.S. world influence should be scaled down in recognition of the need for alternative social and economic solutions.

Controlling Militarism

The simplest, speediest and most readily understandable means of controlling militarism is to *cut military manpower strengths* and to *reduce defense appropriations*.

Since military manpower accounts for about half of the total defense budget, the first move is to reduce military personnel strength. Despite the services' many reasons to the contrary, they can be reduced as rapidly as they were built up, simply by cutting down the input of personnel—reduce the draft, recruiting and officer procurement, reduce force levels by the steady attrition of men leaving the service at the end of their tours of duty without reinlistment or replacement. Reductions can be further accelerated by voluntary early-outs. A million-man reduction can be effected in less time than it took to build up forces from a strength of 2,653,142 in 1965 to 3,477,500 in 1969.

Force levels of the 1963 period should be a reasonable objective for planning purposes and could provide sufficient strength to perform the missions of a new national security policy. The savings could exceed $10 billion a year and would accumulate future savings on veterans' medical and pension benefits.

Military strength levels 1963

Army	975,155
Navy	664,207
Marines	189,683
Air Force	868,644
Total	2,697,689

Source: Executive Office of the President, Bureau of the Budget: *The Budget of the United States Government.*

Reductions in personnel need not cause a loss of combat power. More efficient use of manpower can be attained by reduction of noncombat, base housekeeping, and service-support organizations. More civilians can be employed to perform base maintenance and service tasks. Fewer bases will be needed.

A chain of cost benefits results from any reduction in military personnel. Pay, subsistence, allowances, and transportation costs go down; training, operations, and maintenance costs are reduced; and the needs for consumable supplies and equipment are reduced.

Deputy Secretary of Defense, David Packard, has said that "The level of military spending is determined by the commitments this country makes around the world, by the things we need to fulfill those commitments." The obvious solution is to review commitments *with the firm intention of reducing them,* then reduce the numbers of U.S. forces deployed overseas:

Disengage and withdraw the 530,000-man expeditionary force from South Vietnam.

Reduce the numbers of U.S. air and ground forces stationed in Europe as elements of NATO's collective defense effort.

Reduce or withdraw air and ground units stationed in Korea, Thailand, Japan, Taiwan and Okinawa with an objective of complete withdrawal in the mid-range (three year) period.

Reduce the numbers of American forces on Luzon but continue to man the naval base at Subic in the Philippines.

Withdraw U.S. forces to mid-Pacific bases which meet naval and air requirements to accomplish the missions of an air/sea strategy in the Pacific area.

Reduce the sphere of responsibility and curtail the constant presence of a major U.S. fleet in the Mediterranean Sea. Return the responsibility for that sea to the nations who surround it.

Drastically reduce or eliminate military assistance and advisory missions world-wide.

There should also be a reduction and closer controls of defense material and procurement programs in consonance with a revised national defense policy. The highly dubious and suspect ABM system was examined, debated and questioned by Congress during the summer of 1969 in a way that no other program advanced by the Pentagon in recent years had suffered. Congress has given evidence of its new sense of responsibility "to provide for the common defense." Its future tasks are taking form as the military establishment draws up its latest shopping lists. The Pentagon has warned that the end of the war in Vietnam will not necessarily mean a reduction in defense spending. It has been the Defense Department's contention that, when the war ends, it will need large sums to produce new strategic weapons and to modernize conventional forces. This is the old canard that present strategic weapons which already have a gross overkill capability are not powerful enough. A greater overkill capacity is needed. The world's most modern conventional weapons are, like a perfectly adequate three-year-old sedan, now out of style and must be replaced by the "latest models." Of all the weapons systems, U.S. fleet combatant vessels are the most dated, old, and worn. A long-range program of ship modernization and replacement is necessary for the United States to remain a major sea power and is a pressing matter in the national interest.

Congress and the American people are going to have to determine the true justification and requirements for many other weapons systems and defense programs with far-reaching implications. In addition to the ABM, there are possible savings in controls of proposed programs for:

MIRV, the multiple-headed atomic missile; nuclear aircraft carriers (at over $540 million each); a new advanced manned strategic aircraft (AMSA) bomber (with a ten-year systems cost estimate of $12 billion); a new generation of intercontinental ballistic missiles in super-hard silos; a new intercepter air defense jet; the new M-70 tank (six years behind schedule at a cost of $228 million); a Navy anti-submarine aircraft; a new advanced Air Force fighter aircraft; the Fast Deployment Logistic (FDL) ship (with estimated program cost of $187 million); the chemical and biological warfare projects—a stretch-out and gradual reduction of the B-52 bomber fleet to mention a few.

Further savings can be realized by modifications in the size, nature, and functions of the general purpose forces. These questions should be studied:

Is there a valid need for fifteen naval attack carriers?

Is there a need for expensive high performance jet fighter-bombers in the close troop support role?

How feasible is tactical atomic warfare and what are the requirements for tactical nuclear (surface-to-surface) weapons?

Is the concept of rapid reaction and employment of large numbers of the C-5A cargo air transport based on a sound and desirable strategy?

What size and type of amphibious forces are required

under a strategy of limited forward deployment and reduced commitments?

Why can't American military forces attain a higher ratio of combat unit manpower to overall strength?

Other reductions in cost can result from:

Control of funds requested by the military for modernization of weapons and improved performance through management-control devices such as the trade-off concept (i.e., the principle that for each additional dollar spent on procurement, a dollar must be saved elsewhere).

Rigid control over procurement to minimize "gold plating" (equipment with excessive quality and capability).

Research and development projects of dubious value and relation to improved combat effectiveness should be eliminated.

Those performed by private institutes and contract research centers should be reduced and the defense forces urged to think more for themselves.

Fortune magazine believes that a post-Vietnam defense budget of around $61 billion would allow the U.S. to remain the dominant military power capable of fulfilling its necessary roles and duties and executing the strategies of its basic defense concepts.[11]

Even after cuts and reductions the U.S. can still have a most powerful and diversified military force capable of maintaining a credible deterrent to aggression. The nation cannot and should not revert to isolationism, but it will continue to be isolated while its friends reject its leadership and example. There is no realistic prospect of unilateral disarmament in the world of today or tomorrow, but reduced armaments and controlled militarism can be a constant goal.

There is and has been civilian control of the military services and the Joint Chiefs of Staff, but that does not mean that the armed forces and their leaders do not exert their influence in many

ways—through their Congressional supporters, their industry teammates, their associations, their publications, and their public affairs
offices. Armed forces leaders continue to be influential speech- and
opinion-makers. What remains to be placed under control is the
defense establishment, the Department of Defense civilian officials
and bureaucrats, the military planners, the defense industry, and
all the related vested interests who profit from militarism. The
responsibility of Congress will be to realize that every idea, estimate, and program that comes out of the Pentagon is not oracular
and that because the defense budget comes wrapped in the flag
is no reason not to examine its contents.

James Reston said: "The control of military arms is undoubtedly
the most important political question in the world today, for the
arms race devours the money and influences all other questions
of poverty, race, jobs, and housing, both here and abroad." [12]

The Rulers of Our Own Spirit

The strategic importance of Vietnam, if such ever really existed,
has greatly diminished for the United States since ground combat
troops landed there in 1965. China's increasingly acrimonious
dispute with Russia and its internal disorders have left Peking
with little time or energy to "export revolution." The pseudo-
Communist threat of the Sukarno era in Indonesia has dissolved.
The simplistic "domino theory" that was used to support our
intervention in Vietnam in the early 1960's no longer seems so
valid. Now Laos remains an unstable area, and Thailand faces
possible insurgency, but their futures do not appear to hinge upon
a massive U.S. military presence—and probably never did. The
leaders of these countries seem capable of dealing with their own
problems in their own Asiatic way. In the long run even the existence of the American fleet just over the horizon will probably have
little effect upon the course of events in that part of the world.
The failures and frustrations of the United States in Vietnam have
come about not so much from any incompetence of the military
forces, but rather from a failure of both the top civilian and military leadership to understand the proper role of armed power in
this form of conflict. The military's only solutions have been fire-

power, mobility, and more of the same—and fewer tactical restrictions. The civilian leaders persisted in the pursuit of limited
objectives with limited and graduated combat power.

Eventually in June, 1969, five years after it lost control by
passing the Tonkin Gulf resolution, the Senate began to shut the
barn door. It resolved that the executive branch of government
should not in the future commit U.S. troops or financial resources
to other countries without the approval of Congress. The theories
of limited war and gradual response have not proved appropriate
for the solution of social-political insurgency and civil war in Southeast Asia. The reasons for going to war in 1965 which were recited
by the disciples of militarism have since been discredited by facts
and events. Congress is renewing its grip on its duties to provide
for the common defense.

The changing world demands modification of outworn foreign
and military policies:

> America's world objectives must be reshaped in the
> light of new realities and in recognition of a less polar-
> ized and more pluralistic world.
>
> The limitations of American power must be recog-
> nized. There are problems at home as well as abroad
> that cannot easily be resolved. America does not neces-
> sarily have the proper answers to the difficulties of other
> people—and until it can deal more effectively with its
> own domestic affairs it can hardly expect aliens to accept
> American solutions and values as the ideal.
>
> Greater emphasis must be put on the use of moral
> influence and the examples of understanding, coexist-
> ence, democracy, and freedom as opposed to armed
> power and the threats of killing.
>
> The new world requires that we judge each threat or
> crisis deliberately on its merits without regard for pre-
> conceptions and stereotypes.

President Kennedy said: "We must face the fact that the United
States is neither omnipotent or omniscient—that we are only six

percent of the world's population—that we cannot impose our will on the other ninety-four percent of mankind—that we cannot right every wrong or reverse each adversity—and that therefore there cannot be an American solution to every world problem."

The American people have lived with fears of a Soviet attack for some twenty-five years, and have spent $1,000 billion on defense in recognition of this possible danger. They now know that billions of these defense dollars have been wasted and that other plans, programs, and policies vital to the nation's well-being have suffered. Yet to contemplate hasty and drastic reductions in U.S. armed power is neither wise nor feasible in the foreseeable future. The realities of power in the nuclear age may be unattractive, costly, and dangerous—but they remain realities.

At the same time, however, the national energies, leadership, technological skills, pride, and competitive spirit—which have for so long been directed into the nonproductive fields of militarism and destructive power—should now be redirected into the adventures and exploration of the space frontier, into building better cities, more schools, adequate transportation systems, housing, hospitals, a more attractive, healthier country and curing social ills.

Joseph Schumpeter wrote of the Romans from the Punic Wars to Augustus, and his account bears a startling contemporary relevance to American militarism:

> Here is the classic example of the kind of insincerity in both foreign and domestic affairs which permeates not only avowed motives but also probably the conscious motives of the actors themselves—of that policy which pretends to aspire to peace but unerringly generates war, the policy of continual preparation for war, the policy of meddlesome interventionism. There was no corner of the known world where some interest was not alleged to be in danger or under actual attack. If the interests were not Roman, they were those of Rome's allies; and if Rome had no allies, then allies would be invented. When it was utterly impossible to continue such an

interest—why then it was the national honor that had been insulted.[13]

It is known how the legions extended their power and influence to the far reaches of the empire while, weakened by dissension, Rome rotted and crumbled away behind them.

The sixth President, John Quincy Adams, defined the character of the country most Americans still desire:

> Wherever the standard of freedom and independence has been or shall be unfurled there will be America's heart, her benedictions and her prayers. But she goes not abroad in search of monsters to destroy. She is the well wisher to the freedom and independence of all. She is the champion and vindicator only of her own.
>
> She will recommend the general cause by the countenance of her voice and by the benignant sympathy of her example. She well knows that by once enlisting under other banners than her own, were they even the banners of foreign independence, she would involve herself beyond the power of extrication, in all the wars of interest and intrigue, of individual avarice, envy and ambition which assume the colors and usurps the standards of freedom.
>
> The fundamental maxims of her policy would insensibly change from liberty to force . . . she might become the dictatress of the world. She would no longer be the ruler of her own spirit.[14]

Footnotes

[1] Samuel P. Huntington, *The Soldier and the State,* Harvard University Press, Cambridge, Mass., 1964, p. 257.

[2] "The Battle Over U.S. Policy in Vietnam," *U.S. News & World Report,* February 28, 1966.

[3] *The Bluejackets' Manual,* U.S. Naval Institute, Annapolis, Md., 1967.

[4] A. A. Ageton and W. P. Mack, *The Naval Officers Guide,* Naval Institute, Md., 1967.

[5] Secretary of State Dean Rusk before the Senate Foreign Relations Committee, February 18, 1966.

[6] "The Military: Servant or Master of Policy?" *Time,* April 11, 1969.

[7] Elliot L. Richardson, Under Secretary of State, Speech to the Advertising Council, Washington, D.C., June 9, 1969.

[8] "The Case for Cutting Defense Spending," *Fortune,* August 1, 1969.

[9] "Defense Budget Highlights," *Defense Industry Bulletin,* Department of Defense, Washington D.C., March, 1969.

[10] John D. Hayes, Rear Adm., USN-Ret., "Peripheral Strategy . . . Littoral Tactics," *Army,* September 1954.

[11] "The Case for Cutting Defense Spending," *Fortune,* August 1, 1969.

[12] James Reston, *The New York Times,* March 16, 1969.

[13] Schumpeter, Joseph A., *Imperialism and Social Classes,* Meridian Books, New York, N.Y.

[14] From speech by John Quincy Adams, given at Washington, D.C., July 4, 1821.

Epilogue

On November 6, 1969, Congress approved a $20.7 billion 1970 Defense procurement authorization bill to give the Defense Department almost every weapon it asked for. Despite widespread public concern about defense costs and the growth of militarism— and the tardy but conscientious efforts by Senate critics to get the military machine under political control, the defense establishment and its powerful allies continue to crush their opposition.

Although the sum approved was $1.2 billion less than the Pentagon had requested, it was billions more than the Senate desired and $721 million more than the Senate had originally approved. No major weapon system was left out of the bill and none was seriously restricted.

The major projects which critics had hoped to curtail or cut moved relentlessly forward:

> Funds for the Safeguard anti-ballistic-missile survived intact.
>
> The MBT-70 "main battle tank" will be provided with funds to continue the program.
>
> Money was kept for additional C-5A jet transports.
>
> The planned strategic bomber B-1 (AMSA) will be funded.
>
> A third nuclear-powered aircraft carrier was approved.
>
> Even chemical-biological warfare programs were provided for with only minor restrictions.

Congress gives every indication in its approval that the American war machine will continue to dominate all other national programs, needs, and interests—and that militarism will maintain its rule over the republic's character.

Appendix 1

MILITARY PERSONNEL ON ACTIVE DUTY BY SERVICE
(As of June 30)

	1940	1945	1964	1965	1966	1967	1968 (Est.)
ARMY							
Officers	18,326	891,663	110,276	111,541	117,205	143,425	164,136
Enlisted	250,697	7,376,295	862,169	856,772	1,081,841	1,298,997	1,371,490
Total	269,023	8,267,958	972,445	968,313	1,199,046	1,442,422	1,535,626
NAVY							
Officers	13,604	331,379	76,257	77,720	79,457	81,677	85,597
Enlisted	147,393	3,049,438	590,906	593,289	665,012	669,717	682,603
Total	160,997	3,380,817	667,163	671,009	744,469	751,394	768,200
MARINES							
Officers	1,800	37,067	16,819	17,234	20,485	23,592	25,236
Enlisted	26,545	437,613	172,932	172,953	241,202	261,677	276,686
Total	28,345	474,680	189,751	190,187	261,687	285,269	301,922
AIR FORCE							
Officers	—	—	133,029	131,141	130,285	135,417	137,128
Enlisted	—	—	722,773	692,492	756,065	762,009	747,000
Total	—	—	855,802	823,633	886,350	897,426	884,128
GRAND TOTAL	458,365	12,123,455	2,685,161	2,653,142	3,091,552	3,376,511	3,489,876
FEMALE	—	265,006	—	30,610	32,589	35,173	—

Source: Department of Defense.

Appendix 2

SUMMARY OF MAJOR U.S. MILITARY FORCES: 1965–1967
(As of June 30)

DESCRIPTION	1965	1966	1967
DEPARTMENT OF THE ARMY:			
Divisions	16	17	17
Regiments and regimental combat teams	4	4	5
Armored combat commands	—	—	—
Infantry brigades	7	9	11
Infantry battle groups	—	—	—
Missile commands	2	1	1
Air defense battalions	56¾	55¼	56¼
Special forces groups	7	7	7
Active aircraft inventory	6,933	8,098	9,375
DEPARTMENT OF THE NAVY:			
Commissioned ships	880	909	931
Warships	407	410	419
Other ships	473	499	512
Carrier air groups	17	17	17
Carrier antisubmarine air groups	11	10	10
Carrier antisubmarine squadrons	31	28	28
Marine divisions	3	4	4
Marine aircraft wings	3	3	3
Active aircraft inventory	8,056	8,260	8,417
Operating aircraft	6,620	6,485	6,591
Logistical support aircraft	1,436	1,775	1,826
DEPARTMENT OF THE AIR FORCE:			
USAF Wings	78	74	74
Strategic	28	23	23
Air defense	13	11	9
Tactical (including airlift)	37	40	42
Active aircraft inventory	14,875	14,196	15,017
Operating aircraft	13,094	12,574	13,034
Nonoperating aircraft	1,781	1,622	1,983

Source: Dept. of Defense, Office of the Secretary: annual report, *Selected Manpower Statistics.*

Appendix 3

**MILITARY RESERVE PERSONNEL
NOT ON ACTIVE DUTY: 1967**
(In thousands, as of June 30)

	1967	
BRANCH OF SERVICE	Total	Paid Drill Training
Total	2,758	983
ARMY	1,639	680
Army National Guard	421	418
Officers	35	34
Enlisted	386	384
Army Reserve	1,218	262
Officers	255	35
Enlisted	963	227
NAVY	624	173
Naval Reserve	479	125
Officers	174	22
Enlisted	305	103
Marine Corps Reserve	144	48
Officers	21	3
Enlisted	124	45
AIR FORCE	496	130
Air National Guard	84	84
Officers	11	11
Enlisted	73	73
Air Force Reserve	412	46
Officers	160	11
Enlisted	252	36

Source: Dept. of Defense, Office of the Secretary: *Annual Report of the Secretary of Defense.*

Appendix 4

DESCRIPTION	1967	1968 est.	1969 est.
STRATEGIC RETALIATORY FORCES:			
Intercontinental ballistic missiles (squadrons):			
Minuteman	20	20	20
Titan	6	6	6
Polaris submarines[1]	41	41	41
Polaris missiles	656	656	656
Strategic bombers (wings):			
B-52	12	11	10
B-58	2	2	2
CONTINENTAL AIR AND MISSILE DEFENSE FORCES:			
Manned fighter interceptor squadrons	28	26	19
Interceptor missile squadrons (BOMARC)	6	6	6
Army air defense missile battalions	18	18	18
GENERAL PURPOSE FORCES:			
Army divisions (combat ready)	17	19	19
Army maneuver battalions	201	212	212
Army aviation units	183	218	234
Army special forces groups	7	7	7
Warships[1]	378	379	376
Amphibious assault ships[1]	162	157	166
Carrier air groups (attack and ASW)	27	27	25
Marine Corps divisions/aircraft wings	4/3	4/3	4/3
Air Force tactical forces squadrons	126	136	138
AIRLIFT AND SEALIFT FORCES:			
Airlift aircraft (squadrons):			
C–130 through C–141	44	44	43
C–124 and C–7	16	14	11
Troopships, cargo ships, and tankers	130	130	130

[1] In commission.

Source: Executive Office of the President, Bureau of the Budget; *The Budget of the United States Government.*

Bibliography

Books

Ageton, A. A., and W. P. Mack. *The Naval Officers Guide.* Annapolis: U.S. Naval Institute, 1967.

Almanac and Yearbook. New York: Readers Digest, 1969.

Associates in Political Science, USAF Academy. *American Defense Policy,* Baltimore: The Johns Hopkins Press, 1965.

Barnet, Richard J., *The Economy of Death,* New York, Atheneum, 1769.

Bernardo, C. J., and Eugene H. Bacon. *American Military Policy.* Pennsylvania: The Stackpole Co., 1955.

The Bluejackets' Manual. Annapolis: U.S. Naval Institute, 1967.

Bosch, Juan. *Pentagonism, A Substitute for Imperialism.* New York: Grove Press, 1968.

Coffin, Tristram. *The Passion of the Hawks.* New York: The Macmillan Company, 1964.

Corson, Lt. Col. William R., USMC. *The Betrayal.* New York: W. W. Norton & Company, 1968.

Donovan, Col. James A., USMC Ret. *The United States Marine Corps.* New York: Frederick A. Praeger, 1967.

Duncan, David Douglas. *I Protest!* New York: The New American Library, April 1968.

Duscha, Julius. *Arms, Money and Politics.* New York: Ives Washburn, Inc., 1965.

Esposito, Brig. Gen. Vincent J., USA Ret. *A Concise History of World War II.* New York: Frederick A. Praegar, 1964.

Furniss, Edgar S., Jr. *American Military Policy.* New York: Rinehart & Co., Inc., 1957.

Gavin, Gen. James M., USA Ret. *Crisis Now.* New York: Random House, 1968.

Goulden, Joseph C. *Truth Is the First Casualty.* New York: Rand McNally & Co., 1969.

Halberstam, David. *The Making of a Quagmire.* New York: Random House, 1964.

Heinl, Col. Robert Debs, Jr., USMC Ret. *Soldiers of the Sea.* Annapolis: U.S. Naval Institute, 1962.

————. *Dictionary of Military and Naval Quotations.* Annapolis: U.S. Naval Institute, 1966.

Hoopes, Townsend W. *The Limits of Intervention.* New York: David McKay Co., 1969.

Huntington, Samuel P. *The Soldier and the State.* Cambridge, Mass.: Harvard University Press, 1964.

Isely, Jeter A., and Philip A. Crowl. *The Marines and Amphibious War.* Princeton, N.J.: Princeton University Press, 1951.

Janowitz, Morris. *The Professional Soldier: A Social and Political Portrait.* New York: Free Press, 1960.

Kissinger, Henry A. *The Necessity for Choice.* New York: Harper and Brothers, 1960.

————. *Problems of National Security.* New York: Frederick A. Praeger, 1965.

Leuchtenburg, William E., and the Editors of *Life. New Deal and Global War.* Vol. XI of *The Life History of the U.S.* New York: Time, Inc., 1964.

————. *The Great Age of Change.* Vol. XII of *The Life History of the U.S.* New York: Time, Inc., 1964.

Lippmann, Walter. *United States Foreign Policy: Shield of the Republic.* Boston: Little, Brown & Co., 1943.

Lyons, Gene M., and John W. Masland. *Education and Military Leadership.* Princeton, N.J.: Princeton University Press, 1959.

————, and Louis Morton. *Schools for Strategy.* New York: Frederick A. Praeger, 1965.

Masland, John W., and Laurence I. Radway. *Soldiers and Scholars.* Princeton, N.J.: Princeton University Press, 1957.

Potter, E. B., and C. W. Nimitz. *Triumph in the Pacific.* Englewood Cliffs, N.J.: Prentice-Hall, Inc., 1963.

Powers, Lt. Col. Patrick W., USA Ret. *A Guide to National Defense.* New York: Frederick A. Praeger, 1964.

Pusey, Merlo J. *The Way We Go to War.* Boston: Houghton Mifflin Company, 1969.

Raymond, Jack. *Power at the Pentagon.* New York: Harper & Row, 1964.

Riencourt, Amaury de. *The American Empire.* New York: The Dial Press, Inc., 1968.

Schlesinger, Arthur M., Jr. *The Bitter Heritage.* Greenwich, Conn.: Fawcett Publications, Inc., 1968.

Snyder, Richard C., and H. Hubert Wilson. *The Roots of Political Behavior.* New York, 1949.

Taylor, Gen. Maxwell D., USA Ret. *The Uncertain Trumpet.* New York: Harper and Brothers, 1959.

Articles

"The Advisors Who Shaped the New Vietnam Policy," *U.S. News & World Report,* February 21, 1966.

"Air War in North Vietnam: Adding Up the Score," *U.S. News & World Report,* August 18, 1969.

"American Militarism," Part II: "The Defense Establishment," *Look,* August 26, 1969.

"As Told by Secretary Rusk—Why U.S. Fights in Vietnam," *U.S. News & World Report,* February 28, 1966.

Baldwin, Hanson W., "The Seas Are Our Strength," *Marine Corp Gazette.* March 1960.

"The Battle Over U.S. Policy In Vietnam," *U.S. News & World Report,* February 28, 1966.

"Build-up Is the Keyword in Vietnam: It Started with Mortar Shells on Bien Hoa," *Armed Forces Management,* November 1965.

"Bundy's Second Thoughts," *Newsweek,* October 21, 1968.

Butz, J. S., Jr., "Tactical Air Power in 1965 . . . The Trial by Fire," *Air Force/Space Digest,* March 1966.

"The Case for Cutting Defense Spending," *Fortune,* August 1, 1969.

Colwell, V. Adm. John B., USN, "Naval Action—Vietnam," *Ordnance,* Nov.–Dec. 1966.

"Dominican Action—1965," The Center for Strategic Studies, Georgetown Univ., Washington, D.C., 1966, p. 65.

"The Dominican Republic Crisis 1965," *The Hammarskjold Forums,* New York, May 1966.

Erbsen, Lt. (jg) Claude E., USNR, "Fiscal Year 1965 Flag Officers: A Statistical Profile," *Navy Magazine,* September 1964.

"Esquire's Official Court of Inquiry Into the Present State of the U.S. Navy," *Esquire,* July 1969.

Fulbright, Senator J. W., "The Arrogance of Power" (Address to School of Advanced International Studies at Johns Hopkins University, in Washington, D.C., May 5, 1966).

———. (Owen-Corning lecture at Dennison University, Granville, Ohio, April 18, 1969).

Galbraith, John Kenneth, "How to Control the Military," *Harper's Magazine,* June 1969.

Gavin, General James M., USA Ret., "Hold Enclaves, Stop Bombing," *U.S. News & World Report*, February 7, 1966.

Greene, Jerry, "Airpower's Buildup in Vietnam," *Air Force/Space Digest*, June 1965.

Guelzo, Major Carl M., USA, "Chore or Challenge, A Professional Ethic for the Nuclear Age," *U.S. Naval Institute Proceedings*, May 1964.

Halberstam, David, "The Very Expensive Education of McGeorge Bundy," *Harper's Magazine*, July 1969.

Hayes, Rear Adm. John D., USN Ret., "Peripheral Strategy . . . Littoral Tactics . . . Limited War," *The Army Combat Forces Journal*, September 1954.

Hayward, John T., "The Second-Class Military Advisor: His Cause and Cure," *Armed Forces Management*, November 1968.

Hendricks, James D., "C-5A to Revolutionize U.S. Military Airlift," *Aviation Week & Space Technology*, November 20, 1967.

Hoffman, Fred S., "Airlift/Sealift for a Global 'Fire Brigade,' " *The National Guardsman*, December 1965.

Horowitz, Robert S., "The Week in Congress," *Navy Times*, August 13, 1969.

Johnson, General Harold K., USA, "End of the Vietnam War in Sight," Interview, *U.S. News & World Report*, September 11, 1967.

Just, Ward S., "Notes on Losing a War," *The Atlantic,* January 1969.

Keatley, Robert, "Student Soldiers," *Wall Street Journal*, July 2, 1969.

Kennedy, John F., "Notes for Profiles in Courage," 1955.

Kurtz, Howard G. and Harriet B., "The Collapse of U.S. Global Strategy," *Military Review*, May 1969.

Lippmann, Walter, "The Holding Strategy," *Newsweek*, January 31, 1966.

―――. "The Misconceived War," *Newsweek,* June 6, 1966.

―――. "The Crux in Vietnam," *Newsweek,* December 2, 1968.

"March of the News," *U.S. News & World Report*, June 14, 1965.

"The Military Influence," Editorial, *New York Times*, July 6, 1969.

"The Military: Servant or Master of Policy?" *Time* magazine, April 11, 1969.

"McNamara Speaks on Defense Decision-Making; Cites Chaos of Past," *Army Navy Air Force Journal and Register*, 4 May 1963.

Morgan, Edward P., "Elementary Lesson on the Armed Forces," *Newsday*, 1969.

"The New Pressures to Trim U.S. Defenses," *U.S. News & World Report*, July 21, 1969.

Norman, Lloyd, "Anatomy of a Decision," *Army*, September 1965.

"The Penalty of Power," *U.S. News & World Report*, April 1, 1968.

Powell, Craig, "Civilian/Military Rapport Reaches a New Maturity in the Defense Arena," *Armed Forces Managament*, December 1967.

"The Power in the Pentagon," *Newsweek*, December 6, 1965.

Raymond, Jack, "Growing Threat of Our Military-Industrial Complex," *Harvard Business Review*, May–June 1968.

"Readiness for the Little War," *Military Review*, April, 1957.

Reischauer, Edwin O., "A Broad Look at Our Asian Policy," *The New York Times Magazine*, May 10, 1968.

Roosevelt, Edith Kermit, "The Pentagon's Philosopher Kings," *Navy Magazine*, November 1966.

Schell, Jonathan, "A Reporter at Large, Quang Ngai and Quang Tin," *The New Yorker*, March 9–16, 1968.

Schlesinger, Arthur, Jr., "A Middle Way Out of Vietnam," *The New York Times Magazine*, September 18, 1966.

Sevareid, Eric, "American Militarism: What Is It Doing to Us?" *Look*, August 12, 1969.

Shoup, General D. M., USMC Ret., "Our New American Militarism," *Atlantic*, April, 1969.

Standard Rate and Data Service, Business Publications, June 24, 1969.

Stillman, Richard J., "The Pentagon's Whiz Kids," *U.S. Naval Institute Proceedings*, April 1966.

Stone, I. F., *I. F. Stone's Weekly*, March 4, 1968. Gives details on Tonkin Gulf events of August 1964.

————, *I. F. Stone's Weekly*, 1966–1969.

"The Story of Robert McNamara," *U.S. News & World Report*, July 25, 1966.

Tomkins, Maj. Gen. R. McC., USMC, "Ubique," *Marine Corps Gazette*, September, 1965.

"Top Authority Looks at Vietnam War and Its Future," *U.S. News & World Report*, February 21, 1966.

Trainor, James L., "Navy's Fast Deployment Ships Designed for U.S. Military, Economic Needs," *Armed Forces Management*, February 1967.

Tuohy, William, "Marines May Be Downgraded in Viet Command Structure," *Los Angeles Times News Service*, March 1968.

"U.S. Role in a Changing World," *U.S. News & World Report,* July 18, 1966.

"Vietnam: Let's Not Have More of the Same," Editorial, *Life,* March 15, 1968.

Vietnam 1969, An American Friends Service Committee White Paper on Ending the War, Philadelphia, May 5, 1969.

Wagner, Joe H., "How Well Are We Organized in Vietnam?" *Armed Forces Management,* January 1968.

Wertzman, Bernard G., "Youths' Pacifism Scored in Soviet," *New York Sunday Times,* July 6, 1969.

Wheeler, General Earl G., USA, "Gavin Plan Will Not Work," *U.S. News & World Report,* February 7, 1966.

"Why U.S. Isn't Winning a 'Little' War," *U.S. News & World Report,* April 1, 1968.

"Will U.S. Shrink Its Global Role?" *Business Week,* June 7, 1969.

Wilson, Brig. Gen. C. V., USA, "Weapon at the Ready," *Ordnance,* March–April 1965.

Winn, Bill, "Marching Through Georgia," *Atlanta Magazine,* March 1969.

Witze, Claude, "The Case for a Unified Command: CINCSEA," *Air Force Magazine,* January 1967.

Official Sources

The Armed Forces Officer, The Department of Defense, Washington, D.C., 1950.

Army Information Digest, Department of the Army, Washington, D.C., June 1958.

Commanders Digest, Armed Forces Press Service, Office of Information for the Armed Forces (Official information), Washington, D.C., Weekly, 1966–1969.

Defense Industry Bulletin, Assistant Secretary of Defense-Public Affairs, Department of Defense, Washington, D.C., Monthly, 1965–1969.

"Defense Budget Highlights: Approach to the FY 1970–74 Program and FY 1970 Budget," *Defense Industry Bulletin,* Department of Defense, Washington, D.C., March 1969.

Dictionary of United States Military Terms for Joint Usage, The Joint Chiefs of Staff, Washington, D.C., 1964.

"Fleet Marine Force Pacific—Force in Readiness," *Information Handbook,* Headquarters, FMF Pac Hawaii, 1965.

Harrison, G. A., *Cross Channel Attack*, U.S. Army World War II, Office of the Chief of Military History, Washington, D.C., 1951.

"Hearings," House Armed Services Committee, 85th Congress, Second Session on H.R. 12541, 1958.

"Most Misunderstood War in U.S. History," *Commanders Digest*, Department of Defense, Washington, D.C., February 22, 1969.

Organization for National Defense, Marine Corps Educational Center, Marine Corps Schools, Quantico, Va., 1965.

Statistical Abstract of the U.S. 1968, The Department of Commerce, Washington, D.C., 1968.

Unified Action Armed Forces (UNAAF), JCS Pub. 2, The Joint Chiefs of Staff, Washington, D.C., 1959.

"The U.S. Air Force in Southeast Asia," U.S. Air Force Aerospace Speech Series, Secretary of the Air Force, Office of Information, Washington, D.C., February 1966.

"Why Vietnam?" Official White House review of commitments leading up to the Vietnam intervention, August 20, 1965.

Index